49.95

THE
HISTORY OF
BULGARIA

ADVISORY BOARD

THE HISTORY OF BULGARIA

Frederick B. Chary

The Greenwood Histories of the Modern Nations
Frank W. Thackeray and John E. Findling, Series Editors

 GREENWOOD

AN IMPRINT OF ABC-CLIO, LLC
Santa Barbara, California • Denver, Colorado • Oxford, England

Copyright 2011 by ABC-CLIO, LLC

All rights reserved. No part of this publication may be reproduced, stored in a retrieval system, or transmitted, in any form or by any means, electronic, mechanical, photocopying, recording, or otherwise, except for the inclusion of brief quotations in a review, without prior permission in writing from the publisher.

Library of Congress Cataloging-in-Publication Data

Chary, Frederick B.
  The history of Bulgaria / Frederick B. Chary.
    p. cm. — (The Greenwood histories of the modern nations)
  Includes bibliographical references and index.
    ISBN 978–0–313–38446–2 (hard copy : alk. paper) — ISBN 978–0–313–38447–9 (ebook)
  1. Bulgaria—History. I. Title.
  DR67.C46   2011
  949.9—dc22   2010048660

ISBN: 978–0–313–38446–2
EISBN: 978–0–313–38447–9

15 14 13 12 11   1 2 3 4 5

This book is also available on the World Wide Web as an eBook.
Visit www.abc-clio.com for details.

Greenwood
An Imprint of ABC-CLIO, LLC

ABC-CLIO, LLC
130 Cremona Drive, P.O. Box 1911
Santa Barbara, California 93116-1911

This book is printed on acid-free paper ∞

Manufactured in the United States of America

For Diane, David, Michael, and EllaRose

Contents

Series Foreword

The *Greenwood Histories of the Modern Nations* series is intended to provide students and interested laypeople with up-to-date, concise, and analytical histories of many of the nations of the contemporary world. Not since the 1960s has there been a systematic attempt to publish a series of national histories, and as series advisors, we believe that this series will prove to be a valuable contribution to our understanding of other countries in our increasingly interdependent world.

Some 40 years ago, at the end of the 1960s, the Cold War was an accepted reality of global politics. The process of decolonization was still in progress, the idea of a unified Europe with a single currency was unheard of, the United States was mired in a war in Vietnam, and the economic boom in Asia was still years in the future. Richard Nixon was president of the United States, Mao Tse-tung (not yet Mao Zedong) ruled China, Leonid Brezhnev guided the Soviet Union, and Harold Wilson was prime minister of the United Kingdom. Authoritarian dictators still controlled most of Latin America, the Middle East was reeling in the wake of the Six-Day War, and Shah Mohammad Reza Pahlavi was at the height of his power in Iran.

Since then, the Cold War has ended, the Soviet Union has vanished, leaving 16 independent republics in its wake, the advent of the computer age has radically transformed global communications, the rising demand for oil makes the Middle East still a dangerous flashpoint, and the rise of new economic powers like the People's Republic of China and India threatens to bring about a new world order. All of these developments have had a dramatic impact on the recent history of every nation of the world.

For this series, which was launched in 1998, we first selected nations whose political, economic, and socio-cultural affairs marked them as among the most important of our time. For each nation, we found an author who was recognized as a specialist in the history of that nation. These authors worked cooperatively with us and with Greenwood Press to produce volumes that reflected current research on their nations and that are interesting and informative to their readers. In the first decade of the series, more than 40 volumes were published, and as of 2008, some are moving into second editions.

The success of the series has encouraged us to broaden our scope to include additional nations whose histories have had significant effects on their regions, if not on the entire world. In addition, geopolitical changes have elevated other nations to positions of greater importance in world affairs, so we have chosen to include them in this series as well. The importance of a series such as this cannot be underestimated. As a superpower whose influence is felt all over the world, the United States can claim a "special" relationship with almost every other nation. Yet many Americans know very little about the histories of nations with which the United States relates. How did they get to be the way they are? What kind of political systems have evolved there? What kind of influence do they have on their own regions? What are the dominant political, religious, and cultural forces that move their leaders? These and many other questions are answered in the volumes of this series.

The authors who contribute to this series write comprehensive histories of their nations, dating back, in some instances, to prehistoric times. Each of them, however, has devoted a significant portion of his or her book to events of the past 40 years because the modern era has contributed the most to contemporary issues that have an impact on U.S. policy. Authors make every effort to be as up to date as possible so that readers can benefit from discussion and analysis of recent events.

In addition to the historical narrative, each volume contains an introductory chapter giving an overview of that country's geography, political institutions, economic structure, and cultural attributes. This is meant to give readers a snapshot of the nation as it exists in the contemporary world. Each history also includes supplementary information following the narrative, which may include a timeline that represents a succinct chronology of the nation's historical evolution, biographical sketches of the nation's most important historical figures, and a glossary of important terms or concepts that are usually expressed in a foreign language. Finally, each author prepares a comprehensive bibliography for readers who wish to pursue the subject further.

Readers of these volumes will find them fascinating and well written. More importantly, they will come away with a better understanding of the contemporary world and the nations that comprise it. As series advisors, we hope that this series will contribute to a heightened sense of global understanding as we move through the early years of the twenty-first century.

Frank W. Thackeray and John E. Findling
Indiana University Southeast

Preface

For Americans, Bulgaria is one of the lesser-known European countries. Until recently, very few books about it have been written in English. It is, however, a fascinating land with a long and important history. Throughout the past it has occupied a place in one of the major geopolitical crossroads of cultures and civilizations—the Balkans. In ancient times, the land was the home of the Thracians and Macedonians, who played a role in the Classical Age of Greece. The Bulgarians, an amalgamation of Southern Slavs and Turkic Bulgars, arrived at the beginning of the Middle Ages. Their destiny has been linked to the Great Powers who have fought for control of this vital region.

What little Americans know about Bulgaria has had negative connotations, a phenomenon that American specialists in Bulgarian studies call "Bulgaria bashing." There are several reasons for this. Bulgaria was on the opposite side from the United States in the two world wars. During the Cold War it was the Soviet Union's most loyal ally in the region. Additionally, relatively few Bulgarians have immigrated to the United States, and here they are vastly outnumbered by immigrants who have come from rival Balkan countries. Bulgaria generally has made headlines in the American press when it has been connected to scandal such as the attempted assassination of Pope John Paul II or the infamous umbrella murder of Georgi Markov. In literature, films, and television drama it has been the bastion of villains and assassins. Bulgarians still smart over the manner in which they were portrayed in the James Bond thriller *From Russia with Love*.

In contrast, America has been captivated by the haunting harmonies of "The Mysterious Voices of Bulgaria," a world-class a cappella group. The fortunate few of us who have visited the country have also enjoyed the nation's marvelous mountains, beautiful seacoast, famous opera stars, and tradition of hospitality.

This brief history is a modest attempt to acquaint with its past those who are interested in learning more of this exotic land. It is based principally on scholarly monographs and texts and the author's four decades of research into modern Bulgarian history. The author has visited Bulgaria from 1966 to 2008 on numerous occasions, including four extended tenures as a researcher, lecturer, and visiting professor at Sofia University. I would like to thank my colleagues in America, Bulgaria, and the many countries around the world. As part of the family of Bulgarian studies, they have assisted me in learning about this land that first captured my imagination when I was an undergraduate at the University of Pennsylvania in the early 1960s. I would also like to thank my wife Diane, a journalist and English teacher, who certainly has made my prose more readable.

The transliteration of Bulgarian names and places is generally according to the Library of Congress standard without diacritical marks. An exception is made for well-known places, for example, Bulgaria, not Bulgariia, and Sofia, not Sofiia.

Timeline of Historical Events

10,000 to 3,000 BCE	New Stone Age
3,000 to 1000 BCE	Bronze Age, Thracian Period
356–323 BCE	Alexander the Great
323–146 BCE	Hellenistic Age, Kingdom of Macedonia
146 BCE–circa fourth century	Roman period
325	Beginning of Byzantine Empire
Sixth century	Slavs entered the Balkans
681–1018	First Bulgarian Empire
681	Beginning of reign of Asparuch
803–814	Reign of Krum
852–889	Reign of Boris I
864	Conversion of Boris I to Christianity
893–927	Reign of Simeon I
927–968	Reign of Peter

978–1014	Reign of Samuil
1018–1185	Byzantine occupation
1185–1393	Second Bulgarian Empire
1185–1196	Reign of Peter II and Ivan Asen I
1196–1208	Reign of Kaloian
1331–1371	Reign of Ivan Alexander
1393–1878	Ottoman period
1760s	Paisii Khilendarksi wrote a history of Bulgaria
1835	Gabrovo High School opened
1857–1860	Midhat Pasha was governor of northern Bulgaria
1870	Bulgarian exarchate established
1875–1878	Balkan crisis
1876	April Uprising
1877–1878	Russo-Turkish War
March 3, 1878	Treaty of San Stefano
June 1878	Treaty of Berlin
1879	Turnovo Constitution
1879–1886	Reign of Prince Alexander of Battenberg
1881–1883	Suspension of the Turnovo Constitution
1885	Union of Bulgaria and Eastern Rumelia
1885	Bulgarian-Serbian War
1887–1894	"Dictatorship" of Stefan Stambolov
1887–1918	Reign of Ferdinand
1891	Founding of the Bulgarian Social Democratic Party
1894	Beginning of Ferdinand's personal rule
1899	Founding of the Bulgarian Agrarian National Union (BANU)

1903	Ilinden uprising
1903	Social Democrats split into "broads" and "narrows"
1908	Bulgaria ended ties to the Ottoman Empire
October 1912–May 1913	First Balkan War
May–June 1913	Second Balkan War
October 1915	Bulgaria entered World War I
September–October 1918	Radomir Rebellion
September 1918	Bulgaria left World War I
1918–1943	Reign of Boris III
1919–1923	BANU government
1919	Treaty of Neuilly
June 9, 1923	Coup d'etat against Stamboliiski
September 1923	September Uprising
1923–1931	Democratic Alliance government
1931–1934	Democratic Bloc government
1933–1934	*Reichstag* Fire Trial
1934	Georgi Dimitrov became General Secretary of *Comintern*
May 1934	Zveno-Military League coup d'etat
1935–1943	Personal rule of King Boris III
1940	Bulgaria regained Southern Dobrudja with German help
March 1941	Bulgaria joined Axis and entered World War II
April 1941	Bulgaria occupied Macedonia and Thrace
December 13, 1941	Bulgaria declared "symbolic" war on the United States
March 1943	Dimitur Peshev's intervention prevented the deportation of Bulgarian Jews to the Nazi killing Centers

August 28, 1943	King Boris III died
1943–1947	Reign of Simeon II
September 9, 1944	Fatherland Front government
1947	Republican "Dimitrov Constitution"
1954	Zhivkov became Communist Party First Secretary
1956	April Plenum
1962	Zhivkov won power struggle against Iugov and Chervenkov
1971	New constitution promulgated
1981	1300th anniversary celebration
July 21, 1981	Death of Liudmila Zhivkova
1983–1989	Revival process
December 10, 1989	Zhivkov resigned
January–May 1990	Round Table talks
1990–1997	Zheliu Zhelev presidency
1990	New constitution introduced
1991–1995	UDF government
1995–2001	Socialist government
1997–2002	Peter Stoianov presidency
2001–2005	Government of former King Simeon II
2002–	Georgi Parvanov presidency
2004	Bulgaria joined NATO
2005–2009	Socialist government
2007	Bulgaria joined the EU
2009–	GERB government

Introduction

GEOGRAPHY AND CLIMATE

Bulgaria is located in southeast Europe on the Black Sea. Its area is 42,858 square miles, about the size of Virginia. To the west lay Serbia and the Republic of Macedonia, to the north Romania, and to the south Greece and Turkey. The Balkan mountain range running eastward from Serbia to the Black Sea divides the country in half and embraces the famous Valley of the Roses, the source of oil prized by the international perfume industry. Bulgaria's northern border follows the Danube River until it bends north at Silistra. South of the Balkans, the Maritsa River flows eastward then south into the Aegean, draining the fertile Thracian Plain. In the south, the Rila and Rhodope ranges rise even higher than the Balkans.

Other important rivers are the Iskur in the Rila Mountains, the Arda in the Rhodopes, the Struma in Bulgarian Macedonia, and the meandering Iantra, which cuts through the medieval capital of Turnovo in the north central region. The many different types of soil can be divided into three main areas. In the northern Danubian plain one finds rich black earth and gray forest soil. The mountains have both characteristic forest and meadow soil. The Thracian plain, the most extensive region, also has fertile forest soils. Because of Bulgaria's geographic location at the juncture of several regions of the Eurasian land mass, its native flora and fauna include arctic, alpine, and steppe species.

Most of Bulgaria has a moderate continental climate. The Thracian Plain, however, is more Mediterranean. The country's average temperature is 51 degrees Fahrenheit, although in winter, temperatures can drop to subzero levels and in summer be extremely hot. Temperatures over 100 degrees have been recorded. Annual precipitation ranges from 18 inches in the northeast to more than 45 inches in the mountains. Snow falls on about 20 to 30 days a year. In general, Bulgaria's geography and climate make it ideal for an agricultural and forest economy.

POPULATION

Bulgaria has a population of more than seven and a half million. Eighty-five percent of its people are of Bulgarian ethnicity. Nine and a half percent are Turks, and 4.5 percent are Roma. The remaining 2 percent include a great variety of other ethnicities, the most important of which historically have been Greeks, Armenians, and Jews. The population of the Pirin region of Bulgaria (historically part of Macedonia) is officially Bulgarian.

Since 1969, Bulgaria's population has been more urban than rural. In the twenty-first century that ratio is two-thirds urban. There are about 250 cities and 4,000 villages. The population density is estimated at 174 persons per square mile. Bulgaria has a negative population growth because its death rate (14.31 per thousand) is greater than its birth rate (9.51 per thousand). The rate of loss is about .02 percent annually. Part of the decline may be due to emigration, especially as the young leave and the population grows older.

LANGUAGE

Bulgarian is a South Slavic language closely related to the other South Slavic languages: Slovenian, Serbo-Croatian, and especially Macedonian. It is written in the Cyrillic alphabet. Since language is intimately connected to nationality and, therefore, to the political concept of a nation state, there is a political dimension both to language and to alphabet. Cyrillic, where used, varies from country to country. Bulgarian Cyrillic was modified in the Communist period to bring it closer to the variety used to write Russian. Macedonian Cyrillic is modeled on the variety used to write Serbian.

To native speakers, all South Slavic languages are mutually intelligible. Moreover, it is easier for Bulgarian speakers to understand Serbo-Croatian than some dialects spoken in their own country, for example, that found in the Rhodopes. Bulgarian and Macedonian are almost identical and some Bulgarian linguists refuse to recognize them as separate languages.

RELIGION

Eastern Orthodox Christianity is the historical religion of Bulgarians. Under the Constitution of 1991, Eastern Orthodoxy is characterized as the "traditional religion" of Bulgaria, not the state religion, as it was designated under the pre-Communist Turnovo Constitution. In 1992, there was a dispute over the qualifications of the patriarch, and an alternative church declared itself the true Bulgarian Orthodox Church. In 2004, the government and courts sided with the original church, but the alternative congregations still are disputing the decision and have supporters among congregants abroad.

The constitution recognizes freedom of religion for all Bulgarian citizens, but there have been complaints of harassment and discrimination from those of other faiths, particularly those that are not registered as Bulgarian law requires. There are about 44,000 Roman Catholics in Bulgaria, one quarter of whom practice the Byzantine rite. Protestants also number more than 40,000. The latter include both Bulgarians and some of the non-Bulgarian minorities. Catholicism spread by missionaries has existed since the Middle Ages and also gained converts during the religious struggle against the Greek clergy in the nineteenth century. American and European missionaries converted some Bulgarians to various Protestant sects. There has been a sizeable increase in converts to Protestantism since the fall of Communism, especially among the Roma.

The largest non-Orthodox religion is Islam practiced by Turks, Pomaks (Bulgarian-speaking Moslems), and other Moslem minorities. There are almost a million Moslems in Bulgaria. More than 92 percent are Sunni and the remainder is Shiite. Three quarters are Turks. There are also almost 11,000 members of the Armenian Apostolic Church and even 1,000 Buddhists. The small Jewish community is significant because virtually the entire population of 50,000 survived the Holocaust. Ninety percent of these moved to Palestine-Israel after World War II. Most of the remainder left after the fall of Communism. There are about a thousand Jews still living in Bulgaria.

Despite the religious freedom Bulgarians now enjoy, many are not observant.

REGIONALISM

Traditionally, Bulgaria has seven different regions: Thrace, the Rhodopes, Macedonia, Shopska (Sofia region), North Bulgaria, Northeast Bulgaria, and Strandzha (the southeastern region). These areas differ in folklore (dances, songs, costumes, etc.) and dialect. Modern Bulgaria is a unified nation with a unified language brought together by a national education system.

The only regional area of political importance now is greater Macedonia. Since the fall of the Ottoman Empire, this area has been divided among different countries, and today Bulgaria, Greece, and the Republic of Macedonia share the region. There are ethnic complications as well because Greeks, Albanians, Serbs, and other ethnic groups live in the Greek and Macedonian section. However, aside from Turks and Roma, the rest of the population of Pirin Macedonia, that is, the Bulgarian section, is virtually all South Slavs. The political question is: are they Bulgarians or Macedonians? It was only in 1999 that the Bulgarian government conceded that a Macedonian nation even existed. Officially, Bulgaria concedes that only the people of the Republic of Macedonia are Macedonians. In return, Skopje acknowledged that the population of Pirin was Bulgarian. There are indeed undoubtedly those on both sides of the border as well as their conationalists living abroad who have their own opinion of who is what.

GOVERNMENT

According to the Constitution of 1991, Bulgaria is a democratic republic with a separation of executive, legislative, and judicial powers. All citizens are regarded as equal irrespective of race, ethnicity, gender, or social status. The constitution guarantees the usual accepted civil liberties accorded in democracies in the twenty-first century, for example, speech, assembly, privacy, freedom from unlawful arrest, and so forth. All persons born in Bulgaria are Bulgarian citizens. So are persons not citizens of another country with at least one parent with Bulgarian citizenship. Other persons of Bulgarian origin can apply for citizenship in a manner proscribed by law. The president of the republic along with the vice president running on the same ticket is elected by four-tailed (universal, direct, equal, and secret) ballot for a five-year term. There is a limit of two terms in office. The legislative body is a unicameral chamber, the *subranie*, whose 240 members are also elected by four-tailed ballot. These representatives serve 31 districts for four-year terms. Under certain circumstances, the president may dissolve the *subranie* before its term ends and call for new elections. For special items such as certain amendments to the constitution or changing the territory of the country, a Grand National Assembly of 400 is elected.

The president chooses a prime minister from the political party with the most seats in the *subranie* who is then approved by the assembly. The prime minister chooses a council of ministers, also subject to the *subranie*'s approval. Both the president and the prime minister have executive powers, and difficulties have occurred when the two have different political agendas or opinions.

The independent judiciary consists of a complicated network of courts and judges, much of which has come down through Bulgaria's unique judicial history. There is a Supreme Judicial Council of 25. It consists of members appointed by the *subranie* and the president along with several members who sit *ex officio*. The latter are the prosecutor general and chairmen of the two supreme courts described below. The president appoints the prosecutor general, who is in charge of the state's prosecutors. The office of prosecutor general was established in the nineteenth century and has continued with modifications throughout Bulgaria's modern history. The Supreme Judicial Council appoints the judges. There are two supreme courts: one for cassation (appeals) and one for administrative law (judgments made by offices outside the regular law courts). The chairs of these courts are appointed by the president. The deputy judges, as well as all other judges, are appointed by the Supreme Judicial Council. Chairmen of the supreme courts and the prosecutor general have seven-year terms with a two-term limit. Judges in general have tenure after five years and serve until the age of 65 unless dismissed for incapacitation, criminal activity, or neglect of duty.

In addition, the Constitution of 1991 provided for a Constitutional Court to decide the constitutionality of legislation. One third of this court of 12 judges is appointed by the president, one third by the *subranie*, and one third is chosen by a joint meeting of the Supreme Court of Cassation and the Supreme Administrative Court. The appointments are for nine years in a rotation system of a third every three years. The judges are not eligible for reappointment. The chair of the court is elected by his or her colleagues every three years.

Bulgaria is a unitary state with local self-government. The constitution does not permit autonomous territories within its borders. The country, however, is divided into 31 regions containing municipalities. These units have local government administered by elected officials and councils.

The constitution's Article Eleven concerns political parties, which are permitted to function in Bulgaria on an equal basis. Their formation, dissolution, and activities are proscribed by law. No party can be formed on an ethnic, racial, or religious basis. However, some ethnic parties, such as the Turkish Movement for Rights and Freedom (MRF) and the Roma Party, have managed to compete in elections through legal loopholes. No party can advocate the violent seizure of state power. Only political parties can engage in politics. Other associations may meet and protect their members' interests, but they may not engage in political activity. The constitution specifically mentions trade unions as such associations.

Since the introduction of the 1991 constitution, scores of political parties have participated in Bulgarian elections. More often than not, they have run together in blocs. Between 1990 and 2009, 13 national elections have been held, including the 1990 election for the Grand National Assembly called to write the current constitution. Four were presidential elections (1992, 1996, 2001, and 2006); six, *subranie* elections (1991, 1994, 1997, 2001, 2005, 2009); and two for Bulgarian representatives to the parliament of the European Union (2007 and 2009).

The major Bulgarian parties and blocs, those that have won seats in the parliaments, are listed from political left to right as follows:

Socialists

The Socialist Party is the old ruling Communist Party, which changed its name in 1990. There is a minor party calling itself Communist that has never gained significant support. In 1997, the new Communists ran in the Democratic Left coalition with Ekoglasnost, an environmental group. In the elections of 2005 and 2009, it ran with the Socialists in a bloc called the Coalition for Bulgaria, which also contained a number of other left-wing parties including the Green Party, one of the Agrarian factions, the Roma Party, and others. There were slight changes in the membership in the two elections.

Euroleft

The Euroleft Party spun off from the Socialists in 1997 and won several seats in the 1997 *subranie* elections. In 2003, it changed its name to the Social Democrats and joined the Socialists in the Coalition for Bulgaria.

Bulgarian Agrarian National Union (BANU)

BANU was founded in 1899 and came to prominence in the first decades of the twentieth century under Aleksandur Stamboliiski, who was prime minister of Bulgaria from 1919 to 1923. After his murder and the fall of his government, several parties laid claim to the party's name. One shared power in government with the Communists from 1944 to 1990. After the fall of Communism, BANU ran separately but had only modest success. It joined for a while with members of BANU-Nikola Petkov, a party of dissidents and returning exiles, named after an Agrarian leader executed by the Communists in 1947. This party, called BANU-United, split up after a few years. At least a half dozen other parties also have used BANU in their party names. None of them had much success individually, but they sometimes won running in coalitions and blocs with other parties.

Movement for Rights and Freedoms (MRF)

The MRF was founded in January 1990 before the constitution was adopted. Its principle goal was the protection of the Turkish ethnic community and Moslem rights in Bulgaria. It registered as a party under the constitution and was challenged as violating the document's article forbidding parties based on ethnicity. However, it successfully won the right to register by arguing that it was open to all Bulgarians. It successfully competed in elections, usually winning about 14 percent of the vote. It used its influence as a parliamentary group by swinging votes toward one side or another to gain its objectives.

The Union of Democratic Forces (UDF)

The oldest of the post-Communist political organizations, the UDF, was formed in December of 1989 as Todor Zhivkov was losing power. Its Bulgarian acronym SDS (*Suiuz na demokratichneski sila*) evoked ironic smiles from American Balkanists recalling the student radical group of the 1960s. It has a centrist political orientation and originally contained 11 political parties and organizations. More joined and others left over the following two decades, and in later years it itself joined in new coalitions. Its leaders have twice been elected president and several have been prime ministers.

Democrats for a Strong Bulgaria (DSB)

Ivan Kostov, a former UDF prime minister, formed the DSB with a group of other dissatisfied UDF members in 2004. It had modest success in the 2005 *subranie* elections and then rejoined with the UDF and several smaller parties in the Blue Coalition for the 2009 elections.

National Movement Simeon II (NMSS)

The NMSS was founded in 2001 with the purpose of electing the former king Simeon II to office. They succeeded in winning the *subranie* elections of 2001 and having Simeon appointed prime minister. After his term, Simeon resigned from the leadership, and the party in 2007 changed its name to the National Movement for Stability and Progress. It is a centrist party, liberal in the European sense.

Bulgarian Business Bloc (BBB)

The BBB was founded in 1990 by the Union for Private Economic Enterprise. Its politics were center right, supporting economic freedom and technical progress. Two splinter parties split off from it, and the BBB dissolved in 1997. It won a handful of seats in the parliamentary elections of 1994 and 1997.

Order, Lawfulness, Justice (RZS)

RZS is a center-right party formed in 2005 to fight crime and corruption in Bulgaria and to support conservative politics. It is close to the British Conservative Party. It won 10 seats in the 2009 *subranie* elections.

Bulgarian People's Union (BNS)

The BNS was a center-right political coalition of some Agrarians, members of IMRO, and others that elected a handful of representatives in the 2005 *subranie* election.

Citizens for European Development of Bulgaria (GERB)

GERB, a centrist-right party, was formed in 2006 and rapidly gained popular support. It won a plurality of votes in the 2007 and 2009 elections for the European parliament and the 2009 *subranie* elections. Their leader, Boiko Borisov, became prime minister. GERB has a nationalist and conservative agenda. The Socialists have tagged it as racist, which GERB's leadership denies. It has associated with the conservative European People's Party-European Democrats (EPP-ED).

Attack

Coalition Union Attack or simply Attack (*Ataka*) is an extreme right-wing political party advocating Bulgarian nationalism. Attack has attacked minority groups, particularly Roma and Turks, in its slogans and propaganda. It is also opposed to greater ties between Bulgaria and the West, especially the United States. After its formation in 2005, it gained significant following in Bulgaria.

ECONOMY

Traditionally, Bulgaria had an agricultural economy producing for its own consumption and, under the Ottomans, the Turkish market. In the nineteenth and twentieth centuries, holdings changed from large Turkish estates to small and middle-sized farms. After independence in 1878, there were very few large holdings. Some Bulgarian agricultural produce became known for its quality on the international market. Rose oil supplied the European perfume industry. Tobacco was also exported worldwide. Some of the "finest Turkish tobaccos" advertised by Camel and Chesterfield cigarettes were grown in Bulgaria; however, no camels were used for transport. Other agricultural products were sold abroad in Europe. Industry in Bulgaria was modest and also for internal consumption. Wool was developed with government subsidies for uniforms for the military and civilian services.

In the Communist period, farms were collectivized on the Soviet model and more emphasis was placed on industrialization. The economy remained woefully behind the rest of Europe and even lagged in the Soviet Bloc until reforms began to take hold in the 1960s. In addition to the traditional agricultural products, Bulgarian wine and its high-quality feta cheese made from sheep's milk did well on the international market. The industrial sector, however, did not do well. Especially disastrous was the Kremikovtsi steel complex outside of Sofia. It was ill conceived and never produced anything near what it cost to build, maintain, and run. Bulgaria was able to find a niche in exporting to other Soviet Bloc countries its Balkancar forklifts and to Third World nations its inexpensive electronic items. The government emphasized raising the standard of living of its people by producing and importing consumer goods, thus running up a debt of billions of American dollars. The country also achieved modest success with tourism.

Nevertheless, the economy never achieved a level to bring satisfaction to the people. A series of natural and manmade economic setbacks in the 1980s contributed to the fall of Communism. The new post-Communist circumstances played havoc with the economy further, bringing joblessness, inflation, and scarcities as the country tried to adjust to a market system, privatization, and setting Western European standards for rebuilding the country. Bulgaria remains today one of the poorest nations on the continent.

In the first few years of the post-Communist era, the economy was characterized by slow progress followed by setbacks. Some years saw triple-digit inflation. The lev fell to more than 20 times its artificially pegged value. The standard of living was reduced by almost half. In 1997, the establishment of an independent currency board and other reforms began the long process of stabilizing the economy. By 2004, the standard of living returned to pre-1989 levels. There was steady growth and even budget surpluses, although inflation and unemployment remained problems. The 2008 world economic crisis gave Bulgaria as elsewhere yet another economic shock.

Agricultural produce remains the country's main export. Tourism is again a major sector of the economy, as is foreign investment in land. Bulgaria has yet to develop fully its rich mineral resources because of the lack of necessary equipment and infrastructure to put it on a competitive basis. The country still has an unfavorable balance of trade. It hopes to change its currency from the lev to the euro in the near future, but it still lags far behind in gross domestic product (GDP).

FOREIGN RELATIONS

Since the fall of Communism in 1990, Bulgaria has moved closer to the West. In 2004, it joined NATO and in 2007, the European Union. It participated in the war in Iraq, but there was some opposition to this within the country. Traditionally both before and during the advent of Communism in the country in 1944, Bulgaria was very close to Russia. The ties still exist, but the closeness of relations depends somewhat on which political party is in power. Bulgaria also has reasonably good relations with its neighbors, although some border and minority issues occasionally have caused periods of coolness. Sofia has joined the other Balkan nations in a number of important regional associations and commissions. The problem over Macedonia was resolved in 1999 when Sofia and Skopje agreed to respect each other's borders, and the Bulgarians finally recognized the Macedonians as belonging to a nation distinct from the Bulgarians.

Sofia also recognized the Vatican and Israel after long periods without diplomatic relations. The latter was important because of the large number of Jews whose families emigrated from Bulgaria living there. This policy of reaching out to all nations has been questioned by the ultranationalistic xenophobic political group Attack, which gained significant support in the country after 2005 and is working with GERB, which won the 2009 parliamentary elections.

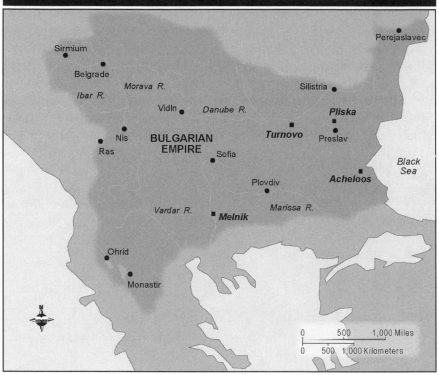

(ABC-CLIO)

1

The First Bulgarian Empire (10,000 BCE–1018)

PREHISTORIC AND ANCIENT BULGARIA

Evidence of prehistoric habitation in Bulgaria includes the remarkable cave drawings in the northwest region of Magura and other drawings and kitchen middens on the Madara plateau near Shumen in the northeast as well as elsewhere in the country. Archeologists have also unearthed beautiful gold artifacts in northern Bulgaria dating to 4000 BCE. In the Bronze Age (circa 3000 to 1000 BCE), Thracians lived there. Much of what we know of them comes from their burial tombs. The famous fourth-century tomb of Kazanluk was unearthed in 1944 during excavation for a bomb shelter, and the world-renowned Thracian Gold—cups and jewelry—was found near Panigiurishte. We also know of Thracian early history from the writings of the Greek historian Herodotus. Thracians maintained a number of tribal communities that interacted politically, commercially, and culturally with the Greek city-states and the Persian Empire during the Classical Age. The Bulgarians claim as their own the mythological Thracian musician Orpheus, who came from the Haemus (Balkan) mountains and entered the underworld to claim his wife Eurydice, who had been taken by Hades. Today every year an Orphic music festival is held in the country. In 475 BCE, the Thracian tribes united in the Odrysian kingdom, only to be captured by the Macedonian king Philip II a half century later.

Philip went on to conquer Greece and his son, Alexander the Great, the Persian Empire. Upon Alexander's death, his generals divided his empire. Macedonia, including Thrace and Greece, became a territory embroiled in constant struggle, wars, and political disputes just as the region has been since the beginning of recorded history and remains to this day. Because of the aid that the Macedonian king Philip V gave to Hannibal of Carthage in his wars against Rome (third century BCE), the latter conquered the region (215–148 BCE), dividing it into a group of Roman provinces—Macedonia, Thracia, and Moesia. Over the next centuries, these provinces became a vital part of the Roman Empire. With the decline of the Western Empire (fourth century CE) and the rise of the Eastern (later called the Byzantine) Empire, the area became even more important and was at some times the seat of the emperor himself. In the part that later fell to Bulgaria, great cities, arose including Serdica (today Sofia), Philippoupolis (Philip's old capital, today Plovdiv), Varna, and Ruse among them. The province was both a border area and a commercial crossroads from west to east. Macedonia continued beyond the end of the Roman and Byzantine empires into a disputed area among the peoples and states of the region. Peoples of all ethnicities and religions entered and populated it. It is no wonder that the word *Macedonia* has come to mean in French and Italian *fruit salad*, just as the word *Balkan*, actually a Turkish word for mountain, has come to mean, in *balkanize, fractional dispute*.

In the fourth century CE as the Roman Empire continued to lose its mastery of Europe and the Mediterranean, hostile tribes entered from the east, replacing the empire in the west with so-called barbarian kingdoms. A new capital, Constantinople, established in 325 by the emperor Constantine I in Byzantium on the Bosporus strait, grew in strength and importance. The empire adopted Christianity as the official, and within a century, the only state religion. In Moesia and Thracia, the most important invaders were the South Slavs.

THE SLAVS AND BULGARS

The Slavs are a branch of the Indo-European peoples who came from the Baltic-Russian area. In the early centuries of the Common Era, they inhabited the area of the Germanic Visigoths. During the migrations beginning in the fourth century, they divided into three major groups: West, East, and South Slavs. The South Slavs entered and settled in the Balkans beginning in the fifth century. There they loosely divided into two branches, the western becoming in later years Slovenes, Serbs, and Croatians and the eastern becoming Bulgarians and Macedonians.

In the Bulgarian lands the Slavs, mainly farmers, adopted the superior Roman technology of the area and were on the point of organizing into states but could not resist the armed might of the Byzantine Empire until a new element entered: the Bulgars, a Mongolian people of Central Asia who moved into the region extending over the Black and Caspian Seas during the great migrations. In 632, the Bulgar ruler Khan Kubrat established himself as an independent ruler, and on his death in 651, his five sons divided his empire. They assigned the third son, Asparuch, the region of the southern Ukraine.

Within 30 years, Asparuch and his *boyars* (nobles) fought their way to the Danube and beyond, where they organized the eastern branch of the South Slavs into a viable state. Earlier in the century, the Byzantine Empire lost much control over these Balkan regions because of their wars with Persians and Arabs in the Middle East, but in the later 600s, they turned their attention back to the Balkans and easily reconquered much of the land, in part of because of the disunity of the Slavs and the latter's inferior arms. The Byzantine army also now began a war against Asparuch's Bulgars, who had moved south of the Danube. Asparuch now offered protection to the Slavs and joined their forces into his army. He also began construction of a new capital in Pliska, located in northwestern present-day Bulgaria. The city was well defended with two surrounding walls and additional walls around the palace. Furthermore, the high bluffs around the town added more protection. In 680, the Bulgar-Slav army defeated the Byzantine forces led by Emperor Constantine IV himself. The next year, Constantinople recognized the control of Moesia by the Bulgars. The treaties between the Bulgars and the Slavs provided for a hereditary monarchy in the line of Asparuch, a noble council of Bulgar *boyars*, and an assembly of *boyars* and Slav chiefs. Thus modern Bulgarians claim the year 681 as the founding of their first medieval empire.

The Slav chiefs maintained control over their own people but were obligated to pay the Bulgars tribute and provide for the army. In the long run, the two peoples merged into one, Bulgarians, and the South Slavic language became their tongue.

Tervel, Asparuch's successor, ruled in the early eighth century. The Byzantine chroniclers record that he supported the deposed emperor

Justinian II and helped restore him to the throne in 705. Justinian granted him the title of Caesar. The Slavic appellation *tsar*, later used by Bulgarian emperors as well as modern Bulgarian and Russian rulers, is generally considered derived from it. The emperor proved to be an unfaithful friend and in 707 attempted to regain the territory he had earlier awarded Tervel, but the latter bested the Byzantine army at the Battle of Anchialus on the Black Sea.

Tervel carved the magnificent Madara horseman, a bas-relief sculpture almost 20 feet high, found in the caves near Shuman. The sculpture shows a knight on horseback piercing a lion. Madara was a place sacred to the Thracians, which the Bulgar khans now adopted for the worship of their own gods, and various Greek inscriptions near it relate events of the early khans. The inscription lists of Bulgarian rulers indicate that 11 more led the state until the advent of the celebrated Khan Krum (803–814); however, historical records are scanty and suspect.

The family background of Krum is uncertain. Paternally, he may have descended from a line of Bulgars that settled in Macedonia, and his mother may have been a Slav. He was all the same a bold and adventurous leader. By this time, the monarchy had become more centralized, and Krum used his position to advantage. In 805, he ventured north and defeated the Avars, absorbing Transylvania and eastern Pannonia into his lands, which then abutted the Holy Roman Empire of Charlemagne as well as the Byzantine Empire. Two years later, Krum then took on the latter, defeating them in the Struma valley. In 809, he besieged the central fortress of Sredetz (a.k.a. Serdica or Sofia), a major point on the crossroads from Western Europe to Constantinople and the Middle East. After failing to take the city for a number of weeks, he promised the garrison, some 6,000 strong, safe conduct, but broke his word and massacred them all when they surrendered.

The emperor Nikephoros I resolved to take revenge. He brought settlers from Asia Minor into Thrace and Macedonia to strengthen the frontier and then advanced on Sredetz but failed to take it back. In 811, the emperor attacked Bulgaria again. He captured and pillaged Pliska, looting Krum's treasury. However, on the Greek army's return south, Krum, who had mobilized the entire population including women, fell upon the Greeks in the mountain passes and defeated them, slaying Nikephoros himself. Legend has it that the khan lined the emperor's skull with silver and used it to toast guests at his feasts. The khan continued to fight the Byzantines successfully, winning wars against the next two emperors, Michael I and Leo V. Yet in addition to his military activity, Krum also took care to improve his government, including instituting a new law code for the state.

Wars with the Byzantines and their other neighbors continued throughout the century, and Bulgarian territory grew. The khans divided their land into administrative districts with appointed governors. Although the Slavs, as well as some others who inhabited the territory, included themselves in the incipient Bulgarian nation, a great number of other ethnicities lived there also. Furthermore, followers of various religions dwelt in the lands: the original Bulgarian and Slavic pagans, Christians, Jews, and Moslems. Missionaries of the three monotheistic faiths came seeking to convert these Bulgarians.

BORIS AND SIMEON

Boris I, who ascended to the khanate in 852, wished to establish a state religion in order to deal with conflicts arising from the different religious, legal, and moral traditions in conflict with the state's centralized code. Furthermore, at the beginning of his reign, the khan found himself involved in wars with the Byzantines and in diplomatic negotiations with the Christian countries of Europe. As a pagan, he found himself in an inferior position. Therefore Boris and the boyar council decided to adopt Christianity as the state religion. However, although in the ninth century there still officially was only one Christian church in Europe, politically, culturally, and economically, conversion of new states and peoples could come from the Byzantine emperor and patriarch or the Holy Roman Emperor and the pope of Rome. With the help of the Roman Emperor Louis the German, Boris agreed to convert to the western brand of Christianity. In response, the Greek Emperor Michael III attacked Bulgaria, forcing Boris to accept the Byzantine version. His country suffering from the consequences of a severe drought and a recent earthquake, Boris could not resist, and with Michael as his godfather, the khan and a number of *boyars* converted. He even added the emperor's name to his own, becoming Boris-Michael, and changed his title to king. Other *boyars*, however, remained loyal to paganism and fruitlessly revolted. Orders were sent throughout Bulgaria to convert all subjects to the new religion. Emperor Michael was overjoyed with the conversion and rewarded his godson with territory in Thrace.

Boris investigated the new religion further and desired to establish an autonomous church in Bulgaria. When Patriarch Photios I was hesitant to help him, he turned back to the pope and sent a detailed questionnaire to Rome. Pope Nicholas also hesitated to give Boris an autonomous church but did send more than a hundred responses to his questions. He also sent missionaries to Bulgaria to turn the country to the Western rite. However, a few years later Boris fell out with Rome when the new pope, Adrian II, refused his nominees for archbishop of Bulgaria. The 870 Council of Constantinople placed Bulgaria under the Greek patriarch, who now granted the king an autocephalous (autonomous) church. Bulgaria was now firmly established in the Eastern Orthodox rite and even a nominal placement of the country under Rome later in the decade could not change this direction.

One result of the autocephalous church was Bulgaria's advantage in preaching the new faith in Bulgarian rather than Greek. Indeed, Medieval Bulgarian became the Old Church Slavonic that the Slavic churches of the Eastern rite use in their liturgy. The development of the liturgical language was aided by the efforts of two celebrated missionaries, the brothers Saints Cyril and Methodius. Although the origin of the pair is somewhat obscure, the sources indicate that they were born into a noble family in Thessaloniki. Bulgarians and Greeks and even others claim them as their nationals. They began their translation of the Bible into Slavonic as missionaries not in Bulgaria but in Greater Moravia (now part of the Czech Republic). Here they developed a new alphabet called *Glagolitsa* based on Greek and Hebrew to fit the Slavic tongue. However, the use of the Slavic language, as well as the brothers' association with the Greek rite, caused difficulties with German princes and the Roman clergy. In the 880s, after the deaths of Cyril and Methodius, their disciples were expelled from Moravia and went to Bulgaria. Two, Clement of Ohrid and Naum of Preslav, revised Glagolitsa into the Cyrillic alphabet, versions of which are used in Bulgaria as well as Russia, Serbia, and some other Slavic countries today. In 889, Boris abdicated to become a monk, handing over the throne to his son Vladimir.

Vladimir, however, remained loyal to the old gods and spearheaded a revival of paganism. Boris returned from his monastery to lead the Christian forces to victory in 893 against his son, whom he blinded (a Byzantine custom applied to defeated rulers), and replaced him with his younger brother. Simeon had been designated for the church and educated in Constantinople. He was therefore personally attuned to Greek culture and as ruler of Bulgaria continued his father's accomplishments, establishing the country as a significant power in European politics. Indeed, it is entirely justified to call the state the First Bulgarian Empire. Simeon styled himself tsar or emperor. He moved the capital away from Pliska with its pagan influences to the garrison city of Preslav, which had a literary school well known for its Christian scholars. The Bulgarian tsar built the new capital into a magnificent city fit for an empire.

The chief focus of Simeon's reign was his conflict with the Byzantine emperors Leo VI and Constantine VII. The struggle involved five wars and began almost as soon as he came to the throne. The initial dispute involved trade. Leo ordered that Bulgarian merchants who had port rights in Constantinople transfer their operations to the more inferior stations at Thessaloniki. Simeon declared war and invaded Thrace. Behind the conflict was the emperor's desire to see Bulgaria remain as a client state, while Simeon followed Boris's outlook that Bulgaria be completely independent of Constantinople.

In the wake of Simeon's success on the battlefields of Thrace, Leo had his allies the Magyars, then occupying the southern Ukraine, attack Bulgaria from the north. Simeon rushed the main bulk of troops to face them, leaving Thrace open to a new assault by the Byzantine army. In 895, the Magyar army circled around the main Bulgarian force stationed in forts along the Danube to besiege Preslav. Once again Boris left his monastery to rally the depleted troops in the capital, including old men, youths, and women. The siege was broken and the Magyar army suffered a catastrophic defeat. The main Bulgarian army rushed into the Magyar lands of the Ukraine, forcing the population to move westward, where they settled in the Pannonian plain and founded modern Hungary. Boris died in 907, and the church canonized him.

Simeon followed this victory with another over the Byzantines and went on to add the western Balkans, the territory of modern Albania and northern Greece, to his empire. In 904, Simeon and Leo signed an armistice. The latter, still at war with the Arabs in the Middle East, agreed to cede to Bulgaria the lands that Simeon won in the recent battles and pay him an annual tribute. However, the Bulgarian ruler had bigger goals: the Byzantine Empire itself.

In 912, Leo VI died, and after a few months of Byzantine intrigue, Constantine VII emerged as emperor. However, before Constantine came to the throne, Simeon invaded Thrace and reached the gates of Constantinople, but the patriarch persuaded him to attempt a diplomatic solution to their difficulties. Simeon then sent envoys to Constantinople, hoping to have the young emperor wed one of his daughters. Constantine's mother, the widow of Leo, prevented the marriage, although Simeon gained recognition of the title *emperor*. He then attacked the Byzantines concentrating in areas west of the capital.

In 917, the Byzantine army allied with Hungarians and Serbs, and the Pechenegs of the Eurasian steppe moved against Bulgaria. The two forces, reputed to be 150,000 troops combined, met at Acheloos near present-day Burgas on the Black Sea. The Bulgarians achieved an overwhelming victory even though Simeon, who led the army himself, was slightly wounded. The Hungarians and Pechenegs withdrew from the alliance and Simeon went west to defeat the Serbs, annexing their territory to his empire.

Simeon now declared the Bulgarian church to be a full patriarchate and styled himself Emperor of the Bulgarians and the Romans, that is, the Byzantines. He continued to successfully attack the Byzantine armies, annexing much of their European territory. But although he approached the gates of Constantinople, his lack of a navy and the strong walled defensives of the city prevented his entering and capturing the Greek capital.

PETER

Simeon died of heart failure in 927 and was succeeded by his son Peter (ruled 927–968), who, after an initial short war with the Byzantine Empire, reigned in peace for four decades, although at the expense of lost territory during his reign. Serbia regained its independence, and its allies the Magyars raided Bulgaria until Peter allowed them to settle in the lands north of the Danube. Furthermore, he faced internal dissention as his brothers unsuccessfully tried to replace him.

Another threat during his reign was the rise of the heretical Christian movement Bogomilism, which translates from the Slavic to "dear to God." In fact, Bogomilism was part of a heretical movement that swept across Christianity in the late Middle Ages, starting with the Paulicians of Asia Minor in the late seventh century, and had versions in Central Europe (Cathari) and southern France (Albigensianism). Its basic premise was found in the old Gnostic and Manichean theologies of dualism: that is, there are two gods at work in the world, one of good and one of evil. As a consequence, the Bogomils rejected the sacraments and the power of the church to grant everlasting life, believing it a tool of the evil god.

The movement had a great appeal to the peasantry, who were upset by the increasing burdens that the landed aristocracy backed by the church placed upon them. The movement also had an appeal to the growing middle class, which found itself politically and socially in an inferior position to the aristocracy. The government and church naturally vigorously fought the heretics.

Still, Bulgaria during Peter's reign enjoyed an age of prosperity. The tsar in turn gave many benefits to the clergy, building new churches and founding monasteries. Some viewed his lavish gifts as excessive, leading to corruption. One cleric who did not live in luxury was the holy hermit and ascetic St. John of Rila, who dwelled in a cave in the high Rila Mountains south of Sredetz. Even the tsar took note of him for his reputation of good works and the miracles attributed to him. After his death, the faithful erected a renowned monastery near his cave, which is regarded today as one of Bulgaria's greatest historical monuments.

Peter married Irene Lakapena, a member of the Byzantine imperial family, which helped maintain peaceful relations between the empires. However, on her death in 963, the emperor Nikephoros II, dismayed over Bulgaria's alliance with the Magyars, stopped paying tribute and threatened war. Nikephoros did not attack but persuaded the Grand Prince of Kiev, Sviatislav, to attack the Bulgarians from the north. Sviatislav seized a number of fortresses, but Peter's allies the Pechenegs drew him off. In the meantime, Peter patched up his dispute with Nikephoros, signing a new treaty that included the marriage of two Byzantine princes to Peter's daughters. In 969, Sviatislav attacked again and occupied Preslav. The tsar suffered a stroke, and the boyars forced him to abdicate in favor of his son Boris II and retire to a monastery. He died the following year.

Peter's reputation is mixed. Contemporaries admired him for ruling his country in peace and prosperity and for his generosity to the clergy. The Bulgarian church canonized him. Some historians have depicted him as a weakling when compared to his father Simeon, the great warrior, and especially with a view to the defeats of his last years. However, other modern historians have reappraised his reign as a successful period in Bulgaria's past.

SAMUIL

Sviatislav forced Boris to add his army to the multiethnic force he now commanded, including East Slavs, Maygars, and Pechenegs in their war against the Byzantine army. However, despite their numbers, the Greeks, led by Emperor John I (Tzimiskes), defeated them and captured Preslav. John stripped Boris of his titles, added Bulgaria to his empire, and took Boris and his brother Roman back to Constantinople as captives. Not all the Bulgarian governors agreed with the Byzantine occupation, especially the governor of Sredetz, Samuil. He and his brothers, also governors, worked together for their own benefit as well as that of the state. In the following years, they proved well able to stand up against the Greeks. With northeastern Bulgaria devastated by Tzimiskes, the brothers shifted the center of power to the southwest, their bailiwick.

Basil II, who succeeded his uncle John Tzimiskes in 976, immediately sent a new army to deal with the brothers, but his main concern was a rebellion by a Greek commander in Asia Minor. Samuil and his brother Aron (his other brothers had died) were able to hold off the Greeks. Roman, who had escaped from Constantinople and was now tsar but childless, gave up the throne to Samuil in 978.

Samuil was the last emperor of the First Bulgarian Empire, and he spent his reign in wars against the Byzantine emperor Basil II. Samuil liberated northern Bulgaria and for 10 years raided Byzantine Thrace and Greece. In 986, Basil was ready to face the Bulgarians and marched through Philippoupolis to Sredetz, Samuil's home base. However, he made too many mistakes to take the city. He divided his troops, leaving a contingent behind to guard his rear. The Bulgarians burned their crops and even managed to steal the cattle the Greeks brought with them, cutting off the Byzantine food supply. The commanders placed their siege equipment in the wrong place and Bulgarians were able to destroy it. The siege lasted less then three weeks before Basil retreated. Furthermore, the commander he left in the rear went back to Philippoupolis, and Basil believed he was going to challenge him for the throne. Samuil, who had been fighting in Thrace, caught the emperor at the Gates of Trajan, a fortification outside of Sredetz. Here rumors and fear overtook the Byzantine troops, throwing them into despair. The Bulgarians seized their opportunity, rushing the Greek camp and winning a great victory, but Basil managed to escape, although the valuables he had brought with him fell to the Bulgarians.

Samuil followed up his victory with more raids into the empire, not only Thrace and Macedonia but also down into the Greek peninsula as far as the Peloponnesian cities and to the Adriatic, capturing Dyrachachium (modern Durrës). He also defeated the Serbs and Hungarians. In 990, he moved his capital to Ohrid in western Macedonia. The city became the seat of the Bulgarian Patriarchate as well. In fact, Samuil, unable during the wars to regain recognition of the imperial crown, asked and perhaps received acknowledgement of his titles from Pope Gregory V. (The church was still nominally united and did not reach an irreparable breach between Eastern and Western Christianity until 1054.)

In 988, Samuil attacked the Serbs to prevent them from joining Basil. The Serbian prince, Jovan Vladimir, retreated into the mountains. Samuil then divided his force—one part to continue the fight against Prince Jovan and the bulk to attack the port of Ulcinj. Jovan refused Samuil's entreaty for his surrender, but a number of Serbian noblemen went over to the Bulgarians in light of the hopelessness of their cause, and Samuil took Jovan prisoner. The tsar then marched up the Adriatic coast through Dalmatia, capturing Kotor and laying waste to the towns and villages around Dubrovnik, although he failed to take the city. He then proceeded into Bosnia and Croatia, where rival dukes were in constant warfare. Siding with some against the others, he was able to win the dukes over as his vassals.

Meanwhile, he allowed his daughter Theodora to marry Prince Jovan, her father's prisoner, who had won her love. Samuil restored Jovan's lands and made him his vassal. He also made a treaty with Hungary by having his son Gavril Radomir marry the daughter of the Magyar grand prince Geza. Thus becoming the master of Bulgaria, Macedonia, Thrace, Serbia, Bosnia, and Croatia, he brought his empire to a renewed height by the end of the century, reversing the disasters of the last years of Peter and the reigns of Boris II and Roman and rivaling the achievements of Simeon.

All this turned from success to failure as the eleventh century opened. Basil, determined to follow up on his uncle's triumphs and reconquer Bulgaria, diverted his forces from his war with the Moslems to attack Samuil. In 1001, he sent a large force to capture the Bulgarian fortresses north of the Balkan Mountains, capturing the old capitals of Pliska and Preslav. The following year, the Byzantines marched to the west, retaking Thessaly. Samuil's' commander Dobromir, related to the tsar by marriage, surrendered and joined his troops to Basil's. Samuil was now on the defensive, and eventually the Greek emperor was able to retake Thessaly and resettle the Bulgarian population farther north.

Samuil's relations with the Hungarians also deteriorated. After Geza died, the Bulgarian tsar supported the rivals of his son, the glorious St. Stephen, regarded as the founder of modern Hungary. The marriage of Samuil's son Gavril to Geza's daughter was dissolved. Stephen, along with the Byzantines, attacked Bulgarian territory on the Danube, and Hungary replaced Bulgaria north of the river.

The war of attrition continued for another decade. Each year Basil would raid into the Bulgarian lands, pillaging the villages. The usual Greek path was north through the Struma River valley, so in 1014, Samuil decided to take a decisive stand at the village significantly named Kliuch, "the key," the gateway to the valley.

Samuil fortified the approaches to the village with wooden walls and stationed an army of more than 15,000 men behind it. While certainly not comparable to the massive walls of Constantinople nor even the fortifications of the Bulgarian capitals, they were strong enough to cause Basil difficulties, and the Greeks suffered many losses in their attempts to breach them.

Despite the Greeks' difficulties, at the end of July, Nikephoros Xiphias, the Byzantine governor of Plovdiv, managed to lead his troops around the walls and attack the Bulgarians from behind. The Bulgarians left their defenses to face the new threat, finally giving Basil an opportunity to break through. The Byzantine army killed thousands of the Bulgarians and took thousands more prisoner, but Samuil managed to escape with the aid of his son Gabriel, who gave up his own horse to his father.

Basil then abandoned his march north, but on the retreat he managed to capture Melnik, another important fortress protecting the route. According to the contemporary accounts, Basil blinded all thousands of the Bulgarian captives, leaving one in a hundred with one eye to lead the others back home. He accomplished this cruelty either as a punishment for the revolt against him, as he regarded himself as their sovereign, or in retaliation for the killing of a Greek commander. The legend further has it that on seeing the pitiful sight when the soldiers returned, Samuel died of a heart attack in October 1014. The war, however, continued with Samuil's son Gabriel Radomir leading the empire. In 1015, Ivan Vladislav, Samuil's nephew, conspired with Byzantine agents to murder Gabriel and took the throne himself. He also murdered his brother-in-law Jovan Vladimir, the duke of Zeta (present-day Montenegro). He did not conclude a peace with Basil but continued the war. However, the losses were too much to bear. Many Bulgarian governors and commanders went over to the Byzantines. In 1018, Basil dealt the decisive blow at Dyrrhachium (modern Durrës). Ivan mortally fell in the battle and his army retreated. The remaining governors and commanders surrendered, and Basil incorporated Bulgaria up to the Danube into his empire, restoring the lands that had been lost since the seventh century. He was awarded the appellation *Bulgaroktonos*, Basil the Bulgarslayer.

This state, this empire, which endured from the arrival of Asparuch to the death of Ivan Vladislav and held at various times territory stretching from the lands of the modern countries of Greece to Hungary, from Albania and Croatia to the Ukraine, historians call the First Bulgarian Empire. Modern Bulgarians have accepted it as the beginning of their national history (although they also like to claim kinship to other peoples that lived there before the arrival of Asparuch, including the mythological Orpheus and the historical Aristotle). This does not preclude others from also laying claim to the state, especially the Slavic Macedonians, who justifiably point out that Samuil had his capital and the church patriarchate in Ohrid. Two modern nations claiming the same past is certainly not unique. Both the Ukrainians and Russians claim Kievan Rus as their medieval legacy. History is not simply the chronology of past events but also how those events affect the present and how persons in the present interpret those events. The First Empire has certainly affected the modern Bulgarian nation. Krum remains a very popular Bulgarian name. Bulgarian literature, culture, and art still glorify its medieval past. By 1018, after three and half centuries, the core of a nation existed with a culture based on the amalgamation of two major ethnicities—the Bulgars and the South Slavs—and contributions from a number of others, including the Thracians who lived there before either of the former two. The population spoke a South Slavic language, wrote in a version of an alphabet created for that language, and practiced the eastern version of Christianity. This was the legacy that the empire left for future generations of Bulgaria.

2

The Second Bulgarian Empire (1018–1393)

Basil lived only a few more years, and then after a short reign by his brother, the empire fell into a half century of chaos, intrigue, and civil war marvelously described by the Byzantine historian Michael Psellus. Basil's nieces Zoe and Theodora, the former's various consorts, and other interlopers ruled off and on until Alexios I Komnenuos ascended the throne in 1081 and established the more stable Komnenid dynasty. After Basil's victory, the emperor initially incorporated Bulgaria into several provinces called themes. The Byzantine aristocracy absorbed the boyars. The Bulgarian church retained its autonomous status, remaining in Ohrid, but as a bishopric rather than a patriarchate. Thus Macedonia remained part of Bulgaria. Constantinople left the Bulgarian tax and land-owning laws intact as well. Bulgarians filled the ranks of the military in the themes. Gradually, however, the emperors passed rule of the land over to Greeks. They shifted Bulgarian boyars to other lands in the empire or bought them out. Greek clerics filled the posts in the churches. Many of the Greeks that came into the Byzantine themes treated their positions as temporary sinecures and had as their first priority exploiting the available wealth. Romanos II (reigned 1028–1034) replaced the Bulgarian tax code with the harsher Byzantine system.

DELYAN'S REVOLT

In 1040, Peter Delyan, claiming to be the son of Gabriel Radomir and hence the grandson of Tsar Samuil, raised the standard of revolt in Belgrade. However, scholars cannot confirm his ancestry. Perhaps he may have been the son of Marguerite, Gabriel's Hungarian wife, which would have made him the nephew of St. Stephen as well. However, some believing that a son of Radomir could not have escaped the murders carried out by Ivan Vladislav think him to be an imposter making the claims to add weight to his rebellion. Delyan had been one of the Bulgarians taken captive after Basil's victory and was a servant to a Byzantine aristocrat. When he escaped, he fled to Belgrade on the Bulgarian-Hungarian border.

Here Delyan won support of the local Bulgarians dissatisfied with Byzantine rule and adopted the name of the sainted tsar Peter I. At the head of a growing army of Bulgarian rebels, Peter moved southward toward Ohrid, killing Byzantine officials along the way. At the same time the boyar Tikhomir, an experienced warrior from Dyrrhachium who heard of the revolt, had himself declared tsar and led a second army eastward to Ohrid. The two armies met and Peter and Tikhomir both appealed to the assemblage to choose which one should rule. Peter's eloquence won the day and the Bulgarians chose him; he then executed Tikhomir. The enlarged army gathered more rebellious Bulgarians and captured territory from Albania, Macedonia, and deep into Greece as far as Corinth.

Another pretender to the crown Alusian, a grandson of Samuil's brother Aron, arose in Armenia, where the Byzantines had transported many Bulgarians after the fall of the First Empire. He had been a governor of an Armenian theme but lost favor during the many twists and turns of the notorious Byzantine intrigues. Learning of the rebellion in the Balkans, he clandestinely made his way to Delyan's camp, where the pretender welcomed him as a cousin and put him in charge of a large force of 40,000 men assigned to attack Thessaloniki. The venture failed, and Alusian lost more than a third of his army.

Relations between the cousins deteriorated, and Peter suspected Alusian of treason. Alusian feared Peter conspired against him. He invited Delyan to a feast and, waiting until the tsar was drunk, had his followers fall on him and take out his eyes. Alusian now took over the revolt, but losing in battle again, he went over to the Byzantines. Emperor Michael V now gathered a large army of Greeks and mercenaries and put down the revolt, decisively defeating the Bulgarians led by the blind Peter Delyan at the Battle of Ostrovo in 1041. The fate of Delyan remains unknown. In the following weeks, the Greeks suppressed the remainder of the rebels.

THE ASENIDS

Toward the end of the century, a number of new revolts broke out, but the Byzantine emperors were able to quash them. The most important was in Skopje led by Georgi Votekh and Prince Michael of Zeta. After initial success in Skopje and elsewhere, however, the Byzantine forces suppressed the uprising. Constantinople suffered more serious problems with the conquest of its southern Italian lands by the Normans and its Middle Eastern territories by the Moslems. Alexios I gave up on hopes for Italy, but he asked for help from the West in retaking Syria and Palestine. The result was the Crusades. The Western crusaders who came east beginning in 1096 came not to return the lands to the Byzantine emperors but rather grab the Moslem (and some Middle Eastern Christian) lands for themselves. The crusading masses in the eleventh and twelfth centuries marched through Bulgaria despoiling the land, believing that because they were on a holy cause, they had the right to take what they needed without payment. By the end of the century, Byzantine rule in Bulgaria was almost nominal and the local Bulgarian aristocracy, in essence warlords, took over.

In the 1180s, a new series of tax riots broke out over levies imposed to finance the marriage of Isaac II of the new Byzantine Angelid dynasty to a Hungarian princess. Two noblemen, the brothers Ivan Asen and Todor, requested that Isaac appoint them autonomous governors of all the Bulgarian lands. The brothers' origins and ethnicity are obscure. Bulgarians maintain that they were descendents of the tsars of the First Empire and therefore had the right to rule as tsars themselves. However, others have raised doubts, especially the Romanians, who claim they were Vlachs and hence related to them.

When Isaac turned down the brothers' request, they returned home and took the lead of the rebels, declaring the older, Todor, tsar Peter II. However, Ivan Asen led the military campaigns and left his name to the new dynasty, the Asenids. With the Angelids engaged in a dynastic struggle, the Bulgarians had great success raiding into Thrace and reestablishing the Bulgarian Empire. The brothers established their capital in the picturesque town of Great Turnovo on the meandering Iantra River. A replica of the castle was built in the late twentieth century and the Bulgarian tourist agency exhibits a laser light show to demonstrate to native and foreign tourists its pride in its Medieval past.

Asen, too, was given the title of tsar in 1188, the two brothers ruling together. The war against the Greeks continued for a decade, during which despite several reverses the tsars were able to consolidate their rule. In 1196, however, Asen was assassinated by a relative angered over a private matter, and assassins also murdered Peter the following year. The throne next fell to a younger brother, Kaloian, who continued the war against the Byzantines, capturing Macedonia and Greek cities along the Black Sea coast and defeating the Hungarian allies of Constantinople, adding land north of the Danube to his empire.

KALOIAN

Kaloian began negotiations with both Pope Innocent III and Emperor Alexios III for recognition of his title. The churches had by now split and the rivals were anxious to have the new powerful ruler on their respective sides. Thus Kaloian received recognition from both. Furthermore, the Byzantine Empire met with disaster. The Angelid family squabble brought in the crusaders of the infamous Fourth Crusade, who, instead of going on to Palestine after restoring their Angelid sponsors, installed one of their own, Baldwin of Flanders, as Emperor Baldwin I of the Latin Empire, which lasted in Constantinople until 1265. The Byzantine themes now became more than a dozen feudal fiefs in the Western style awarded to other crusader nobles, now vassals of Baldwin. In addition, other powerful states grew on the borders of the Byzantine Empire. The Greek emperors established their new empire in Nicea across the Bosporus until their return to Constantinople in 1265. The Ottoman Turks would appear later in the century. The Norman kingdom of Sicily also staked it claims. The Republics of Venice and Dubrovnik (Ragusa) appeared as wealthy mercantile states. The Serbian kingdom reached its zenith, and there were even more that would complicate the affairs of the Balkans and the Eastern Mediterranean, making it one of the most vexing shatter belts of world geopolitics for the rest of history.

Kaloian sent envoys to draw up the border between Bulgaria and the new empire, but Baldwin contemptuously dismissed them and vowed that he would retake the renegade state. Kaloian's appeal to Pope Innocent III was of no use because he had already condemned the crusaders for their attacks on Christian states. The Bulgarian tsar then fomented a revolt among the Greek nobles of Thrace, and when Baldwin marched to Adrianople, he found the city loyal to Kaloian, who soon arrived with his army. The Latin troops then attacked the Bulgarian forces but suffered a humiliating defeat. Kaloian captured Baldwin and carried him off to Turnovo, where he died (perhaps being executed). Legend has it, however, that the tsar imprisoned him in his castle, a remnant of which, as mentioned above, survived through the centuries, and the locals called one part of the edifice "Baldwin's tower."

Kaloian followed his victory with further attacks on the Latin Empire, conquering all of Thrace. Boniface of Montferrat, the king of Thessalonki, the last surviving leader of the Fourth Crusade, died in the battle. However, Kaloian himself died as well, perhaps murdered by one of his own allies. His nephew Boril (reigned 1208–1217) succeeded him.

However, while Kaloian's reign ranks as one of the greatest and most celebrated in Bulgarian medieval history, his nephew's was a significant disappointment. His ineptitude in political and military affairs led to the loss of Thrace and an invitation to invasion from both the Latins and Hungarians, only resolved by papal mediation and diplomatic marriages. In Bulgaria itself, a number of governors unhappy with the tsar and suspecting him of being involved in the demise of Kaloian plotted against him in 1217. Ivan Asen's son overthrew Boril and assumed the crown as Ivan Asen II.

Tsar Asen was able to restore Bulgarian territory by diplomatic treaties, including his marriage to a Hungarian princess. When a Greek pretender to the Byzantine throne attacked him from Epirus on the Adriatic coast, Asen defeated this foe and restored Bulgarian power in the western Balkans. The Second Empire became a force to be reckoned with in European affairs and a commercial epicenter for southeast Europe. The decline of the church in Constantinople and Kiev made the Bulgarian patriarchate an ecclesiastical power as well. However, his successors could not hold the state's dominant position. Bulgaria not only suffered from internal revolts and coups but also faced foreign enemies again, especially the restored Byzantine Empire and the Mongols, whose raids were devastating all of Eastern Europe.

The Bulgarians kept their lands intact, although they paid tribute to the Mongols and fought them in a number of battles. In 1277, one Ivailo defeated the Mongols and briefly became tsar. His importance is not his reign but his legend. Although his origin is obscure, and he may even have been a boyar, the Bulgarian myth is that he was a peasant. The story of the peasant king resonated to modern times when the country had no native aristocracy, and everyone was of peasant origin. Thus they placed the mantle of hero around Ivailo's shoulders.

IVAN ALEXANDER

At the beginning of the fourteenth century, Mongol control over Bulgaria loosened, and the new tsar Todor Svetoslav (reigned 1300–1322) defeated the weakening Byzantine Empire, restoring Bulgaria to its former strength. In 1331, Ivan Alexander, the governor of Lovech, descended from the Asens on his mother's side, assumed the throne after a dynastic struggle. Under him the empire reached a new peak, its last in the Middle Ages. Having trade connections with the Italian and Adriatic mercantile republics, Turnovo became a cosmopolitan commercial and cultural center. Indeed, the tsar sent his first wife to a convent and chose a new bride, Sara, from the large Jewish mercantile community in the capital. Unhappily, however, Sara—or Theodora, as she was called after her conversion to the Christian faith—was not kind to her former coreligionists and joined the priests and bishops in their campaign against Jewish influence. Turnovo at this time was also a major religious and cultural center with many churches and monasteries. The most famous religious artifact of Medieval Bulgaria is Tsar Ivan Alexander's Tetraevangelia, the four gospels, illustrated and translated into Medieval Bulgarian. One of the illustrations is that of the tsar and his second wife Sara-Theodora and their two sons. The tsar had several sons, whom he established as corulers, and several daughters, one of whom married the Byzantine emperor Andronikos IV Paleaologus and another who was sent off as a hostage concubine to Sultan Murad IV of the Ottoman Turks.

The latter now became the major factor in the power struggle of the Balkans. While the remnants of the Latin Empire, the various Slavic lords, the Italian princes, the Hungarians, and others fought each other for territory and influence, the Turks gradually increased their hold on Asia Minor and then Europe. The struggle would reach its culmination in 1453, when after his predecessors had conquered virtually all of the Balkans, Sultan Mehmed II finally took the decrepit Byzantine capital. The struggle among the Christians took the form of a religious battle over loyalty to Pope or Greek emperor symbolized by which version of the Apostles' Creed their subjects should follow. (The difference centered merely on a three-letter suffix of a single word.) However, the real issues were wealth, land, and power, and the kings, dukes,

Tsar Ivan Alexander, Tsarina Theodora (Sara) and sons from his Tetraevangelia. (StockPhotoPro/The British Library)

and lords would change church and alliance as the politics dictated. The fratricidal struggle gave the Turks ample opportunity to move in and take over.

Ivan Alexander, as did all other rulers, took part in these wars and intrigues. Sending Kera Tamara, his daughter, off to Murad's harem was just another alliance. Obviously, political *realpolitik* took precedence over religious conviction. To deal with the complex situation resulting from the fragmentation of power in the Balkans in 1356, Ivan Alexander set up his son Ivan Strashimir as independent tsar of Vidin in northwest Bulgaria.

In 1363, the Turks established their base in Europe in Adrianople (Edirne) and the next year invaded Bulgaria and captured Thrace, including the important center of Philippoupolis (Plovdiv). A coalition of Bulgarians and Serbs prepared to meet the Turks in battle in 1371. Ivan Alexander died before the conflict began, and the Turks won a great victory at Chernomen near Adrianople. Ivan Shishman succeeded his father as tsar of Bulgaria in Turnovo. The Ottomans followed up their victory with new incursions into the Christian states, forcing Ivan Shishman into vassalage. The princes and rulers of Hungary and the Italian states and cities also moved in for the kill, taking over parts of the area. The Turks won a crucial and a legendary victory against the powerful Serbs in 1389 at Kosovo Field. They followed this up by capturing Turnovo in 1393 and Vidin in 1396. Although a few Bulgarian commanders were able to hold out for a few more years, the Second Empire came to an end.

3

Bulgarian Revival (1393–1878)

BULGARIA UNDER THE OTTOMANS

The Ottoman conquest of the Balkans provided a degree of security for its inhabitants, even though the Turks continued their military campaigns. They regularly marched north through Bulgarian lands while Christian armies invaded southward, as in the crusades of John Hunyadi of Hungary in the 1440s. The constant warfare between the numerous princes and the ever-changing borders and alliances that preceded the Turkish takeover continued. The Turks divided the conquered peoples into religious communities called millets, which handled many of their internal affairs. Thus, Bulgarians were part of the Orthodox millet, which also included the Greeks, many of whom lived in the coastal cities. In addition, there were other ethnicities in Bulgaria. However, modern Bulgaria is more ethnically homogenous than other Balkan countries. Greeks, Jews, and Armenians moved into the Bulgarian cities as tradesmen and artisans, and much of the commercial activity that characterized the Second Empire remained. Furthermore, the sultans welcomed the Sephardic Jews expelled from Spain in 1492 into the Ottoman Empire. Thessaloniki became a Jewish city, and many of their brethren moved into Sofia, Plovdiv, Varna, and other Bulgarian cities. The Jews and Armenian Christians had their own millets. The Bulgarians and Greeks, as mentioned above, belonged to the same millet and were controlled by the Greek Orthodox patriarch in Istanbul—the Turks' name for Constantinople, literally "the city." Greek liturgy replaced Old Church Slavonic in Bulgarian churches, and Greek clergy were sent to officiate in these churches. However, some remnants of Slavic culture remained alive in monasteries such as Rila and Bachkovo.

Most of the peasants were Bulgarians. The native aristocracy disappeared. However, some minor chiefs remained, though under Turkish control. Now the Turks were the lords. A feudal aristocracy called *spahi* (knights) served as the Turkish cavalry and ruled over estates called *timars*. The *spahi* provided laborers from the peasantry as the state needed them. Ottoman officials, *beys*, administered the territory. While forced conversion to Islam occurred on rare occasions, the amount of voluntary conversion was significant. Nobles and even whole communities who wanted to retain their property became Moslems. They kept, however, their Bulgarian tongue. Today's Pomaks may trace their roots to those Bulgarian converts in Thrace.

Life under the Turks could be harsh. The *devshirme*, a gathering up of European Christian children, occurred at regular intervals. The Ottomans selected boys from 7 to 14 and converted them to Islam. The brightest of the boys became the sultan's civil administration and often held the higher posts, including that of grand vizier. Since this was a life that a Balkan peasant could only dream of obtaining, it was not unusual for the Christians' Moslem neighbors to sometimes try to substitute their own children for the collection. The remainder of the boys entered the famous Janissary corps, the infantry of the Turkish army. Since the civil servants and janissaries were the slaves of the sultans, they could not employ freeborn Moslems. Girls, too, were sometimes taken for the harems of the sultan and the *beys*. Thus they became concubines and mothers of future sultans.

To escape Ottoman rule, whole villages of Bulgarians sometimes left the country for other Orthodox lands. Large numbers went to Bessarabia (modern-day Moldova). Others resisted. Significant uprisings occurred, usually in conjunction with the wars between the European countries and the Turks. Of particular note were the uprisings of the 1680s, which were connected with the climactic struggle between the Turks and the Christian coalition led by Austria. The failure of the Turks to take Vienna a second time in 1683 led to a change in the balance of power. For the next two and a half centuries, the Ottomans found themselves on the defensive.

DECLINE OF THE EMPIRE

Inside the empire, things changed. The sultans became more and more isolated inside the palace and the chambers of the harem. The "wives" and mothers of the sultan, the eunuchs who guarded them, and government officials thus controlled the Sublime Porte, the Ottoman government. Many if not most of these women and officials were the children gathered in the *devshirme* or their descendents. Outside of Istanbul, the sultan's power waned as well, and the *beys* who ruled the provinces became virtually independent. By the early nineteenth century, Bulgaria, like the rest of the Balkans, was ruled by warlords and autonomous *beys*. The *timor* system became less important as private individuals found ways to own land. New estates called *chifliks* arose. For Bulgarians, this meant harsher conditions. Landlords demanded new obligations in addition to government taxes often collected by corrupt tax gatherers. A number of men reacted by turning to banditry. These *haiduks*, or highwaymen, fell on the rich merchants, Turkish or not. Bulgarians have mythologized these folk heroes as Robin Hoods whose exploits helped preserve the country's spirit and bring about its independence. One of Bulgaria's favorite folk songs, "Hadji Dimitur," by the renowned poet Hristo Botev (1848–1876), celebrates such a *haiduk*.

During the two centuries of Ottoman decline, Bulgaria, the closest province to Istanbul, increased its commercial wealth. Bulgarian artisans and merchants rose in stature, especially dealers of wool, tobacco, and rose oil. Artisans appeared in the towns and villages, forming various guilds and building shops.

In the eighteenth century, the Turks fought a series of unsuccessful wars with the Austrians and Russians. In 1774, the Treaty of Kuchuk-Kainardzhi gave St. Petersburg the right to intervene on behalf of the Orthodox Christians in the Balkans. The Bulgarians, therefore, looked to Russia as a protector. However, Orthodox Christianity in the Ottoman Empire remained in the hands of the Greeks, who had nationalistic stirrings of their own. By mid-century, many Bulgarians had become enamored with Greek nationalism, having yet no national identity of their own. The Greek clergy furthermore pushed to suppress the Slavic elements under their control. The patriarch in Istanbul abolished whatever independent and autonomous patriarchates and bishoprics there were. Orthodox Patriarch Samuel ordered the burning of Slavonic liturgical texts. Yet a number of religious books, especially those written by monks for the common people, circulated through the seventeenth and eighteenth centuries. These used Bulgarian rather than Old Church Slavonic. There were also a few histories.

PAISII AND SOFRONII

One of these histories found its way to the Zograf monastery, established by monks from Turnovo, located on Mt. Athos in Greece, a holy retreat. In the 1760s, a Bulgarian monk named Paisii, who lived at the Hilendar monastery at Athos, used it to write his landmark book: *A Slavonic-Bulgarian History of the People, Tsars, Saints, and of all their Deeds and the Bulgarian Way of Life*. In it he urged Bulgarians to remember their past.

Paiisi left the monastery to travel around the country and preach his message of Bulgarian nationalism. His disciple Stoicho Vladislavov, better known by his clerical name Sofronii Vrachanski, the son of a wealthy cattle drover who studied with Paisii on Athos, became the bishop of Vratsa. There he also preached the message. Sofronii defied the Greek clergy and preached in Bulgarian. Others also promoted the need for Bulgarians to remember their past and honor their culture, but the effort was slow and only began to show results in the nineteenth century after both Serbia in 1804 and Greece in 1829 established states independent from Constantinople.

From 1700 to 1860, Russia and Turkey fought seven wars that involved battles on Bulgarian soil. The disruptions of this incessant warfare caused, on the one hand, the displacement of the Bulgarian populations. In some cases, even some migrations of whole villages occurred within and outside of the country. On the other hand, Bulgaria came in contact with foreign modernizing forces.

OTTOMAN REFORM

In particular, the bond between Russia and Bulgaria mentioned above grew stronger. Beginning in 1792 with the sultanate of Selim III, the Porte began its attempts at reform (*Tanzimat*). This movement reached a critical point during the Greek War of Independence under Mahmud II.

Mahmud's destruction in 1826 of the Janissary corps, which had by that time evolved from a devoted military corps to a virtual independent disruptive element, heralded a new day in Turkey. Then followed two major edicts of reform—the *Hatt-i-Sherif* of Gülhane in 1839 and the *Hatt-ı Hümayun* in 1856. The reforms were in part a response to international demands but also were pushed by a growing number of younger Turkish intellectuals. The latter saw the only hope for the decaying empire in modernization and allowing Christians to enjoy the same rights as Moslems.

Now Bulgarians could own property, and soon a class of small farmers populated the land. The old Slavic tradition of communal farming (*zadrugi*) remained only a minor element in the Bulgarian countryside. Furthermore, as the century wore on and the countries of European Turkey gained their independence, Bulgaria and Macedonia remained key economic resources of the empire. In the 1860s, one of Turkey's greatest statemen and reformers, Midhat Pasha, was governor in Bulgaria. He further encouraged the small farmers by extending cheap credit. The institution he created has evolved and remained through all the various state changes into the twenty-first century as the Bulgarian Agricultural Bank.

The Turkish reformers hoped that not only modernization but also tolerance would preserve the empire, but they were fighting a losing battle. The new driving force in Europe was nationalism—nationalism linked in the early nineteenth century to classical liberalism. The French Revolution ignited the spark and the French Emperor Napoleon Bonaparte fanned it into a flame that spread throughout the continent.

THE EMERGENCE OF BULGARIAN NATIONALISM

Count Klemens von Metternech of Austria hoped to reverse the nationalistic tide with his Concert of Europe, created in 1815 at the Congress of Vienna after Bonaparte's defeat. His vision of a restored *Ancien Regime* (Europe before the French Revolution), however, failed.

The drive for constitutional nation-states would continue throughout the nineteenth and twentieth centuries. The great autocratic multinational powers of Eastern Europe could not hold it back no matter what they tried. Russia hoped to do so by a policy of Russification, turning all ethnicities into Russians. It failed. Austria and the Ottomans tried tolerance, allowing cultural diversity but keeping autocratic nonconstitutional rule. It failed as well. Nationalism is an ideology based on common cultural characteristics and sentiments. In the nineteenth and twentieth centuries, these were primarily based on language, but other factors—such as religion, perceived historical memories, and geographical concentration—played a role. The national myth assumes that all members of the nation have a common ancestry. The nations of Europe in the nineteenth century desired above all the formation of independent nation-states. The now wealthy and mature bourgeoisie—the middle class—who were the core of the nationalist movement fuel by the ideas French Revoltuion wished the states to be based on liberal constitutions. An independent state can determine which dialect will be the language of the nation. "A language is a dialect with an army and a navy" is a common aphorism that bears a kernel of truth. The state, after all, can establish an education system that will teach its children the "proper" language and the "correct" history of its nation. The middle class turned the national and liberal constitutional ideologies into political action, which culminated in the revolutions of 1830 and 1848.

In Germany and Italy, nationalism and liberalism led to successful movements for unification of the dozens autocratic states and dependencies left over from the *Ancien Regime* or established by the Congress of Vienna. If the Germans and Italians could create nation-states based on a common culture and ancestry, despite various dialects and regional customs, some Slavs believed that they, too, could build a common nation-state based on their common "language," that Russian, Polish, Serbian, Bulgarian, and all the other Slavic languages were perhaps dialects ready to be changed to one language. The revolutions of 1848 had only minor repercussions in the Balkans, but Balkan representatives came to the Pan-Slav Congress in Prague that year to discuss a united Slavic nation. However, the Slavs proved too diverse. They had no vibrant middle class to carry the torch as the Germans had in 1848 and no leading state—like Prussia in Germany and Savoy in Italy—capable of accomplishing the task later on. Some looked to Russia, but others, like the Poles oppressed under Russia, objected. When Russians did take up the cause in the 1860s and 1870s, concentrating, as we shall see, on Serbia and Bulgaria, the other great powers prevented it, although modern political scientists argue that the "Soviet Empire" of post-World War II Europe reflected the goals of the Pan-Slavic movement. A variety of Pan-Slavism, Yugoslavism—literally "South Slavism"—based on the kinship of the South Slavs, has had a more fruitful history. Yet with the failure of the Pan-Slavs to unite all Slavic peoples, about a dozen Slavic groups have emerged as nations in the nineteenth and twntieth centuries—all claiming the right of national identity and the right to a nation-state of some sort.

For Bulgaria, the national movement was spurred by the new reforms and improved economic situation and validated by the historical memory recalled by Paisii, Sofronii, and their followers. Under the new conditions, the Bulgarians built churches and schools in their towns and villages. Elected communal councils connected to the churches served as intermediaries between the townsfolk and the authorities—both Turkish adminstrators and Greek clergy. The wealthier peasants, called *chorbadzhi* (literally "meat-eaters") because they could afford richer fare for their meals, came to dominate the councils, and while they took up the Bulgarian cause, they were often villified by the common folk both out of jealously of their wealth and for sometimes neglecting the interests of the poor or exploiting them for their own benefit.

Another important aspect of the Bulgarian national movement was the establisment of an educational system. Before the nineteenth century, the only schools in Bulgaria were monastery schools emphasizing religion. A few of these located in towns began teaching other subjects as well. At the beginning of the nineteenth century, there were also Greek schools reflecting the Greek national movement. Wealthy Bulgarians enrolled their sons in them.

Starting in 1815, a number of Greek-Bulgarian secular schools were established, including one where the monk Neofit Bozveli (1745–1848), a student of Sofronii, became a teacher. While most of the lessons in these schools were in Greek, some Bulgarian was introduced, and many of the leaders of the national liberation movement attended these schools. The first secular high school opened in Gabrovo, a noted center of the wool industry. By mid-century, the towns across Bulgaria built schools for educating their children—both boys and girls—in Bulgarian. Foreign missionaries who began coming to Bulgaria in the mid-nineteenth century also established schools with lessons in their own languages: French, German, and English. Bulgaria was a popular place for the missionaries because they could more easily convert Bulgarians. The Turks would impose a capital sentence on anyone trying to convert a Moslem, while the Jews and Armenians rejected their efforts out of hand. The Bulgarians, dissatisfied with the Greek clergy, however, listened. While only a few converted, many more welcomed the schools they established. The American schools were especially favored because they offered a modern curriculum that included sciences, in contrast to the classical curriculum of the European schools. The American College (really a high school), founded in 1860, still operates today, although it was closed during the Communist period. The American Robert College in Istanbul, although a college preparatory school today, did offer higher education in the nineteenth century and was another favorite for Bulgarians going on to university. Before independence, many Bulgarian merchants sent their sons and a few daughters to be educated abroad. Although Russian universities were popular, more students actually went to other European countries and to Istanbul. In addition to the schools, the Bulgarians adopted the *chita-lishte* (reading rooms) from Serbia. These were places where people could sit and read or hear someone else read newspapers, books, and journals. They also provided classes in reading and writing. Together with cultural clubs and societies as well as libraries, these *chitalishte* spread across the county and helped foster a slowly growing literacy. Although only about 20 percent of the population, mostly male, was literate by the end of the nineteenth century, it was the highest percentage in the Balkans. From the first in 1861, Bulgarian Cyrillic printing presses also slowly appeared in Bulgaria, although a few earlier ones had been established in other cities in Turkey. Along with presses came newspapers. All these educational and cultural institutions prepared the way for the national revival and the demand for a nation-state.

THE STRUGGLE FOR A BULGARIAN CHURCH

However, the first move was not toward an independent country, but toward an independent church. A revived national Bulgarian church replaced the one dominated by Greek clergy. There had been autonomous and autocephalous churches in the empire in the past, but the Turkish authorities had united these for efficiency. In the 1830s, with the growing national movements, both the patriarch and sultan, under Russian pressure, permitted renewed autonomy for churches in Serbia and Greece, both independent states (although Serbia was still *de jure* part of the Ottoman Empire). At that time, the conflict between Bulgarians and the Greek clergy was at a high point, mainly over the venality of the clergy and the heavy tithing burden they put upon their congregations. The patriarch and the bishops smoothed things over for a while, but in the 1840s, the conflict flared up again. This time it had nationalistic overtones as the cultural revival made the Bulgarians sensitive to the inferior status in which they were being held by the Greeks. Many of the concessions that the clergy had earlier permitted—such as using Bulgarian in the liturgy—they now revoked. Furthermore, Bulgarian clergy who had studied in Russia were now prepared to move into clerical vacancies. When the patriarch insisted on nominating Greek clergy or only those Bulgarians willing to preach in Greek, protests and even riots broke out. The monk and educator Neofit Bozveli, whom the patriarch rejected as a bishop, led the call for Bulgarian religious autonomy. Ilarion Makariopolski (1812–1875), a leader of the Bulgarian community in Istanbul, supported Bozveli's request. Bozveli and Makariopolski presented a list of demands to the Porte, including a call for religious autonomy and a Bulgarian church to serve their community in Istanbul. The patriarch protested and exiled the pair to Mt. Athos. However, an influential Bulgarian group of manufacturers kept up the demand for a separate Bulgarian church in the Ottoman capital, which the sultan finally granted in 1849. It was named St. Stefan's.

The revolutionary fervor in Europe, the Crimean War, and the new reforms of 1856 fanned the flames of Bulgarian nationalism even more, and the call for an independent Bulgarian church became more and more strident. On Easter Sunday, 1860, Makariopolski, who was preaching mass in St. Stefan's, broke a time-honored custom. He prayed directly to God for the health of the sultan. By tradition, only the patriarch could offer such a prayer. Thus Makariopolski dramatically signaled Bulgarian ecclesiastical independence. Both the sultan and the patriarch refused to acknowledge this declaration for a decade, but by 1870 Sultan Abdül Aziz granted a Bulgarian Exarchate headquartered in Istanbul. In part, this was because of a war that Turkey then waged with Greece. The exarch was still under the patriarch. Nevertheless, the patriarch refused to recognize the exarchate and in 1872 declared the Bulgarian church schismatic. The first and only Bulgarian exarch was Antim I (born Atanas M. Chalukov, 1816–1888). After his death the post remained vacant. The exarchate covered not only Bulgaria but also Thrace and Macedonia, and the church could establish schools there. Over the next decades, South Slavic children would grow up in those regions learning that they were Bulgarians, a point that seethes with controversy even today.

THE APRIL UPRISING

Many Bulgarians, particularly the *chorbadzhi*, the wealthy merchants, were satisfied with religious independence. Commercial opportunities for Bulgaria, after all, had increased with the empire's loss of other European territories. Therefore, they did not push for an independent Bulgarian nation-state. Nevertheless, a vibrant movement for complete independence had arisen in the land. Radical journalists like Georgi Rakovski (1821–1867) and Liuben Karavelov (1834–1869) spread the word, while the daring exploits of *haiduks* like Hadzhi Dimitur (1840–1868), Stefan Karadzha (1840–1868), and Philip Tot'o (1830–1907) inspired the masses. They were, after all, fighting now for Bulgarian independence, not just personal gain. Bulgarians at home and abroad formed secret societies and planned for rebellion. In 1862, Rakovski founded a Bulgarian Legion in Belgrade with hopes of stirring up military action against the Turks, but the Serbs expelled him. He then set up the Secret Central Bulgarian Committee to continue his plan and aid the *haiduks*.

Although these initial efforts failed, other leaders emerged. Prince Michael of Serbia, who wanted a general uprising of the Slavs against the Ottomans in European Turkey, enlisted Bulgarians in his cause. His plans, however, ended with his mysterious assassination in 1868. Other committees were formed in Odessa, Bucharest, and Istanbul. Two were the most important: the Bulgarian Secret Central Committee (BSCC) in Bucharest and the even more influential Bulgarian Revolutionary Central Committee (BRCC). Karavelov and Vasil Levski (nee Vasil I. Kunchev, 1837–1873), the Apostle of Freedom, led the latter. It had branches in both Romania and Serbia and hundreds of followers in Bulgaria itself. Karavelov spent some time at the University of Moscow and in the 1860s had worked for Russian newspapers as a Balkan correspondent. Like Rakovski, he agitated for Bulgarian independence in Serbia; also like Rakovski, he ran into trouble with the authorities. He was swept up in the broad net of radicals after the assassination of Prince Michael and briefly sent to prison. He then went to Bucharest, where he met Levski and Hristo Botev. Levski would clandestinely travel through the country enlisting followers and assigning tasks to "apostles," preparing for the day of uprising. On one trip, the Turks caught and hanged him.

In the summer of 1875, while the Bulgarian revolutionaries were secretly preparing for an uprising, one broke out in Bosnia. Although

Vasil Levski. (Vasil Levski Museum—Karlovo)

the Great Powers tried to defuse the situation, the fires of rebellion spread, and the Bulgarians planned to act in the spring of 1876. When the Ottoman authorities got word of the plans, the rebels moved at once. The first shot occurred in the mountain village of Koprivsthitsa on May 2. However, the event is called the April Uprising because according to the religious Julian calendar then in use by the Bulgarians, the date was April 20. The Bulgarian rebels fared badly and the Turks soon subdued them. In another attempt at rebellion, Botev commandeered a ship on the Danube and, with a small detachment, invaded from the north, where his band was defeated and he was killed. According to some rumors, his own men did it. Some of the rebels raided the Moslem towns in Thrace. In retaliation, Ottoman irregular troops, the Bashi-Bazouks from the Caucuses, which were stationed there, pillaged the Bulgarian villages to the north, raping and murdering thousands. In Batak they burned down the church with the inhabitants huddled inside. Their bones are still on display for visitors today.

While the revolt in Bulgaria failed, the ones further west flourished. In the summer of 1876, Serbian and Montenegrin forces invaded Turkey. In Russia, the Pan-Slav movement also had received new life with the goal of uniting the Slavs under the tsar. One of the devotees to the Pan-Slav cause was the Russian ambassador in Constantinople, Nikolai Ignatiev, who aided the rebels with weapons and diplomacy. Russian Pan-Slavs surreptitiously sent arms to the rebels and spread propaganda on their behalf. Meanwhile, the Great Powers continued to press for a peaceful resolution. Tsar Alexander II refused to send the army into Turkey as the Pan-Slavs urged. The war went badly for the Slavs despite having Russian officers who had resigned their commissions to lead them. Furthermore, the English prime minister Benjamin Disraeli took up the cause of the new Sultan, Abdul Hamid II, and Midhat Pasha, now the Turkish vizier, in keeping the empire intact. The powers agreed to resolve the issue at a conference in Istanbul in December. By that time, the news of the massacres in Bulgaria had been revealed to the world in graphic fashion by the American newspaperman Januarius A. MacGahan (1844–1878). Bulgarian students at Robert College had told their professors of the massacres, and George Washburn, president of the school, brought the news to Eugene Schuyler, the American representative in Istanbul, who asked the British ambassador to investigate. Disraeli, anxious that nothing untoward come of this, arranged to have an inexperienced team investigate the charges. They, of course, found nothing serious. However, Washburn and Schuyler pressed the issue, and a more prepared group including MacGahan went to the villages. Soon the massacres became front-page news. Interest in the Balkans switched to the Bulgarians. English Liberal Party Leader William Gladstone used the "Bulgarian Horrors" in his attacks on Disraeli. When the Istanbul Conference failed, Tsar Alexander prepared for war. Beginning in June 1877, the Russian advance initially moved rapidly across the Danube. Thousands of Bulgarian volunteers joined them. British warships entered into the straits in order to prevent the fall of Istanbul, and a "jingoistic" atmosphere arose to fever pitch in London, where a war against Russia was expected. However, the Turks stymied the Russian advance at the battle of Pleven, and while the Bulgarian volunteers performed majestically at the Shipka pass in the Balkan mountains, the war was not concluded until the spring of 1878, leaving Istanbul in Ottoman hands.

Russia and Turkey signed a peace treaty, ending the war in the Istanbul suburb of San Stefano on March 3, 1878—today Bulgaria's national day. The treaty granted full independence to Serbia, Montenegro, and Romania, ceded Bessarabia and territory in the Caucuses to Russia, and granted autonomous status (*de facto* independence) to Bulgaria. Its boundaries would include the area of the exarchate, that is, not only the present-day boundaries of Bulgaria, but also Thrace and Macedonia. St. Petersburg must have realized that the treaty would not stand. They had created a large Bulgaria, which conflicted with treaties they had signed with Vienna before the war, so that concessions could more easily be made. However, for the Bulgarians the cry of "San Stefano Bulgaria" would echo for more than a century as an expression of their natural and historical right. However, as was expected, the Great Powers and Bulgaria's neighbors demanded a revision of the treaty. The powers met in June in Berlin, hosted by German chancellor Otto von Bismarck, who claimed to have no interest in the Balkans and would be an "honest broker."

The Congress of Berlin kept most of the Treaty of San Stefano intact except for the sections dealing with Bulgaria. The fear that an enlarged Bulgaria would upset the balance of power led to dividing the province into three parts. The northern section was to be autonomous as specified by San Stefano; a middle section, Eastern Rumelia, less autonomous with Plovdiv as its capital and a governor approved by the sultan and supervised by a commission with representatives of the Great Powers; and the southern section, Macedonia and Aegean Thrace, reincorporated into Turkey. Russia was to administer Bulgaria for nine months, and the Bulgarians were to elect a Christian prince approved by the powers but not a member of any of their ruling houses. Thus blessed by the powers, Bulgaria, after five centuries, reentered the panorama of nations.

4

Modern Bulgaria until the Balkan Wars (1878–1911)

THE TURNOVO CONSTITUTION

The first order of business in the new state was writing a constitution. The leaders of the revolution, the Liberals, now controlled politics as well. Unhappy with the Treaty of Berlin, they talked of boycotting the constitutional assembly, but cooler heads prevailed. General Prince Aleksander Dondukov-Korsakov, the Russian administrator, supervised convocation of the assembly, which met in the medieval capital of Turnovo, even though Sofia, centrally located in the San Stefano boundaries, had already been selected as the country's new capital. Most of the delegates were notables who took their seats *ex officio*. Dondukov-Korsakov appointed some. Only 89 of 231 were elected. The bishops were also seated in recognition of the role the church played in the liberation. However, the Treaty of Berlin had provisions requiring equality of religion, and the Moslem chief mufti and the Jewish grand rabbi also sat in the assembly. Indeed, the tolerant Bulgarians had no problem with this. Freedom of worship was guaranteed, even though the Turnovo Constitution, which the assembly drafted, recognized the Eastern

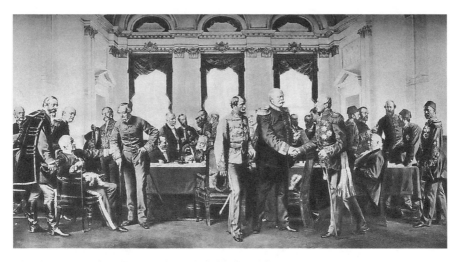

The Congress of Berlin which settled the fate of Bulgaria in 1878. (Singer, Isadore, ed. *The Jewish Encyclopedia*, 1901)

Orthodox Church as the state religion. Although the delegates were unhappy with the exclusion of Macedonia, this new rump Bulgaria was, for the Balkans, distinctly ethnically homogenous. Eighty percent of the population was Bulgarian. Turks were the largest minority, although many fled the war, especially the landlords. Only 16 members of the assembly were not ethnically Bulgarians. Most of these were Turks appointed by Dondukov-Korsakov. There were also representatives from Bulgarian communities in Eastern Rumelia and Macedonia as well as in Bessarabia and elsewhere.

The first days of the assembly were taken up denouncing the Treaty of Berlin and the exclusion of Eastern Rumelia and Macedonia. It was during these debates that the core of the Liberal Party emerged. It included Petko Karavelov (1843–1903), the brother of Liuben; Dragan Tsankov (1829–1911); and the poet Petko Slaveikov (1827–1895). All had played prominent roles in the liberation struggle. Their opponents were the Conservatives, who were willing to work within the framework of the new Treaty and were favored by Dondukov-Korsakov. Their leadership included Dimitur Grekov (1847–1901) and Konstantin Stoilov (1853–1901), and they tended to represent the interests of the *chorbadzhi*. In fact, after the unification debates, the most contentious issue was the adoption of a Senate to counteract the *subranie* (popular assembly) that the new constitution included as a legislature. The Liberals defeated the proposal for a senate and gave Bulgaria a unicameral parliament. The Liberals dominated the convention and Bulgaria's Turnovo Constitution was one of the most democratic in Europe.

Besides the usual civil liberties including freedom of speech, press, and assembly, the constitution banned slavery and provided for free compulsory primary education for boys and girls. All citizens were equal—with the exception, of course, of the prince, required by the Treaty of Berlin. All male citizens over 30 could vote in four-tailed elections (secret, universal, direct, and proportional). All literate male citizens over 30 were eligible for election. (Female suffrage was introduced later in the 1930s.) There were provisions for special Grand National Assemblies—twice as large as the ordinary *subrania*—to meet on special occasions. These would be called to amend the constitution and to deal with questions regarding succession to the throne.

However, the constitution suffered a major weakness. The prime minister and cabinet were chosen solely at the discretion of the monarch. The assembly could only pose questions to the members of the government. It was inevitable that conflicts would develop between the conservative governments chosen by the prince and the liberal and often radical assemblies elected by the people. These conflicts wreaked havoc on Bulgarian politics from the start. In its short run (1879–1947), monarchs suspended the constitution twice and disregarded it in asserting their rule. Furthermore, the resulting fragmentation of Bulgarian political life caused by the constitution's imperfection created so many rival parties that the rulers were able to bend the law to their whims.

ALEXANDER OF BATTENBERG

These problems appeared in the very first government of the country. During the constitutional assembly, Dondukov-Korsakov recommended Prince Alexander of Battenberg from Hesse as the new monarch. The choice was popular with the assembly because he had served in the Russian army during the war and with the powers because he was related to the houses of England, Germany, and Russia. However, there was one important exception: the heir to the Russian throne, the future Alexander III, an ardent Pan-Slav, distrusted his cousin, whom he considered to be too oriented toward western Europe. In the first elections, however, the Liberals handily won control of the assembly, which chose Tsankov as their leader. Prince Alexander, as expected, chose as his prime minister a conservative, Todor Burmov (1834–1906). The assembly and cabinet argued vehemently, chiefly over various economic issues, and soon both Burmov and Tsankov left their posts.

Alexander, now with Russian approval, wished to change the constitution to strengthen his position. He appointed as his prime minister Kazimir Ehrenroth, a Russian general who had been serving as minster of war, and called for a Grand National Assembly. (Under Russian supervision, several cabinet ministers were not Bulgarians.) The prince also introduced authoritarian measures and used the army, which also had Russians in leading posts in the officer corps, to force a conservative outcome in the elections for the Grand National Assembly.

Alexander's new constitution reduced the *subranie* to 70—about half its original size—elected by indirect ballot. It also created a second body, the State Council, which acted as an executive. Civil liberties were also reduced, and the prince would have authoritarian rule for seven years. At that time, a new Grand National Assembly would assess the constitution.

The new system seemed initially to work to Alexander's liking. Many leading liberals left for Eastern Rumelia, but Tsankov remained in Bulgaria, agitating with much popular support for a restoration of the Turnovo Constitution. In addition to the Conservatives in the government, Alexander placed more Russians in the cabinet. These included two generals: Leonid Sobolev, who served as minister of interior, a position that in European countries handled police powers, and Alexander Kaubers, who served as minister of war. These new ministers acted so high-handedly that they soon found themselves in conflict with the Conservatives as well as the Liberals. Soon Prince Alexander himself was losing control of the government. The arguments between the Conservatives and the Russians, in fact, became so intense that both turned to the Liberals for support. Tsankov sided with the Conservatives and in September 1883, the Turnovo Constitution was restored. St. Petersburg agreed that while Russian officers would remain in the Bulgarian army, they would stay out of politics.

The Liberal Party itself was split and Tsankov became prime minister. Dissatisfied with the compromises that Tsankov had made with the Conservatives, Karavelov fled to Plovdiv, where he formed his own party—the Democrats. Soon Karavelov would serve as Prime Minister.

UNIFICATION WITH EASTERN RUMELIA

The issue of unification, however, was very much alive and now took center stage. The Bulgarians argued about how they should approach the question. Which of the two remaining portions of San Stefano Bulgaria left out by Berlin should they go after first, or should it be both of them? Some suggested that Eastern Rumelia and Macedonia should be united first, but they settled on Eastern Rumelia as the easiest to unite to Turnovo Bulgaria because it was the most ethnically Bulgarian. Many still worked for unification with Macedonia as well. Bulgarians in Bulgaria and Eastern Rumelia worked together to prepare for unification. They planned for a coup d'état in Eastern Rumelia in the fall of 1885. That summer, Prince Alexander went to London to attend his brother Henry's wedding to Princess Beatrice, the daughter of Queen Victoria. When he returned, he faced the unexpected *fait accompli* a few weeks earlier than the Rumelians had planned for. They announced in Plovdiv on September 6 that Eastern Rumelia and Bulgaria were united. Stefan Stambolov (1854–1895), who was then the president of the assembly, told Alexander he could either accept the unification or his reign would be over. Alexander chose acceptance and rode into Plovdiv as its prince, despite his earlier assurance to Tsar Alexander III that this would not occur. The tsar for his part feared that the plot of unification was actually discussed with the British by the Bulgarian prince while he was in England. He ordered all the Russian officers in the Bulgarian army to return, leaving the Bulgarians with few, if any, officers above the rank of captain.

Austria, meanwhile, suspected that Russia was behind the plot or at least feared that an enlarged Bulgaria could be a tool used by Russian Pan-Slavs for the subversion of the large and diverse Slavic populations in the Austro-Hungarian Empire. Vienna sparked this fear in its own Slavic ally, King Milan of Serbia, and urged him to attack Bulgaria. Without the Russian officer corps in Bulgaria, St. Petersburg, Vienna, and King Milan expected an easy Serbian victory; but the outcome surprised them. The Bulgarian army daringly performed better than expected, and the Serbian soldiers, told that they would be fighting Turks, not brother Slavs, hesitated. The great Bulgarian victory at Slivinitsa was one of the first national mile markers in the march toward a new state.

In *Arms and the Man*, the Irish playwright George Bernard Shaw used the Bulgarian-Serbian War as a background for his comedic satire on the futility and stupidity of war. Bulgarians were furious. Twenty years later when the Bulgarian National Theater dared to perform a different play by Shaw, students from Sofia University and other outraged citizens rioted in front of the theater.

However, the war accomplished the goal of unification. The powers allowed it to stand, with the fig leaf that Alexander was now both prince of Bulgaria and governor of Eastern Rumelia. Yet Alexander's problems increased. Though in control of Bulgarian politics, the Liberals continued to argue among themselves, causing more parties to appear.

Meanwhile, the Conservatives reconstituted themselves as the National Party. The Liberals divided over Russophiles, including both Tsankov and Karavelov, and Russophobes led by Stambolov. The latter looked for more concessions from Istanbul. There were also differences between those from the Turnovo principality and Eastern Rumelia.

STEFAN STAMBOLOV

The question most on the minds of Bulgarian politicians after unification was: what about Macedonia and Thrace? In many ways unification made this more difficult. On the one hand, the Great Powers were now more vigilant about Bulgarian expansion and on the other, Bulgaria's neighbors—Serbia, Greece, and Turkey—began to push forward their own claims to the multiethnic region. Even Romania claimed interest on behalf of the numerous Vlachs who lived there. The Bulgarians responded with secret committees just as they had with the liberation movement preceding the uprising of 1876 and the unification of Eastern Rumelia. Often at odds with each other, the two most important were the Internal Macedonian Revolutionary Committee (IMRO), based principally inside the region, and the Macedonian Supreme Committee in Sofia. IMRO has had many different names through its history and survives today as the Macedonian Patriotic Organization in Fort Wayne, Indiana.

Many of the Russophiles felt that only Russia could liberate Macedonia because it had liberated Bulgaria originally. They further believed that Prince Alexander's hostility to St. Petersburg was ruining not only this opportunity but other Bulgarian policies as well. In August 1886, a group of army officers forced Alexander to abdicate and he left for Romania. Such events were unfortunately not uncommon in the Balkans. Stambolov demanded that the abdication be rescinded, and Alexander had more popular support than the Russophiles imagined, but the prince said he would return only with the approval of Tsar Alexander III, who did not support him. The abdication stood.

Now Stambolov, who formed his own National Liberal party, was in control of Bulgaria. Constitutionally, the country had to find a new prince. This was not an easy matter. Russian and Bulgarian relations and minor uprisings by Russophile officers threatened the country's stability. Under these circumstances, candidates for the Bulgarian throne were hard to find. Finally in August 1887, a year after the coup against Prince Alexander, Ferdinand of Saxe-Coburg-Gotha accepted the throne and the Grand National Assembly confirmed him.

Like much of European royalty of the time, he had good family connections. He was related to the German, Austrian, and English nobility. He was a grandson of Louis-Phillipe of France to boot and a cousin of the King of Portugal and the Emperor of Brazil.

He was also an accomplished botanist. His major drawback was his Roman Catholic religion. Furthermore, many stories and rumors of his peccadilloes circulated at home and abroad. It was said that he always wore gloves so he would not have to touch his subjects' flesh while shaking hands and that he kept a revolver in his desk drawer in case he had to shoot one of his ministers. Abroad, the rumors spread that he was a homosexual, but Bulgarians whispered about his many female conquests and illegitimate children. Another story claimed that he bought a costume of Byzantine imperial robes from a traveling theatrical company to prepare for the day that the powers would solve the Eastern Question by giving Istanbul to Bulgaria.

For the first seven years of his rule, Stambolov ran the country, and Ferdinand, while making his wishes known, remained in the background. The prime minister ran the country as a dictatorship. Although force and chicanery had been used to control elections before, the National Liberal leader perfected it, and his party would be associated with authoritarian rule even after his death. However, Stambolov and Ferdinand still faced a series of external enemies as well. Russophiles in the army continued to plot revolt. Macedonian irredentists were unhappy with the government's passivity toward union with that province. The church disliked Ferdinand for his Catholicism and Stambolov, the former seminarian, for his anticlerical views. Above all, Russia not only withheld recognition of Ferdinand but also persuaded the Porte to declare his election illegitimate.

Stambolov's ruthless dealing with the rebels— especially the pro-- Macedonian Kosta Panitsa (1855–1890)—persuaded the Porte to come to settlement with Sofia, which included concessions from Istanbul favoring Bulgaria in Macedonia. The prime minister also made concessions to the church that alleviated problems the government had with it. Now Stambolov had the backing of the country, and Ferdinand was soon able to gain recognition abroad as well.

However, now Ferdinand wanted to detach himself from his prime minister. This proved an easy matter as Stambolov's enemies united against him, and when the prince found an excuse, he forced him to resign from office in 1894. Less than a year later, assassins, most likely Macedonian irredentists, attacked him in the street, and he died from his wounds. Ferdinand turned the government over to the Nationals.

Before Stambolov's resignation, a crisis erupted over the prince's marriage to Marie Louise of Bourbon-Parma, a Roman Catholic. Both the family and Pope Leo XIII insisted that the children of the union be raised as Catholics. While the Bulgarian constitution permitted Ferdinand to keep his religion, it required all subsequent monarchs to be Orthodox. Stambolov had resolved the issue by convincing a Grand National Assembly to revise the constitution, permitting Ferdinand's heir to be a Catholic also. Later in 1896, in order to resume relations with Russia, the prince, however, agreed to convert his son Boris to Orthodoxy despite the objections of the pope.

FERDINAND'S PERSONAL RULE

Without the domineering authoritarian hand of Stambolov, Ferdinand found it easy to introduce his "personal rule." The division of the Liberals into several parties made it even easier to play one off against another. He would appoint a prime minister from one party and then wait a few months, find some excuse to appoint another from a different party, and manipulate the whole political system. By the early years of the twentieth century, there were 10 major parties in Bulgaria: the conservative Nationals, the Liberals, the National Liberals, the Progressive Liberals, the Young Liberals, the Democrats, the Radicals, the Social Democrats (Broad), the Social Democrats (Narrow), and the Agrarians—and some minor ones as well.

One problem this political situation raised was the tremendous amount of money needed to keep the politicians in line. The "outs" would sit around in the Sofia cafés waiting for their term in office. The "ins," realizing that their tenure in government might be short, created an overblown government bureaucracy and civil service. This was matched by a huge military, which Ferdinand and the politicians created in preparation for the day they would regain San Stefano Bulgaria. Bulgaria became known as the Prussia of the Balkans. Where did the income come from to support these bureaucracies? Bulgaria's industry was insignificant, and that which did exist depended to a large degree on government contracts, such as uniforms. Its external trade was important in areas such as rose oil and tobacco, but it had no large farms to export significant agricultural products. Most Bulgarians were small- and middle-sized farmers, whose output was for the domestic market or themselves. The major source of revenue for the governments in the 1890s were the onerous taxes imposed on these farmers, including the hated "tithe in kind," which had been one of the major complaints against the Ottomans.

The reaction brought about the creation of radical parties on the left, which championed the farmers and others of the lower classes. The Radical Party, led by Naicho Tsanov (1857–1923) and Todor Vlaikov (1865–1943), split from the Democrats in 1901 to champion these. In addition, in 1891 a group of teachers, students, lawyers, and others familiar with the ideologies of Karl Marx and other European socialists started the Bulgarian Social Democratic Party. It soon became embroiled over the question of revisionism dividing socialists all over Europe. That is, could socialism be achieved through the ballot box rather than armed revolution? In 1903, this new party split into the "Narrows" led by Dimitur Blagoev (1856–1924) and the "Broads" led by Ianko Sakuzov (1860–1941). The Narrows believed in Orthodox Marxism, that their party must concentrate its efforts on Bulgaria's small urban working class, and that it must promote a proletarian revolution. By sheer coincidence, 1903 was the year that the Russian Social Democratic Party split into Mensheviks and Bolsheviks over similar issues, a fact to which the Narrows would later attach great importance. They did bring into their ranks a young printer, Georgi M. Dimitrov (1882–1949), who would, in 1933, become the most famous Bulgarian in the world. The Broads spread a wider net and gained some significant support among Bulgaria's few unions, particularly the schoolteachers, railway workers, and other members of the civil service. They, like the radicals and unlike the Narrows, reached out to the farmers.

ALEKSANDUR STAMBOLIISKI AND THE BULGARIAN AGRARIAN NATIONAL UNION

The farmers, however, created their own organization. In the 1890s Bulgarian farmers suffered from a series financial setbacks. In addition to the tithe, bad harvests combined with the worldwide depression had forced them into debt to local moneylenders, typically the village innkeepers, at usurious interest rates. Another disaster was the phylloxera parasite, which was destroying the European grape crop and wine industry. The continent, including France, had to import new resistant root stock from America and wait for vines to mature. One of the Bulgarian agricultural journals advised, in the meantime, that the farmers should grow poppies for the lucrative opium trade.

Teachers at the Bulgarian agricultural schools called for the formation of a farmers' union to improve the lot of Bulgarian landholders. They themselves were members of the Bulgarian teachers' union linked to the nation's Social Democratic Party. Although the teachers had a great admiration for modern European socialists, the planned union was not Marxist in its orientation because it stressed the private ownership of farms. The first meeting held in 1899 was a great success, and representatives from all over Bulgaria attended. There were some who wished the newly founded Bulgarian Agrarian National Union (BANU) to become a political party, but the conference declared it to be a purely economic union. Representatives of the other Bulgarian parties came to the conference hoping to gain the farmers' votes.

By 1901, the editor of the Union's newspaper *Agrarian Banner* (*Zemledelsko Zname*), Alexander Stamboliiski (1879–1923), a former teacher at one of the agricultural schools, emerged as the leader of the organization. Stamboliiski's rousing speeches as well as his organizational abilities in creating union cells throughout the country raised the union to the largest economic-political association in the country. Furthermore, despite the votes of the early congress, Stamboliiski was determined to make the Union a political party, and he did so with great success. In the elections of 1902, BANU won 14 seats, making it one of the largest opposition groups in parliament.

Initially, the other parties tried to outlaw both BANU and the Social Democrats, claiming they were economic organizations, not political parties. The attempt failed. In 1903, however, the prince gave the National Liberals political power again, and they used it to shut out the Agrarians and Socialists at the polls mainly by strong-arm tactics. Stamboliiski was determined that BANU would return in greater numbers than ever. During the next five years he not only built up BANU's strength through its local cells but also aroused the Bulgarian farmers through his stirring speeches and articles, which blamed their problems on Bulgaria's bloated bureaucracy and military.

Ferdinand's and the National Liberals' major problem was not with BANU but with the Macedonian irredentists. At the turn of the century, they carried out two daring operations that garnered worldwide attention. In 1901, leaders of the Supreme Committee kidnapped Ellen Stone, a teacher at the American missionary school in Samakov. Afterward, Miss Stone became a champion for Macedonian independence. The second operation was organized by IMRO. In August 1903, IMRO coordinated an uprising on St. Elijah's Day (Ilinden). IMRO, in fact, emerged as the major organization seeking independence from the Ottomans, although there was an internal dispute over whether the province should be part of Bulgaria or stand as a separate state.

The National Liberals signed a treaty with Turkey recognizing the existing borders, and Istanbul agreed to an international treaty promising reforms in Macedonia. IMRO reacted to the Bulgarian agreement by assassinating the National Liberal prime minister, Dimitur Petkov. Ironically, both his sons became leaders of BANU and both met tragic ends like their father. Macedonian terrorists assassinated Petko Petkov in 1924, and the Communist government executed Nikola Petkov in 1947 because of his political opposition.

Ferdinand's move toward Macedonia was spurred not by terror but by revolution in Turkey in the summer of 1908. The establishment of constitutional rights in the Ottoman Empire gave the Slavs of Macedonia new liberties, but this was not enough for the irredentists, who wanted either independence or union with another country. We should note here once more that this concerned not only Bulgaria, for both Serbia and Greece laid claim to Macedonian territory and its inhabitants. Furthermore, there were enough Moslems there to wish it to remain in Turkey. Albanians undergoing their own national awakening also viewed parts of Macedonia as their land. These claims were complicated further by the fact that Albania included Moslems and both Western and Eastern Christians.

As we have seen, Bulgaria, while *de facto* independent, was still *de jure* part of the Ottoman Empire. Ferdinand used the Young Turk Revolt to declare Bulgaria's complete independence. Austria-Hungary invited him to be part of a plot in which Sofia would sever the country's relationship with Istanbul while Vienna seized Bosnia-Herzegovina, a province which in fact it controlled already but that like Bulgaria was legally part of the Ottoman Empire. Meanwhile Ferdinand, now proudly assuming the title of king, had replaced the pro-Turkish National Liberal government with the Democrats. Once again, the same electoral tactics of intimidation and gerrymandering prevailed. Many from the other parties jumped to the Democrats. However, the party applied less pressure at the polls than did the National Liberals, and Stamboliiski's preparations over the previous years bore fruit. BANU received 24 out of 204 seats, making it the largest opposition group in the parliament and the most vocal in the 1911 Grand National Assembly, which changed the constitution to reflect Bulgaria's new status. Stamboliiski, true to his unrelenting railings against the military bureaucracy, opposed Ferdinand's new plans for war and expansion.

5

Wars and the Peasant State (1911–1923)

THE FIRST BALKAN WAR

The 1908 revision in the Balkans embarrassed Russia, which was unable to gain any advantage while its rival, the Austro-Hungarian Empire, made more inroads into the peninsula. St. Petersburg, fearing the possibility of Vienna becoming a champion of the Slavs, now moved to help Serbia and Bulgaria form an alliance with the goal of driving the Turks out of Europe and dividing Macedonia among the Christian countries. The Russian representative in Istanbul, Nikolai Charykov, suggested this to the two Balkan states, and with this goal in mind, Ferdinand changed governments once more. Although the king favored the Democrats more than any other party, they did not suit his new plans for a Balkan alliance. Alexander Malinov (1867–1938), the Democrat leader and prime minister, had cooperated with Austria in the crisis of 1908. He rebuffed Serbia's plan. Ferdinand now chose as prime minister Ivan Geshov (1849–1924), a man whom he detested because of his criticism of the crown but who was willing to work with Russia and Serbia. Geshov formed a black-red coalition cabinet of Nationalists and Liberals.

The Italian victory over the Turks in a brief war in 1911 had also given heart to the Balkan countries. Events in Macedonia made the Bulgarians anxious, too. Riots and fights between Slavs and Moslems in the province aroused consternation in Bulgaria. Mass protest meetings were held throughout the country. Geshov and the king decided that now was the time for war. After preliminary talks by Sofia and Belgrade, Geshov and the Serbian prime minister, Milovan Milovanović, met on a train traveling from Belgrade to Nish in February 1912 to discuss the final arrangements. Geshov wanted an autonomous Macedonia, which he believed would later join Bulgaria as Rumelia had in 1885. Milovanović, however, insisted that the land be divided, and Geshov had to give in. The prime ministers and kings of the two countries signed a treaty providing for a war with the Ottoman Empire. The public portion of the agreement called for mutual aid should either country be attacked by one or more states. The "secret" part called for war against Turkey if conditions would threaten the security of either, meaning, in fact, events in Macedonia. They loosely divided European Turkey between themselves. Bulgaria took most of the eastern portions, including Thrace and Eastern Macedonia, while the west, including Albania, went to Serbia, satisfying its goal to gain access to the Adriatic. A small central part was put on the table for later discussion with the arbitration, if necessary, of the Russian tsar. Greece and Bulgaria began negotiations at the end of February but could not agree on territorial agreements. In May, the two countries signed a treaty for mutual assistance in case of war. King Nicholas of Montenegro had, in 1911, been the first to suggest a war with Turkey but was only informally brought into the alliance after the other arrangements were made. The participants signed the military accords during the summer months.

The war began in late September 1912 with the Montenegrins attacking first. Closest to Istanbul, Bulgaria bore the brunt of the battles. Sofia mobilized well over a half million men, and thousands of Macedonian volunteers joined in. Most of the Bulgarian troops fought in Thrace, except for two divisions that joined the Serbs in the Struma valley. The troops approached Adrianople (Edirne) from the north and the west and surrounded the city in a little more than a week. Within another week, the Bulgarians won a decisive victory at Luleburgaz, and the Turks retreated to Istanbul. The Allies won elsewhere as quickly. Shortly all but four cities—Istanbul and Adrianople in the east and Ioannina and Scutari (Shkodër) in the west—lay in Allied hands. Ferdinand and

Geshov wanted to move on Istanbul, but the Bulgarian military commanders hesitated. The army was exhausted, and some soldiers suffered from cholera. They advised accepting a Turkish offer of armistice, but King Ferdinand now dreamed more than ever of adding *Tsarigrad*, the city of the emperor, as Istanbul was called in Bulgarian, to his realm. He ordered the army to attack. The assault failed, and Bulgaria and Turkey agreed to an armistice on December 3.

Desiring a port on the Aegean, the Bulgarians wanted Thessaloniki as well. They believed they had an advantage there because of the Jewish officers in their army, and they ordered them to go to the city to impress the majority Jewish population. However, the Greeks beat them into the city and their forces occupied it.

Peace talks arranged by the powers began in London but failed as the Turks refused to budge on surrendering Adrianople. The war resumed in February 1913 with more Turkish troops arriving from Asia Minor. The Bulgarians brought in their divisions from Macedonia, and some Serbian troops arrived to help as well. For the first time in Europe, bombs were dropped by Bulgaria from aircraft. (The Italians had used them in 1911 in North Africa.) The Turks had some successes at the front. However, in spite of suffering heavy causalities, Adrianople fell in March to the Allies. Ioannina had fallen to the Greeks in February and Scutari to Montenegro in April.

Serbia moved into the territory assigned to it by the treaty, the unresolved area, and also part of the land assigned to Bulgaria. Greece occupied parts of Macedonia and Thrace. The talks in London resumed, but the Balkan allies could not agree on the division of the captured territories. Finally, the British foreign secretary demanded that they sign a treaty and the war ended in May 1913. Now Greece and Serbia did not want to give up the lands they occupied. Greece (we recall) was not party to the territorial agreements. The powers had cut Serbia out of a major portion of its share by insisting on the demand by Austria-Hungary and Italy that Albania be created along the Adriatic coast, limiting Serbia's access to the sea. Furthermore, Romania demanded compensation for its neutrality in the war by acquiring the rich farming land of Dobrudja in northeast Bulgaria.

THE SECOND BALKAN WAR

Ferdinand decided on action to take Macedonia from his former allies. Serbia and Greece had signed a secret treaty just to prevent such a move, and the Bulgarian king, learning of it, feared an attack. He therefore agreed with those military and political advisers who wanted war to strike first. He replaced Geshov, who favored negotiations with the country's former allies, with the Progressive Liberal leader Stoian Danev (1858–1949), more amenable to war. In June, the Second Balkan War began. For Bulgaria, it was a disaster that lasted only a month. While the Bulgarian army moved into Macedonia, Romania and Turkey attacked westward from the rear on Bulgaria's undefended borders. Sofia capitulated and sued for peace. A new treaty reduced Bulgaria's holdings even more. They also had to cede Dobrudja to Romania and give back Edirne to Turkey.

The Second Balkan War cost Bulgaria more than the loss of territory. Although it retained some of its gains from the first war, the disaster of the second nearly negated the whole purpose of going to war in the first place. The loss of Dobrudja with its rich farmland was not compensated by the poorer land in the south. The loss of the province also affected the grain export trade through the port of Varna, which the country had been building up since liberation. Now it had to make costly investments, which would require foreign loans, for its new southern ports on the Aegean.

Furthermore, the Bulgarian attack that started the second war tarnished relations with St. Petersburg, who blamed Bulgaria for breaking up the alliance it had forged. Russia looked now to Belgrade as a more reliable Balkan Slavic ally against Vienna. The Bulgarian Russophiles saw Russia as their great friend, but from the Russian point of view, this had changed. There remained the problem of Ferdinand's Catholicism and connections to the Hapsburgs. Also, in 1903 in Serbia, the pro-Russian Karadjeordjević dynasty had replaced the pro-Austrian Obrenovićes. Finally, Bulgaria's cooperation with Austria in 1908 embarrassed Russia. This diplomatic shift would add further problems for Bulgaria both internally and internationally as World War I approached.

Ferdinand now handed the government over to a coalition of Liberal parties under Vasil Radoslavov (1854–1929) and in November 1913 called for elections. However, while the politicians and military seethingly hoped for revenge, the farmers were angry at the government. The wars had some popular support at the start, but now that support was dashed on the rocks of reality. The government mobilized the farmers when they should have been in the fields and then requisitioned their grain and livestock for the war effort. The farmers now looked to those who had opposed the wars—the socialists and BANU, especially the latter.

Stamboliiski had continued to rail against the government's abuse of the farmers as Ferdinand and his prime ministers entertained

BALKAN FRONT, 1914 – 1918

(ABC-CLIO)

expansionist ideas and maintained a bloated military. Over the years he had won support for his party by organizing the villages into BANU cells, but now his pacifist platform won even more backers. The unprecedented happened. The opposition won the elections with 109 seats to the government's 97. Of the 109 seats, BANU won 47 and the various socialists 37. The king hastily prorogued the assembly and called for new elections. The government party then gerrymandered the districts, especially those in the new territories that did not participate in the earlier voting. Still the vote was a draw with both the government and opposition winning 116 seats. BANU won 50 and the socialists 21. Clearly Stamboliiski was the most popular man in Bulgaria. The government then nullified 16 of the opposition districts and handed them over to its own supporters. Because part of the government's victories in the new territories was obtained by pressuring Moslem voters, the opposition derided it as a "Turkish" majority.

The first order of business for the government was securing a foreign loan to improve the harbor of Port Lagos in Thrace, which was needed to replace Varna as an export depot for Bulgarian grain. A raucous debate over the issue took place during July 1914 as the Great Powers faced down each other in preparation for war. France could not afford Bulgaria's request and Russia demanded the country adhere to the Triple Entente (Russia, France, and Great Britain). Sensing an opportunity, Germany offered the money. In a disputed vote by a show of hands, the German loan passed by a mere seven votes.

WORLD WAR I

When World War I broke out in August 1914, the king, the government, and the opposition were not anxious to join in. Wearied by their experiences in the Balkan wars, all were exhausted. The government thus declared its strict neutrality. However, when both sides began to court Sofia, the opportunity to regain the territories lost in the Second Balkan War—especially Macedonia—was too much to resist. But Stamboliiski remained adamant against the war policy. When members of the assembly jibed at him for his lack of patriotism, asking if he were or were not a Bulgarian, he shouted back, "I am a Yugoslav"[1]—a South Slav. In a public speech from the balcony of the parliament building, he said that if King Ferdinand led the country into war once more, the people would hang him from the statue of Tsar Alexander II, the liberator of Bulgaria, which stood across the square.

The War initially pitted the Central Powers (Germany and Austria-Hungary) against the Allies (England, France, and Russia and also Serbia, over which the conflict had begun). Both sides expected a quick

Alexander Nevsky Cathedral. (Corel)

resolution, as had been the case in most European wars since the Napoleonic age. But as the war dragged on, both camps sought to bring other countries in on their side by promising territorial gains. When Turkey joined in on the side of the Central Powers, Bulgaria more than ever became a key target for both warring factions as a link between the Ottoman Empire and Central Europe. The Allies and the Central Powers approached Bulgaria promising territorial adjustments to the Balkan Wars treaties. But Berlin and Vienna had more to offer, namely Serbian-occupied Macedonia. Furthermore, both the king and Radoslavov preferred the German-Austrian side and, in addition, in 1915, the Central Powers appeared to be winning.

Just before Bulgaria joined the Central Powers in the war, the king called in the leaders of the parties to discuss the move. As the politicians left the audience, Ferdinand turned specifically to Stamboliiski and, because of his speech in Parliament Square, warned him, "My head is old. Yours is young. Watch out for it."[2] Shortly afterward, the Agrarian leader was arrested and sentenced to death. But pressure forced Ferdinand to commute the sentence to life imprisonment.

The government had to prepare the Russophile Bulgarians for its decision to join the Central Powers. Although the Bulgarian public did not want to go to war, they celebrated early Russian victories. The government declared a state emergency in order to exercise its right to shut down newspapers and limit public assembly and political meetings. It started a pro-German propaganda campaign and stressed the Bulgar aspect of the nation to stress the Bulgarians' relation to the Turks and Magyars. The German army made Ferdinand an honorary field marshal. Older Russophile officers were retired, but in some ways this added to the government's problems because many of their younger replacements favored the more progressive Democrats led by Malinov, Radoslavov's chief rival. Bulgaria also decided at this time to change from the Julian to the Gregorian calendar, putting them on the same schedule as Germany and Austria. It was a move that they had previously considered, but the opportunity at this time made it possible and convenient.

On the heels of the Austrian army, Bulgaria joined in the fighting in September 1915 by invading Serbia. Flush with success in that campaign, the Bulgarian generals wanted to go on to Greece, remembering the humiliating defeat of 1913. Although Athens was officially neutral, Allied forces occupied Thessaloniki in anticipation of such an invasion from the north or their own decision to attack. Germany preferred to keep the Allied soldiers in Greece rather than have them move to the western front. This delayed any invasion by Bulgaria. A year later, unable to convince the King of Greece, the German kaiser's brother-in-law, to join in on their side, the Allies engineered a coup d'état and helped establish a rival Greek government in Thessaloniki under the great national leader Eleutherios Venezelos. Venezelos immediately joined the Allied side. The Allies attacked north, but the Bulgarians drove them back and took several cities in Thrace, including Drama and Kavala. In the meantime, Romania also joined the war in 1916 on the Allied side and Bulgarian troops joined the Turks in taking Dobrudja. Toward the end of the year, the Allies fought back and the front line in Macedonia stabilized until the summer of 1918. Although the king, the generals, and the politicians enjoyed the victories of the first years, the civil population suffered considerable hardship because of the demands placed on it. Requisitions from the farms were so severe that the population was on the brink of starvation. Because of conscription, the labor shortage ruined the harvests. Germany demanded more and more foodstuffs while it took over vital areas of the country's infrastructure, like the railroads and telephones. Inflation climbed year by year in an ever-expanding spiral. Food and clothing were in short supply and could only be found for exorbitant prices on the black market. The wheat and corn flour mixture the government used for bread was so indigestible that some people even died from it. The towns were worse off than the countryside, but the requisitions from the farmers made their lot intolerable as well. The economic situation was compounded by the corrupt war profiteers in charge of many areas of supply and distribution.

Riots broke out in several places and, on occasion, even the army threatened mutiny. Opposition in the *subranie* grew as well, although Radoslavov had originally managed to guarantee a majority there by the usual electioneering methods. His opponents, particularly the Democrats led by Alexander Malinov, who had favored the Allies, of course opposed him. Some of the government supporters now turned against him, too. In June 1918, Berlin and Vienna refused to give Bulgaria full control of Dobrudja, Radoslavov resigned, and Ferdinand handed power to Malinov. Malinov tried to build a broader coalition and even spoke to Stamboliiski, still in prison, but the Agrarian leader said he would join the government only if Bulgaria left the war. Ferdinand refused.

The situation was beyond repair. When the Allies attacked from Greece in mid-September, the Bulgarian army dissolved and fled. Soldiers in Radomir, 50 miles south of Sofia, rebelled and demanded a BANU government. Raiko Daskalov (1886–1923), an Agrarian leader, joined them and declared Bulgaria a republic. The Radomir army moved toward Sofia.

In the meantime, the government released Stamboliiski and sent him with a delegation to the Allies to sue for peace. The delegation also included the American consular officer, because Washington never declared war on Bulgaria. Ferdinand reshuffled the cabinet once again under Todor Todorov (1859–1924) of the National Party, who included Agrarians and Broad Socialists in his cabinet.

The Radomir army neared Sofia. Meanwhile, loyal troops were bolstered by Macedonians, who hated the Agrarians for their acceptance of the Balkan Wars treaties. Germans, too, joined the loyalists. In September, the rebels met defeat. The monarchy was saved. However, by terms of the peace treaty negotiated with the help of the American consul, Ferdinand had to leave the country. He abdicated in favor of his son, who took the title Boris III in remembrance of the medieval tsars of that name.

The government blamed Stamboliiski for the rebellion, although he was only indirectly involved and denied fomenting it. When the authorities refused to accept his excuses, he sought help for a full-scale revolution from the Narrow Socialists. However, they were inspired by the success of Vladimir Lenin and the Bolsheviks in Russia. Expecting to come to power shortly themselves, they refused to join the Agrarians in revolution or even as partners in a Bulgarian cabinet. In fact, the Narrows soon joined the Communist International (*Comintern*) established by Lenin and changed their name to the Bulgarian Communist Party. They saw Stamboliiski as the Bulgarian Alexander Kerensky, the Russian Socialist Revolutionary, leader of a peasant party that held power in Russia in the summer and fall of 1917 just before the Bolsheviks took over. Instead of revolution, Stamboliiski came to power via the ballot box.

In the elections for a new parliament in 1919, the Agrarians won a plurality of 85 out of 236 seats. The Communists, buoyed by the success of the Russian Revolution and the country's discontent, came in second with 47 seats. Russia had many sympathizers in Bulgaria because of Slavic kinship and the role it played in winning Bulgaria's liberty. The fact that the first Marxist revolution occurred in Russia was no barrier to the Communist cause in Bulgaria as it was in other Eastern European countries where tsarist Russia had been viewed as an oppressor. Indeed, the major landmark in Sofia is its great cathedral built by the Russophile parties when they held power. Topped with golden domes, it bears the name of the sainted Russian grand prince Alexander Nevsky. The

Communist Party always did well in Bulgarian elections between the world wars when the elections were not manipulated or the party banned. In 1919, the Broad Socialists won 38 seats; the remaining parties that had controlled Bulgarian politics since 1878 won only 66.

STAMBOLIISKI'S FIRST GOVERNMENT

Stamboliiski was now charged with leading a government, but since he had only a plurality, he needed partners. He preferred the Communists, but they preferred to wait for his collapse and their turn. He also distrusted the Socialists because much of their support came from the government unions that BANU would have to confront when he took on the civil bureaucracy about which he had been complaining for almost two decades. Furthermore, the Socialists lost favor with the public when, before the elections, one of their leaders, as minister of interior in the previous cabinet, used force to suppress a demonstration against the country's economic plight. This was another reason for the Communists' success at the polls. The Agrarian leader then had no choice but to invite into his cabinet members of the other parties who had supported the war. In addition to his five Agrarians, he chose two Nationalists and the leader of the Progressive Liberals.

Stamboliiski's first task was to go to Paris and get the best deal he could in the peace treaties that concluded World War I. The Bulgarians hoped that the fact that they were a revolutionary government would help them in the settlement, but all the Central Powers had gone through revolutions except Turkey, where one was imminent. This made no difference to the victors, who wanted revenge. The countries of the Central Powers were not permitted to negotiate on the treaties but had to sign documents prepared by the victors. Peace was dictated. The Allies dealt with each country individually in five different suburbs of Paris. (Austria was separated from Hungary.) The main settlement was with Germany in Versailles. Bulgaria's was sited in Neuilly.

The losers hoped that the peace would be based on Woodrow Wilson's 14 points, which he forged after America joined the war, especially the principle of the self-determination of nations. Bulgarians believed that if this principle were applied truthfully, they would be allowed to keep Dobrudja and be given a larger share of Macedonia and Thrace than they received as a result of the Balkan Wars. Not only did the countries of the Central Powers have hopes for a fair settlement based on self-determination, but colonies and holdings of the victors such as Ireland, India, Indochina, and the Philippines also hoped for independence. However, the victors wanted vengeance and gain, not justice. Decisions were made by the big four: Wilson (USA), David Lloyd George (England), Georges Clemenceau (France), and Vittorio Orlando (Italy). Any attempts by Wilson to seek moderate terms were overruled by the others, especially Clemenceau. While new nations were created on the basis of nationality, they arose on the lands of the defeated Eastern Europe empires, including tsarist Russia. Thus Poland was reborn from German, Austrian, and Russian territory. The Austro-Hungarian Empire was completely dissolved, although a rump Austria and a small Hungary remained. Two new Slavic states emerged: Czechoslovakia and the kingdom of the Serbs, Croats, and Slovenes—Yugoslavia, as it was officially renamed in 1929. England and France divided the Asian territories of the Ottoman Empire in accordance with secret treaties they made during the war. (Another of Wilson's 14 points called for "open covenants . . . openly arrived at.") The powers also seized for themselves the German colonies in Africa and the Pacific. They established a League of Nations based on Wilson's last point, which the president idealistically had hoped would serve as means of peacefully resolving disputes. In fact, the victors used it as an instrument to guarantee their hegemony over Europe. Ironically, Washington did not officially join the League because Wilson's opponents in the American senate refused to ratify the treaty. In practice, however, America followed London's lead and did everything in the League except vote.

The five treaties were similar and meted out proportional penalties. The Central Powers had to agree that they alone were responsible for the war—the infamous "war guilt" clause added by the American delegation in exchange for a lesser reparations payment. The clause would be used as a rallying cry by a later German, Adolf Hitler, in his rise to power. The three major penalties in the treaties were loss of territory, the payment of reparations to the victors, and the reduction of armed forces for the losers. The Treaty of Neuilly required Bulgaria to give up all land it occupied, including Dobrudja. Bulgaria also gave up some small additional territories to the new Serbian kingdom and the rest of Thrace to Greece. Greece was to give Sofia access to the Aegean, but it never did. Some 90,000 Bulgarians now lived in their neighbors' territories. Most Bulgarians also considered the South Slavs of Macedonia to be Bulgarians, too, although some but not all Macedonians thought of themselves as Macedonians. The Serbs now thought of Macedonia as south Serbia. The Greeks looked at the Macedonians as Greek Slavophones belonging to the Greek patriarchate. In any case, there were hundreds of thousands of South Slavic speakers in the region.

In addition, the treaty limited the Bulgarian armed forces to 20,000 volunteers. It restricted armament in number and kind. Bulgaria had to pay reparations in both material and gold. The original sum of the latter was 2.5 billion French francs to be paid over 30 years. Stamboliiski tried to get a reduction as he learned that other countries like Hungary were able to do so. However, at first he failed until he investigated and learned that he neglected to bribe the proper negotiators in charge. Naively, the Agrarian leader thought that this kind of *baksheesh* was practiced only in the Ottoman Empire, not in the "civilized" West. In 1932, reparation payments by the losers ceased, but Bulgaria had already paid 40 million francs.

Stamboliiski made an impression at the conference. "A peasant with a king in his pocket"[3] was how Ernest Hemingway described him later, but the Bulgarian prime minister failed to lessen the harshness of the settlement. His only hope was that in 1919 the Allies preferred a peasant revolution to a Communist one. He was willing to work within the bounds of the treaty in the hopes that in the future the conditions would be alleviated. Before the treaty was signed, Allied troops occupied Bulgaria. The Balkan soldiers were not kind, but the Italians went out of their way to court Bulgaria as a potential ally in the region. Of all the big four nations, Italy received the least of what it desired from the settlements and looked for new opportunities. It made headway in Bulgaria particularly within the court circles, among the military, and especially the Macedonian irredentists, if not with the Agrarians. When Benito Mussolini came to power in 1922, these connections grew stronger.

THE BANU GOVERNMENT

When Stamboliiski returned from Paris, he faced an immediate crisis caused by the unrest among the urban workers, who were staging demonstrations urged on by the Communists and Socialists. The food crisis was still a major problem for the Bulgarian towns and cities even though the war was over. American shipments of wheat provided some relief, but hunger still stalked the streets. Prices had risen by a factor of 12 since 1914, and wages could not keep pace. Demobilization of the military brought with it unemployment, which also added to the country's problems. Workers, disgruntled army officers, civil service workers, pensioners, and others joined in the demonstrations. The failure of the Socialist ministers in the Todorov government to deal with these problems meant that many of their supporters in the Unions and the civil service went over to the Communists.

However, the Socialists and the Communists agreed to act together in a 1919 Christmas Eve demonstration. Stamboliiski ordered the police to use force and arrests, if necessary, to break up the crowds. The response was a call for a general strike, and the government acted with harsher measures. Not only the police but also the new limited army and a BANU paramilitary force called the Orange Guard attacked the strikers. (Orange was the color of Agrarian ballots in elections.) The guard was similar to other political paramilitary detachments that appeared all over Europe after World War I, such as the German *Freikorps*, various Communist red guards, and the Italian Fascist Black Shirts. BANU used them in the following years to enforce its policies in an extralegal fashion and to harass its enemies at political meetings and elections. Stamboliiski obviously learned from his enemies how to deal with critics and win Bulgarian elections. In any case, the strike was broken.

In March 1920, Stamboliiski now called for a new parliamentary election including compulsory voting. BANU won with a greater plurality, but not yet a majority. The Communists won the second most seats, with almost half the number of BANU. The Socialists and the other parties were far behind. Stamboliiski then tried another trick that Ferdinand's Liberal government pulled on him in 1913. He prorogued nine Communist delegates, a move that allowed the Agrarians then to gain a bare majority. He formed an exclusively BANU government, the first one-party cabinet since Stambolov's in 1894.

Stamboliiski still railed about injustices and promised benefits to the farmers, but his reforms were rather modest. In part, he was hampered by the Allied commission still keeping watch over his government. Although it approved of the way he dealt with the Communists, it did not tolerate harsh dealings with Bulgaria's urban middle class, such as his planned property tax, or his desire to establish diplomatic relations with Soviet Russia. Furthermore, the peace treaty required Bulgaria to deliver fuel and livestock to Serbia, Romania, and Greece. This hampered redistribution within Bulgaria.

Stamboliiski hired women in civil service and diplomatic posts not because he was a champion of women's rights but because he reasoned that he could pay them less and save on government expenses. Although BANU had campaigned for female suffrage, it was not adopted in Bulgaria until 1938, long after BANU fell from power. The BANU-controlled legislature passed laws limiting the role of lawyers as elected and appointed officials. The assembly also created a series of courts to deal with farmers' issues such as boundary disputes in which the judges were elected and before which the farmers could plead their own cases.

Stamboliiski also instituted a modest land reform program to redistribute acreage to the poorer farmers. There were similar programs elsewhere in Eastern Europe, but because Bulgaria really did not have large estates after the Turks left, there was not much to give out. Land was taken from the minority of farmers who had more than 75 acres, from absentee landlords, and from uncultivated monastery lands. State land was also distributed. The government compensated the owners according to a schedule that discriminated against the wealthiest owners. The decree was popular and continued even after BANU fell from power.

In another measure, BANU hoped to collect and store grain to hedge against the world market. Part of the Agrarian program had always been to encourage agricultural cooperatives both for buying farm equipment and supplies and for selling produce. This was just a measure in accordance with that practice. However, the Allies took a dim view of controlling markets and interceded to stop the program.

Stamboliiski also planned to put those responsible for Bulgaria's entry into World War I on trial, but the Allies intervened here and would not let the trials take place. One of his most innovative programs was the Compulsory Labor Service. Young men and women were drafted into a civilian corps for a year of service to the public. On the one hand, this served as a substitute for military conscription banned by the Treaty of Neuilly; on the other hand, and more to the point for Stamboliiski and BANU, it fostered the ideal of cooperative labor favored by the Union. The boys worked on infrastructure projects building rural roads and pathways and shelters in the mountains. They helped turn Mount Vitosha, which overlooks Sofia, into a lovely national park where inhabitants of the city today still go to in droves to enjoy a Sunday outing. The women made uniforms for state workers, such as postal and railway employees, and for the labor service itself. The Allies objected because it smacked of a way to outmaneuver the military restrictions, and they made the government modify but not eliminate the program. Moreover, during the Great Depression of the 1930s, American President Franklin Roosevelt's administration studied it as a model for the Civilian Conservation Corps.

Stamboliiski also dealt with overcrowding in Sofia and other cities. The Allies tried to solve the national crisis in Macedonia in the wake of the Balkan Wars and World War I by transferring thousands of people between Turkey and Greece and between Greece and Bulgaria based on declared nationality. Large numbers of South Slavs moved from Macedonia into Bulgaria, particularly Sofia and the Pirin area (Bulgarian Macedonia). This caused a major problem for Stamboliiski and the succeeding governments because of the irredentist movement (discussed later), but another problem was the shortage of living space.

To deal with this, the government limited the number of rooms a family could have and sent inspectors to insure compliance. There was naturally a hostile reaction by the urban population, who had to give up their homes. This contrasted with the public's general acceptance of the redistribution of land. The government also began a program of building apartment complexes, a more acceptable solution, which continued after the fall of the BANU government.

Stamboliiski wished to revamp the education system to suit the farmers' needs. The BANU government built hundreds of new schools, especially at the elementary level, in rural areas. He added a department of veterinary science to the university and established colleges of forestry and commerce. He also established teacher reviews by the rural communities. When his minister of education, Stoian Omarchevski (1885–1941), however, interfered in the affairs of the university, the academic aroused the ire of his fellow professors. Omarchevski wanted to de-emphasize both the extreme nationalism and Marxism that had become prevalent in a number of areas of the curricula. Professors belonging to the Communist Party were fired. Omarchevski also proposed changes in the Bulgarian alphabet. It is no wonder that members of the faculty who might have sympathized with some of the modernizing reforms of BANU joined in the opposition against him.

Some of Stamboliiski's greatest challenges were in foreign affairs. He wished to work within the framework of the peace settlement, hoping that some adjustments could be made in the future. He realized that a new military solution based on Bulgarian expansion was impossible, so he sought accommodation with Belgrade. Because the government of the Yugoslav kingdom was pressuring the Slavs of Macedonia to claim they were Serbs, the Macedonian irredentists, of course, bitterly opposed Stamboliiski's policy.

Furthermore, after the war the Allies, particularly France, set up a network of treaties and alliances in Eastern Europe to contain both Germany and Soviet Russia. Called the *Cordon Sanataire*, it included a treaty with Poland and a series of mutual treaties among France, Czechoslovakia, Yugoslavia, and Romania. The latter three were known as the Little Entente. They were more interested in not losing the land they had gained from the peace settlements back to Hungary and Bulgaria. Later on, Yugoslavia and Romania joined Greece and Turkey. The new agreement, the Balkan Entente, directed specifically toward Bulgaria, was a more relevant one for Frances's allies.

Another aspect of Stamboliiski's foreign policy was the establishment of the Green International, an association of the peasant parties that rose to prominence in the 1920s in Eastern Europe. Stamboliiski's peasant international included Wincenty Witos's Polish party, Iuliu Maniu's Romanian, Milan Hodza's Czechoslovak, and Stjepan Radic's Croatian, among others. The success of the movement led to Moscow's establishing a rival Communist peasant international, the *Krestintern*.

Stamboliiski made a tour of European capitals in 1920 in order to show the country's desire to live as a peaceful member of the European community. The kingdom was welcomed into the League of Nations, the first of the defeated powers to be so admitted. Stamboliiski wanted to use the League and the promised provisions in its charter regarding minority rights to establish a Balkan federation where the South Slavs of Macedonia could exist along with Serbs and Bulgarians. This had always been one of his goals for solving the Balkan question and avoiding the wars promoted by the ultranationalists. We remember that in the debates in the *subranie* over Bulgaria's entry into World War I, he had answered the jeering question whether he was a Serb or Bulgarian by replying that he was a Yugoslav, a South Slav.

THE COUP D'ÉTAT OF 1923

Although the majority of the country supported him, Stamboliiski had powerful enemies. Many had backed him because of his antiwar policies; now that the war was over, this was no longer an issue. Furthermore, Stamboliiski, in order to cut government expenses, refused pay raises to state employees. These included members of the powerful Socialist unions like the schoolteachers and postal and railway workers. The old parties opposed him for cutting them out of government jobs. The victorious allies opposed him because of the war crime trials, which they judged unfair. They also feared him because of his revolutionary Agrarian policies but yet embraced him as a possible bulwark against Communism. However, the newly formed Communist Party refused his overtures for alliance because they compared him to Alexander Kerensky, a precursor to a Communist revolution in Bulgaria, and hence they thought that they would take Stamboliiski's place. The new king Boris III opposed him because he feared that he was planning a republic.

Most of all, the Bulgarian Macedonians opposed him because he was willing to accept the territorial changes of the Treaty of Neuilly and make peace with Belgrade. IMRO, led by Todor Aleksandrov (1881–1924) and General Aleksandur Protogerov (1867–1928), who had suppressed the Radomir rebellion, was now the main Bulgarian organization. It agitated for an independent Macedonian state rather then union with Bulgaria as a more realistic goal. Factions in IMRO developed over personalities, policies, and goals. Some wished to join with the Communists while others did not. There were branches that concentrated their efforts in Thrace. The factions carried out open warfare among themselves. As mentioned above, many of the Macedonian refugees from the population exchanges with Greece and Turkey had settled in the capital. The murderous activity of these feuding groups brought mayhem to the streets of Sofia for more than a decade. The Macedonian terrorists did not confine their violence to their rivals but went after politicians and others whom they saw as obstacles to a free Macedonia. In 1921, they gunned down Alexander Dimitrov (1873–1921), Stamboliiski's minister of war.

The Macedonians, as noted, also controlled the Pirin area, Bulgaria's section of the province centered in Petrich. There they laid a heavy tax on the tobacco growers of the area. There was little that the government could do to stop them. Indeed, many Bulgarian officials looked the other way because they sympathized with the Macedonians' goals. One of the criticisms of Stamboliiski was that he left intact sections of the civil bureaucracy—especially the police forces and the military. Especially with regard to Macedonian irredentism, the army still held the beliefs about which Stamboliiski complained before he had come to power. From its base in Bulgaria, IMRO *cheta* (guerilla groups) raided into Greece and Yugoslavia, killing rival national gangs, officials, and police or demanding "taxes" from the inhabitants. The government in Belgrade refused to deal with Stamboliiski unless he stopped the raids.

Another problem that caused the prime minister grief was the 30,000 Russian soldiers from the "white" (anti-Communist) army of General Peotr Wrangel seeking refuge in the country. They had come to Bulgaria after their defeat in the southern Ukraine in 1920 and interfered in the politics of the country. They despised Communists but had little sympathy for other radicals like Stamboliiski, either. Their close connections with Bulgaria's reduced military presented a possible armed threat to state security. In May 1922, the government disbanded Wrangel's army. Many Bulgarian officers turned against Stamboliiski because of this and also because of his Macedonian policy. Yet that same month Bulgaria held elections for the *subranie* and BANU received an overwhelming majority.

Despite Stamboliiski's complaints about corrupt government when he was out of power, in power the Agrarians did not take the high road. Corruption and shady dealing were rampant. Stamboliiski blamed these problems on his inability to replace the bureaucracies with untrained peasants until a period of transition should pass, but he himself absconded illegally with funds available from the state coffers. Furthermore, his many mistresses and sexual appetites became fodder for the gossipmongers of Sofia. Thus, despite the Agrarian victory at the polls, opposition began to grow against the BANU government.

In 1922, Stamboliiski lifted the state of siege that had been in effect since the strikes of 1919. The old governing parties regrouped as the Constitutional Bloc around the newspaper *Slovo* (*The Word*). Other groups, too, became disgruntled with the Agrarian government. One was the Military League, an organization founded after the Balkan Wars. During the BANU period, General Protogerov, one of the leaders of IMRO, led it. Obviously, it was not friendly toward Stamboliiski or his government. Some members of the League also belonged to the new *Naroden Sgovor* (National or Popular Alliance), an organization of professors and other professionals, some of whom were Socialists.

The Alliance planned a series of antigovernment meetings. The first was scheduled for September in Turnovo, but the Orange Guard took over the city while the government banned public assembly. The Guard also threatened the Alliance members with bodily harm as they arrived in town, and only Raiko Daskalov, the leader of the Radomir Rebellion and a member of the BANU cabinet, prevented violence. He ordered them jailed, however, for their own "protection." The next month Benito Mussolini carried out his famous March on Rome, and the Alliance considered imitating him with a March on Sofia, but fear of the Orange Guard prevented it.

The *subranie* ordered the arrest and trial of more than 30 members of the wartime governments. Although the chief leaders of the Radoslavov cabinet had been tried in 1919, these broadening indictments involving other parties threatened the entire opposition. The trials went forth and the leaders were convicted, although the fall of BANU in 1923 saved them from punishment.

In December, the government faced another crisis. Stamboliiski had just come back from a meeting in Belgrade where he had begun negotiations for ending the impasse over Macedonia. He publicly denounced IMRO and the other extreme nationalists and promised to do something about the raids into the Serb kingdom and Greece. In retaliation, IMRO took over the town of Kiustendil. They set up a tribunal and condemned Stamboliiski and members of his government to death. The Orange Guard moved in and drove the Macedonians back to Petrich. The Guard then moved on Sofia and raided the opposition's party and newspaper offices. The Alliance feared that Stamboliiski would install the Guard as the state's official police authority.

In 1923, the tension increased. In March, Sofia and Belgrade agreed to the Nish Convention, which provided for cooperation against the IMRO raids. Stamboliiski banned the Macedonian terrorist organizations, closed their offices, shut down their newspapers and periodicals, and imprisoned their leaders in detention camps in Eastern Bulgaria. Earlier in the year, the Macedonians failed in an assassination attempt on the premier's life. Stamboliiski entrenched his power. He dismissed Agrarians who opposed his policies and called for a new parliament based on plurality vote instead of proportional representation. This insured an overwhelming BANU victory. Indeed, the Union won 212 representatives against 31 opposition: 16 Communists and 15 from the Alliance.

He then purged even more dissident Agrarians and began even to imitate Mussolini. Members of BANU took an oath to die for the Union if necessary. In a grand parade of the Orange Guard, Stamboliiski reviewed his troops while seated on a white stallion.

Opponents of Stamboliiski and BANU, particularly the Military League and the Macedonians, had plotted and conspired against the Union from the beginning of the Agrarian government. Now, in the spring of 1923, more moderate opponents feared the end of constitutional government. They believed that even if Stamboliiski himself would not attempt a dictatorship, some of the more radical members of BANU might oust him.

The National Alliance now joined in with the Military League and IMRO. King Boris gave tacit approval to the plot. On June 9, while Stamboliiski was vacationing in his home village Slavovitsa near Pazardzhik in Southern Bulgaria, the conspirators seized power in Sofia and arrested the government. Stamboliiski tried to raise an army to fight back. He asked the Communists to join in, but they still refused, thinking that at long last the expected turn to them would occur as it had in Russia in 1917. In fact, when local Communists in Pleven joined the Agrarians, word came from Sofia to stop.

The situation between the Communists and BANU was more complicated. A number of Bulgarians had become important leaders in the *Comintern*, especially Vasil Kolarov (1877–1950), who had recently become close to Lenin after Kolarov ruled in Lenin's favor over a challenge from within the Russian party. The *Comintern* decided that the Bulgarian Communist Party should support Stamboliiski against the coup, which the international labeled fascist. The arguments between Moscow and Sofia continued all summer until the Bulgarian Communist Party carried out a revolt on behalf of themselves and the Agrarians.

The meager force that Stamboliiski was able to raise only held out for a few days. Then the Macedonians captured him and brought him back to his home in Slavovitsa. The terrorists brutally tortured him, castrating him and cutting off his head and the hand that signed the Treaty of Neuilly. Before he died, he wrote his name in blood on the wall of the cellar where he was imprisoned, where it is still there for visitors to see. The conspirators arrested thousands of BANU leaders and the coup easily succeeded, but the travails for Bulgaria had just begun.

NOTES

1. J[oseph] Swire, *Bulgarian Conspiracy* (London: Robert Hall, 1939), 142.

2. Aleksandur Stamboliiski, *Dveti mi sreshti c Tsar Ferdinannd* [*My two meetings with King Ferdinand*], 3rd ed. (Sofiia: BZNS, 1979), 10–17.

3. Hemmingway wrote this about him at the later 1922 Genoa Conference, *Toronto Star*, April 10, 1922.

6

Two Coups d'Etat (1923–1935)

Other opponents of the Stamboliiski regime joined the National Alliance, renamed the Democratic Alliance. Two contending factions led by veteran politicians dominated the party. Andrei Liapchev (1866–1933) and Atanas Burov (1875–1954) led one group, and the new prime minister, Aleksandur Tsankov (1879–1959), headed the other. Liapchev was a member of the Democrat Party and served in a number of important ministerial and diplomatic posts. Burov, a financial expert, who also had served in a number of cabinet positions, was a member of the conservative National Party. Aleksandur Tsankov was a flamboyant Socialist professor of economics at Sofia University. The strengths as well as the flaws of the Democratic Alliance lay in the broad political views of its members, ranging from socialism on the left through both standard liberal and conservative ideologies to admiration of the new fascism that European politicians were now embracing in the 1920s. The coalition simmered with internal disagreements.

The charismatic Tsankov now appeared front and center on the Bulgarian stage. Tsankov was a man who fit the era. Like the two progenitors of Italian Fascism—the poet Gabriele d'Annuncio and Benito Mussolini—Tsankov moved from the extreme left to the extreme right. While Liapchev and Burov wanted the Alliance to reestablish constitutional law in Bulgaria, Tsankov opted for an authoritarian regime in the manner of Stambolov and Stamboliiski.

Tsankov gained the top position with the aid of General Ivan Volkov (1875–1962), the minister of war. Volkov represented the Military League, another part of the Alliance. Volkov, like most members of the League, did not trust the old politicians like Liapchev and Burov, who were part of the "party" system that controlled Bulgaria before World War I. Furthermore, Volkov was very close to both IMRO and Mussolini's Italy, where he would later serve as the Bulgarian plenipotentiary. Italy continued to look on Bulgaria as a likely ally in the Balkans to oppose its rivals, Greece and Yugoslavia. In 1930, King Boris married Ioanna (Giovanna), the daughter of King Victor Emmanuel III of Italy. Volkov saw Tsankov as a partner in bringing strong rule to Bulgaria.

Initially, the Alliance reestablished the rule of law and made concessions to the more liberal members of its party despite the desires of Tsankov and Volkov. Elections were held for a new *subranie*, which agreed to work with the Alliance. It kept the BANU land distribution program with some adjustments and, in fact, gave out more acreage than the Agrarians had. It increased the wages of civil servants, allowed labor unions, and retained the social legislation introduced by Stamboliiski. It also reinstated those who had lost their jobs for opposing Stamboliiski's government. Although many BANU leaders were arrested at the time of the coup, most were soon released, and BANU would soon split into a multitude of factions.

THE SEPTEMBER UPRISING

Then, in the fall of 1923, a new crisis arose that plunged Bulgaria into a virtual state of civil war. As indicated earlier, the Bulgarian Communist Party and the *Comintern* had spent the summer arguing whether the Communists should support BANU in fighting the National Alliance's coup. The international Communist movement, which had been buoyed up in the previous two years by the success of Russia in its Civil War against the "whites" and the creation of the Union of Soviet Socialist Republics, now faced defeats. A worldwide Communist revolution, which Russia had hoped it would spark, did not occur. The hoped-for success of a German revolution that once had seemed promising had failed in three attempts. Bulgaria seemed a likely place for a victory.

The *Comintern* ordered the Bulgarian Communist Party to begin its action on September 23. The prospects were not good. Time for preparation was limited, supplies were short, and many of the Communists and the Agrarians were in no mood to cooperate. The government learned of the plans and declared martial law. While there was some success in a few cities, the fighting lasted less than a week. Tsankov outlawed the Communist Party and its labor unions and confiscated its property. The Communist leadership fell into disarray and broke into factions. Some of this mirrored the struggle for power, which now began in Moscow with the death of Lenin. In the end, Dimitrov and Kolarov, with the support of Josef Stalin, who won out over his rivals in the USSR, would come to lead the BCP. In the meantime, sporadic fighting continued for two years. In 1925, the *Comintern* ordered the party to cease, but there were those who continued and carried out the spectacular bombing of the Holy Sunday church, in the center of Sofia, just before the king arrived for a funeral service. More than 100 people were killed. The government reacted with ferocious reprisals, which brought about international condemnation. Thousands were arrested, and many were never heard from again. Tsankov carried out widespread public executions. Although the "September Uprising" failed, it remained legendary in Communist lore and later became celebrated by the government when the Communists came to power after World War II. The party labeled it "the first antifascist uprising in Europe."

IMRO

The Communist uprising was only one aspect of violence that shook Bulgaria in those years. More significant was the warfare carried out by IMRO, the Macedonian organization that had helped in the coup of 1923 and, in fact, had murdered Stamboliiski. IMRO had many friends in the Alliance. Volkov was a leading supporter, but even Liapchev, who was from Macedonia, tolerated its outrages. IMRO continued the same activities it had carried out under Stamboliiski: it raided into Yugoslavia and Greece and "taxed" the peasants of Macedonia, both those inside Bulgaria and when, possible, in the other countries. It also trafficked in opium. In 1925, Greek troops, in an attempt to occupy Petrich, invaded Bulgaria. The League of Nations resolved the dispute and forced Greece to withdraw and to compensate Bulgaria.

In 1924, the *Comintern* had tried to woo the Macedonians. While it had gained some supporters, Todorov and Protogerov had refused to cooperate. When Kolarov tried to embarrass the two by publishing documents showing that IMRO had signed agreements with the *Comintern*, the leaders publicly rejected their authenticity. Shortly after that, Todorov was mysteriously assassinated. Ivan Mihailov (1896–1990), one of his assistants, took his place as leader of IMRO.

Throughout the 1920s, IMRO continued to carry out revenge assassinations and executions of Balkan officials who opposed it. High on its list were leaders of BANU. In 1923 in Prague, it gunned down Raiko Daskalov, who led the Radomir Rebellion that Protogerov had put down in 1918. In 1924, it also murdered Petko Petkov, the Agrarian representative in parliament and the diplomat in the BANU government mentioned earlier. (He was the son of the prime minister murdered by Macedonian irredentists in 1907.) Hundreds were killed, mostly other Macedonians from rival factions. IMRO ordered the assassination of those who signed the agreement with the Communists. In 1925, the left wing of the movement formed as IMRO-United. These Macedonians worked with the *Comintern* and the Communist parties of Bulgaria, Greece, and Yugoslavia in advocating a federation of Balkan states including Macedonia. However, they found little sympathy in the Balkan countries because of their Communist affiliation and the opposition to them by mainstream IMRO. IMRO-United's headquarters, located originally in Vienna, moved to Berlin in 1928.

In IMRO itself, a major split developed between Mihailov, supported by Liapchev, and Protogerov, supported by Tsankov. Murders increased as the two factions went after each other and the politicians who supported their rivals. Young toughs hung outside the *subranie* building in wait for some representative to hire them as bodyguards as they walked the two blocks to the café of the Hotel Sofia for their daily coffee. In 1928, Mihailov's group killed Protogerov, and the former emerged as the sole leader of the organization. Mihailov moved IMRO toward the extreme right and allied, through Volkov, with Mussolini and Italy. The Italians, who felt cheated at the Paris Peace conference, joined the "revisionist" camp of European countries. These were those who wanted to revise the Peace of Paris, mainly the losers—Germany, Austria, Hungary, and Bulgaria. They opposed the French alliance system—Poland and the Little and Balkan Ententes. Italy had an advantage the other revisionist countries did not. Since it had been on the Allied side, it did not suffer the arms restrictions of the treaties and could secretly send weapons to other revisionist countries. It did so to Hungary in 1928, causing an international scandal. Rumors were that Italy was also supplying IMRO. Since Italy regarded Yugoslavia as one of its chief rivals to expansion in the Balkans, IMRO was a natural ally. So was the Croatian fascist organization *Ustaše*. This group found support not only from the Italian Fascists but also from the Vatican, because part of the *Ustaše* program was an extreme Catholic opposition to the Orthodox Serbs who controlled Yugoslavia. IMRO and the *Ustaše* cooperated in terrorist activities, most infamously the 1934 assassinations in Marseilles of King Alexander of Yugoslavia and French Foreign Minister Louis Barthou. The *Ustaše* planned the operation, but the gunman was Mihailov's driver, Vlado "the Chauffer" Chernozemski.

THE LIAPCHEV GOVERNMENT

International pressure mounted on the Tsankov government to do something about IMRO. He went before the League, arguing that Bulgaria needed a loan to ease the refugee problem brought about by the exchange of population which, he said, was the source of not only the Macedonian terror but of the Communist uprising as well. The League agreed, but he could not convince the Western bankers. A loan could only be raised if he resigned as prime minister, and so he did. Andrei Liapchev replaced him, and the Democratic Alliance remained in power.

Striding around the streets of Sofia with his bodyguards and a contingency of German shepherds, Tsankov remained a flamboyant figure in Bulgarian politics. He formed his own fascist organization, the Bulgarian National Socialist Party, which was closer to Mussolini's ideology than Hitler's despite the name. He continued as a *subranie* representative.

Liapchev and Volkov did nothing to curb IMRO, which continued its slaughter inside Bulgaria and raids into the country's neighbors. The government also favored Macedonians in employment, which raised a great deal of resentment among other Bulgarians. Liapchev did grant amnesty to many Agrarians and Communists, who now formed new parties in order to participate in Bulgarian politics. The Communists reformed themselves as the Bulgarian Workers Party (BWP) and also reestablished their trade unions and other organizations. BANU split into a number of separate parties. The two main ones were the left wing BANU-Alexander Stamboliiski, sometimes called BANU-*Pladne* after its newspaper. It split from the moderate BANU-*Vrabcha 1*. (*Vrabcha 1*, literally "Sparrow Street No. 1," was the address of the Agrarian headquarters in Sofia.)

THE POPULAR BLOC

After the fall of Stamboliiski, the party system that existed before World War I reappeared with old and new alliances. Once again, a multitude of politicians looked for ways to feed at the government trough. To deal with this, Liapchev tried to introduce a system that Mussolini created in Italy and was in effect in neighboring Romania. The party receiving a plurality of votes in the parliamentary election was given the majority of seats. In return, parties and politicians opposed to the Democratic Alliance formed their own blocs and coalitions. They made all sorts of deals, and once again Bulgarian politics was marked by corruption and strange bedfellows. Furthermore, the onset of the worldwide depression hurt Bulgaria as elsewhere very hard, and times were ripe for the replacement of Liapchev and the Alliance. The most effective opposition group was the Popular Bloc, the core of which was an alliance between Malinov's Democrats and BANU-*Vrabcha 1*, led by Dimitur Gichev (1893–1964). When opposition arose in the *subranie* to the Alliance government, Liapchev called for new elections in 1931, which the Popular Bloc won. Malinov assumed the premiership with Gichev as the minister of agriculture. Malinov resigned in October 1931 because of ill health, and Nikola Mushanov (1872–1951), also a Democrat, succeeded him.

King Boris gave tacit approval to the new BANU. The farmers considered him complicit in the murder of Stamboliiski, and he was anxious to win them over. In the spring of 1931, he toured the country, visiting the villages and listening to the questions and complaints of the population. He made a point of visiting with Raiko Daskalov's father. He also stopped to praise the late Tsanko Bakalov (1869–1926) in his home village. Bakalov was one of BANU's founders, a theoretician of the Union and a beloved poet who wrote under the name of Tserkovski.

Despite a good beginning bolstered by much popular support, the Popular Bloc could do little in the face of the Great Depression. The farmers held back their crops in hope that prices would rise, but the shortages in the towns just made the situation worse as food was imported at great cost. The banks refused to extend needed credit, and farm income dropped by 30 percent over the next three years. Workers in the towns went on strikes and carried out demonstrations demanding government action. By 1933, farmers were reduced to subsistence existence with their personal income cut in half. In the cities, workers' salaries dropped by almost 30 percent.

Whatever the government tried had little effect because Bulgaria was entirely dependent on the world situation. Before it left office, the Democratic Alliance had established a grain-purchasing agency to buy the farmers' surplus grain, but that did not help until later in the decade as the depression began to ease. The Popular Bloc began regulation of both the production and mercantile trusts that had controlled the Bulgarian market since the nineteenth century. The government gave the Bulgarian National Bank a near monopoly on transactions in foreign currency. It also introduced measures of individual relief and price controls, but the effects did not outweigh the country's desperate situation. Furthermore, to balance the state budget as demanded by the League of Nations and the international financial community, the government dismissed thousands of civil servants.

While the new BANU participated in the government, the new Communist Party, the Bulgarian Workers Party (BWP), did well as opposition. It won 29 seats in the *subranie* compared to 75 for BANU. (The Popular Bloc received 152 total.) The BWP also did well in the local elections held in 1931 and 1932, winning in fact the Sofia City Council. Following the *Comintern* policies of the early 1930s, the BWP raided socialist organizations for members, gained strength in the workers' unions and organizations, and led strikes and demonstrations. The Popular Bloc government, like its predecessors, used strong-arm tactics to counter the Communists. While not outlawing the BWP, it closed its clubs and banned its meetings. It also dissolved the Sofia city council and expelled 15 Communist deputies from the *subranie* on the somewhat spurious grounds that they were really members of the Communist Party, still "officially" illegal, and not the legal Bulgarian Workers Party.

THE *REICHSTAG* FIRE TRIAL

However, in 1933, events in Germany put Bulgaria on the front pages of the world press, and a Communist Party leader became the most famous Bulgarian of the twentieth century. After the failure of the September Uprising, the Bulgarian Communist Party came under the leadership of a younger generation that blamed the old guard for the party's failures. Kolarov and Dimitrov, old-guard leaders, however, became even more prominent in the *Comintern* and closer to Stalin in Moscow. Yet the younger Bulgarian Communists were able to push them aside by giving them international assignments. Dimitrov became head of the *Comintern's* Western European Bureau headquartered in Berlin.

In January 1933, Adolf Hitler, through backstairs politics with the conservative leadership of Germany, became Chancellor of the

Weimar Republic. He needed some dramatic event to consolidate his power. It came in February when Marinus van der Lubbe, a Dutch arsonist, burned down the German *Reichstag* (parliament) building. Although Van der Lubbe had at one time been a member of the Dutch Communist Party, at the time of the arson he was not. He probably acted alone, but this is a subject of ongoing debate.

Hitler declared the arson to be a Communist plot and convinced the German president, Field Marshal Paul von Hindenburg, to give him dictatorial powers through a special clause in the German constitution. This enabled Hitler to carry out mass arrests of Communists and to have the Nazi party win new elections for the *Reichstag*. As for the fire, the police arrested four others besides Van der Lubbe—a leading German Communist, Ernst Torgler, and three Bulgarians: Blagoi Popov (1902–1968), Vasil Tanev (1897–1941), and Georgi Dimitrov.

Blaming Bulgarians added a certain sense of the exotic and mysterious Balkans to the accusation. Western Europeans remembered too well that it was a Balkan crisis that ignited World War I and that the Macedonian terror apparently emanating from Bulgaria was still disturbing the peace of Europe. In an odd foreshadowing, the "mysterious and dangerous" Bulgarians would also be falsely accused of being involved in the assassination attempt on Pope John Paul II in 1981.

The trial took place in Leipzig, and Hitler wanted to use it as propaganda. The world press turned out and radio broadcasted the trial. The judges were members of the German high court. Van der Lubbe, who had been tortured in prison, repeated his confession, and Popov and Tanev meekly accepted their fate. Dimitrov, however, defended himself and acted as his own attorney. His defense was so forceful and defiant, especially when he was questioning Hermann Goering, that he gained worldwide sympathy. He blamed the Nazis themselves for starting the fire. This was generally accepted as true until historical research after the Second World War suggested that Van Der Lubbe probably acted alone, although some still argue that the Nazis did indeed set the fire. In any case, Dimitrov became a heroic figure not only in Bulgaria but also throughout the world. "Countertrials" were held in various countries defending Dimitrov and accusing the Nazis. Books were published with the same goal.

In the end, Van der Lubbe was found guilty and executed, but the other defendants were acquitted on the grounds of insufficient evidence. The Bulgarians were expelled from Germany and went to the Soviet Union. They may have been saved in part because Stalin threatened to retaliate against Germans in Soviet hands. The Soviet

Communists did not receive Popov and Tanev well. Dimitrov was welcomed as an international hero and made General Secretary of the *Comintern*. The coolness toward his codefendants may have come about because they were, in fact, part of the opposition in the Bulgarian party to Dimitrov and Kolarov, who were now clearly the leaders of the Bulgarian Communists. Popov spent time in the notorious "Gulag" labor camps. During World War II, Tanev parachuted back into Bulgaria with other Bulgarians to fight in the resistance and was shot on landing.

GEMETO

It should be noted that Georgi Dimitrov's real name was Georgi Mihailov and he went by Georgi M. Dimitrov. Bulgarians did not adopt last names until the nineteenth century, and well into the twentieth the practice was still quite fluid. Members from the same family would often adopt different last names based on patronymics or some other family distinction. It is something coincidental but typically Bulgarian that one of Dimitrov's most important political rivals was an Agrarian leader also named Georgi M. Dimitrov (1903–1972), designated "Gemeto" to distinguish him.

Gemeto joined BANU in the late 1920s after earning a medical degree. He was one of a group of Agrarians who founded the newspaper *Pladne* in order to unite divisions that were growing in BANU-*Vrabcha 1*. He also became the secretary of the Agrarian Youth Union and organized the Bulgarian Academic Agrarian Union. He particularly stressed the importance of continuing the Agrarian ideology that Stamboliiski and Bakalov had developed at the beginning of the movement. He felt that in this way BANU could compete with the Marxists and anarchists for Bulgaria's radical youth. In the 1931 elections, he won a seat in the *subranie* from the Lovech district. However, disagreements between Dimitrov's group and the BANU-*Vrabcha 1* leader Gichev were already developing. Gemeto objected to the high-handed policies that Gichev used against his opponents in the Union, and while Gemeto agreed that BANU should support the Popular Bloc in the assembly, he did not want Agrarians to enter the cabinet, but Gichev and two others took portfolios.

The issue that ultimately divided the *Pladne* group from BANU-*Vrabcha 1* was amnesty for the BANU leaders still in prison or exile. Many *Pladne* members also wanted to punish those responsible for the 1923 coup against Stamboliiski. Gichev, however, advocated forgiveness for the Democratic Alliance. The issue of amnesty for the

Agrarians became the divisive one. By the end of 1931, Dimitrov was attacking the government both in the pages of *Pladne* and in the assembly. Amnesty was finally granted. The exiled leaders who had been closest to Stamboliiski and the most radical of the Agrarians returned. Gemeto worked with them, causing even more rancor with Gichev. In March 1932, Gemeto and Nikola Petkov (1889–1947) formed the new party BANU-Alexander Stamboliiski. (Petkov was the son of the slain prime minister Dimitur Petkov and the brother of the Agrarian Petko Petkov, who IMRO assassinated in 1924.) Thus the Communists were now united behind the Dimitrov-Kolarov group and BANU was divided.

THE 1934 COUP D'ETAT

The Popular Bloc government could do little to restore either political or economic stability in Bulgaria. IMRO still controlled the southwest of the country with the connivance or indifference of the government. It still harassed the inhabitants for "taxes," raided Yugoslavia and Greece, and dealt in illegal arms and drugs. Government corruption still ran rampant. Ministers and bureaucrats still enriched themselves by stealing public funds, none more than the Agrarians, who hypocritically complained the loudest about it. The constitutional system was stagnant and seemed incapable of dealing with Bulgaria's problems. The alternative lay in one of two directions: the king or the military. These were the alternatives that appeared to be working for Bulgaria's neighbors. In the 1930s, in both Yugoslavia and Romania, the kings became royal dictators, and in Albania, President Ahmed Zogu declared himself king and also ruled as a royal dictator. In Turkey and Greece, military leaders ruled in one form or another as dictators. It should not be surprising that Bulgaria should seek a similar solution. The transition began in 1927 when an elitist political group formed called *Zveno*, the link.

Zveno was founded by intellectuals like the Social Democrat Dimo Kazasov (1888–1980) and members of the Military League, most prominently the colonels Kimon Georgiev (1882–1969) and Damian Velchev (1883–1954). The group opposed the party system, government corruption, and the terrorism of IMRO. It also opposed the Communists and Agrarians. King Boris was wary of the organization because of his political disagreements with some of its leaders, and the *Zveno* leadership feared the king would act to limit its power in the army. Some members of *Zveno* even favored a republic.

In 1934, the organization briefly split. Kazasov, who had served in the Tsankov cabinet as minister of telephones, posts, and railroads, broke from *Zveno* and led a group into the former prime minister's National Socialist Movement. Kazasov's decision is puzzling. There is no doubt that Tsankov's movement was fascistic in nature. Despite its name, it was more similar to Mussolini's Fascism than Hitler's Nazism. Kazasov, however, was definitely left of center in his political views. He was a highly respected journalist, the editor of *Zveno*'s organ, and one of the best chroniclers of Bulgaria in the years between the wars. In the post-World War II era, he continued to be a respected individual in the country and even served in some Communist-controlled governments. He was enlisted in the Garden of Righteous Among the Nations in *Yad VaShem* as one who protected the Jews during the Holocaust. On the other hand, it might be noted that in 1934 even President Franklin Roosevelt was studying Mussolini's governmental solutions.

The Georgiev-Velchev wing of *Zveno* was solidly opposed to IMRO and also to Tsankov. Despite *Time* magazine labeling them as "fascist,"[1] Georgiev and Velchev, like Kazasov, were also left of center. Tsankov's movement did well in the elections of February 1932. He was planning a great rally in Sofia for May 21, 1934, when Georgiev and Velchev decided to act. On May 19, the military members of *Zveno* arrested the government and swiftly took control of the country. Kimon Georgiev became the new prime minister while Damian Velchev remained in the background. Kazasov soon rejoined his old comrades and became ambassador to Yugoslavia, with which the Georgiev government hoped to improve relations. Before the coup, the two countries were already making cultural exchanges and holding joint sporting events. The kings exchanged visits. Georgiev's government also recognized the Soviet Union for the first time, as did a number of other countries during this period, including the United States.

One of the first acts of the new government was to ban political parties. Georgiev ordered their offices closed and their presses stopped. The *Zvenarists* dissolved the *subranie* and planned to reorganize it on a mixed political and etatist basis, that is, with some members representing different classes in society. They wanted to change the trade unions as well, limiting their functions and making them voluntary. The government also centralized the administration of the country, reduced the number of provinces, and replaced local elected officials with appointed ones. It reduced the civil service by a third.

Some of *Zveno's* greatest efforts were dedicated to the control of IMRO and its outrages. It sent the army into its base in Petrich and also into other strongholds of the organization. While it could not eliminate IMRO completely, the government succeeded in weakening its activity. The raids into neighboring countries and the murders inside Bulgaria diminished.

The *Zvenarists*, nevertheless, were still Bulgarian nationalists. They strengthened the role of the church and put restrictions on other religious sects. They also changed a number of Turkish place names to Bulgarian variants. The major problem that Georgiev and Velchev had to deal with was dissention in their ranks. Although Kazasov had shown that he was willing to work with the colonels, there was still a division between the Military League members of *Zveno* and their civilian counterparts, who wanted to build a mass organization based on the group. There was also dissention in the Military League over attitudes toward the king. Velchev, who had stated that he would not work against the monarchy, nevertheless was known to hold republican views. These opinions disturbed some in the League. King Boris feared Velchev would decide to use the republican officers to take over the government. Working with the monarchists in the League, Boris was able to oust Georgiev as prime minister and replace him in January 1935 with General Pencho Zlatev (1881–1948), the minister of defense. Still not satisfied with the Military League in power, the king, after only three months, replaced Zlatev with Andrei Toshev (1867–1944), a diplomat staunchly loyal to the king. Toshev had served Boris's father. He had served as ambassador to Serbia at the time of the Balkan Wars and to the Ottoman Empire from 1913 to 1914. As prime minister, Toshev created a civilian cabinet, leaving the Military League out of power.

THE PERSONAL RULE OF BORIS III

The king was now a royal dictator in the mode of monarchs King Carol II of Romania and the late King Alexander of Yugoslavia. Remember that the latter had been assassinated in France the previous year by the Croatian *Ustaše* and an IMRO gunman who pulled the trigger. Alexander's son Peter II was too young to rule, but the regent, the late king's cousin Prince Paul, had assumed the role of royal dictator.

The new Bulgarian regime kept much of what the *Zvenarist* coup had accomplished. Political parties remained banned and the policy of closer ties with Belgrade continued. It also reined in IMRO. On accepting the premiership, Toshev announced that he and the king would try to revise the Bulgarian constitution and produce one more suitable to modern times. However, they never got around to doing this. In the end, Toshev proved unsuitable for the task. He had too many disagreements with the king and other members of the new government. Furthermore, his past associations with IMRO made him unsuitable for executing the new policy toward Yugoslavia. In November 1935, Boris appointed his court chamberlain Georgi K'oseivanov (1884–1960) the new prime minister, a man completely under his thumb. K'oseivanov would hold the position for the longest period in Bulgarian history except for the tenure of the post-war Communist leader Todor Zhivkov (1911–1998).

Despite the new nonparty policy, the men who filled the cabinet were from the old political parties. K'oseivanov himself took the portfolio of foreign affairs. Of particular note in the cabinet was the Minister of Justice, Dimitur Peshev (1894–1973), whose role in Bulgarian politics over the next decade would earn him an honored place in his country's history. Peshev was born in Kiustendil in Bulgarian Macedonia in 1894 and finished Sofia University in law in 1921. He served as a judge in his hometown, Kiustendil, and later in Plovdiv and Sofia. In 1932, he went into private practice and gained the reputation as an honest and sagacious lawyer. He did not enter politics until after the coup of 1934. The Georgiev government appointed him chairman of the governing board of the new central state bank, Bulgarian Credit. On September 23, 1935, Toshev appointed Peshev minister of justice in his new cabinet, where he remained until July 4, 1936. It was in this post that he made his first important moral decision involving the case of Damian Velchev.

Velchev had left the country after Zlatev replaced Georgiev, and the government declared him a fugitive. The king suspected him of planning a new coup to establish a republican government. We can note that a similar, if opposite, reversal occurred at this time in neighboring Greece, where the monarchy was brought back to replace the republic, which had ousted the king in 1924. Velchev secretly returned to Bulgaria in November 1935 but was captured and put on trial for treason. He was convicted and sentenced to death. However, Bulgarian law required that the minister of justice sign the death warrant. Peshev refused to do this because he believed the sentence was procedurally flawed, and Velchev was spared. Boris commuted his sentence to life imprisonment. Peshev's decision brought him into conflict with both the king and the right-wing extremist minister of war General Hristo Lukov (1887–1943), but the minister of justice stood his ground. K'oseivanov shortly dismissed Peshev from the cabinet.

Still, Boris was now in charge of Bulgaria and ruled the country according to his will. His prime ministers were chosen, like K'oseivanov, to do his bidding. He met regularly with them to discuss and direct state policy. He was a man greatly influenced by his upbringing and swayed by those in his immediate circle. These included his Italian wife and his younger sister Eudoxia (1898–1985). Boris was raised very strictly as a child and became suspicious and cunning. He also, like his father, was very superstitious and often used numerology to determine some of his decisions in life and politics. He sought the approval of the Bulgarian people and wished to avoid the mutual distrust that his father had with the population. This was the reason he never had a formal coronation and instead proclaimed himself the "democratic monarch." He could also be charming and friendly. Before a reception, he would apprise himself of his visitors' interests so that he might be able to engage in impressive conversation. The king had his own locomotive, which he liked to drive around the country's railway tracks, often stopping in villages to greet the locals and to present them with gifts of cash and small trinkets.

Although Boris gladly continued the *Zveno* policy of outlawing political parties, the royal family had close relations with the Democrats. Ekaterina Karavelova (1860–1947), the widow of Peter Karavelov, one of the party's founders, was the chief lady-in-waiting to Queen Ioanna (1907–2000), and Aleksandur Malinov, the party's chief, was the godfather of royal princess Maria Louisa (b. 1933). Boris avoided making difficult decisions and sometimes left crucial items to his prime minister or one of his advisors. He was more reserved in his private life than his father had been. Although rumors of romantic liaisons circulated, nothing much appeared in print, in contrast to the large amount of gossip about Ferdinand. Boris's circle of friends came from the social, political, and cultural elite of Bulgaria. He particularly enjoyed the company of military officers. In addition to his daughter Maria Louisa, he had a son, Simeon (b. 1937), named after the great medieval Bulgarian tsar.

In addition to Eudoxia and his wife, Boris surrounded himself with a coterie of other advisers. Among them were Major Liubomir Lulchev (1892–1945) and the architect Iordan Sevov (d. 1945), an *éminence grise*, whose importance and mysterious influence earned him the sobriquet "the Bulgarian Rasputin."

Opposition to Boris remained mainly from the Communists and Agrarians, whose status in the state varied from illegal to tolerated, with various amnesties granted for individuals. The old politicians, whose parties were now illegal, still played roles as individuals in Bulgarian politics, and some went along with the king and K'oseivanov while

King Boris III, Queen Ioanna, Prince Simeon II,
and Princess Maria Louisa. (Bettmann/Corbis)

others were opposed. Many would change from support to opposition depending on their ambitions and goals. Apart from Tsankov's National Socialist Movement, there never developed a strong fascist movement in the country. A number of politicians held ideas close to Mussolini's Fascism and some even to Hitler's Nazism, but only a few small groups imitating these developed. At best they were a collection of squabbling comic-opera actors led by would-be *führers*.

Two right-wing associations emerged in the 1930s with more than passing stature. One was the Union of Bulgarian National Legions, or simply Legionnaires, and the other the Guardians of the Advancement of the Bulgarian National Spirit, or more simply *Ratnitsi* (Guardians). Minister of War General Hristo Lukov and General Nikola Zhekov (1864–1949), who commanded the Bulgarian troops in World War I, led the Legionnaires. The third leader who founded the university branch was Ivan Dochev (1906–2005). He later gained notoriety after World War II as the head of a Bulgarian anti-Communist organization supported by the United States. Professor Asen Kantardzhiev founded the *Ratnitsi*, but its most important leader was attorney Petur Gabrovski (1898–1945). The Legion and the *Ratnitsi* adopted an ideology that was close to German Nazism and included anti-Semitism, a prejudice generally lacking in Bulgaria. They maintained connections with Berlin, as did Tsankov.

Furthermore, Bulgaria's economic plight moved Sofia closer to Germany. Of course, there were other connections between Germany and Bulgaria as well. They had fought together in World War I and both followed revisionist foreign policies after the war. There were also cultural connections because many Bulgarians had studied at the German church and secular schools in the country as well as in Germany itself. However, the same was also true for other countries. Other powers had their champions among the people, the different layers of society, and the political parties. Boris supposedly once remarked, "My people are pro-Russian, my army is pro-German, my government is pro-English. I am the only true neutral in the country."

Before the Great Depression, many European countries as well as the United States had invested in and traded with Bulgaria. The Rockefeller Foundation sponsored a number of health and agricultural projects in Bulgaria, as it did elsewhere in the Balkans. While some of this activity continued, it declined in the 1930s. Berlin saw an opportunity to move not only into Bulgaria but also into the whole peninsula. With the authoritarian governments, smacking of fascism and anti-Marxism, emerging in Balkans, the National Socialist regime in Germany was further encouraged. Germany had a further advantage because the Danube Valley was a natural trade route from Central Europe into the Balkans. The Third Reich (Hitler's empire) could exchange the region's rich raw materials and agricultural produce for German manufactured goods. Barter was preferred because cash was in short supply in Germany as elsewhere. However, as time went by, Germany built up a huge debt in marks to many countries including Bulgaria, making all more dependent on Berlin if they wanted to protect their economies from collapse. By 1939, Germany owed Bulgaria more than $21.5 million. At the time, Western observers said that Berlin was swindling these small countries, taking their resources in exchange for cheap items that were of little use to them. In fact, however, it was the only significant foreign trade that these small countries had.

We see from the chart that from 1929 to 1932, German and Austrian imports represented from a fifth to a quarter of all goods brought into Bulgaria and more than a quarter of all exports. For Italy, the figures were an average of 10 to 15 percent of imports and somewhat less than 10 percent of exports. England, France, and the United States combined accounted for about 20 percent of imports and less than 10 percent of exports. As the effects of the depression worsened, the balance in favor of Germany increased. In 1933 and 1934, both imports

Table 6.1. Imports to and Exports from Bulgaria[i] (Percentage of Total for Bulgaria)

| | Imports to Bulgaria | | |
Year	From Germany (and Austria after 1938)	From Italy	From United Kingdom, France, and United States
1929	22.2%	10.7%	20.4%
1930	23.2	13.6	19.4
1931	23.3	13.7	21.3
1932	25.9	15.6	18.7
1933	38.2	12.7	13.5
1934	40.1	7.8	12.5
1935	53.5	3.2	7.4
1936	61.0	0.6	8.0
1937	54.8	5.0	10.1
1938	52.0	7.5	13.5
1939	65.5	6.9	6.3

| | Exports from Bulgaria | | |
Year	To Germany (and Austria after 1938)	To Italy	To United Kingdom, France, and United States
1929	29.9%	10.5%	8.4%
1930	26.2	8.3	8.3
1931	29.5	5.8	5.8
1932	26.0	12.5	6.0
1933	36.0	9.1	6.2
1934	42.7	9.2	4.8
1935	48.0	8.8	7.2
1936	47.5	3.6	16.3
1937	43.1	4.2	19.2
1938	58.9	7.6	9.7
1939	67.8	6.1	7.4

[i]Bulgaria, Direction Générale de la Statistique, *Annuaire Statistque du Royaume de Bulgarie*, 26 (1934), pp. 176–77; 30 (193), pp. 486–87; 32 (1940), pp. 300–01. Published in Frederick B. Chary, *The Bulgarian Jews and the Final Solution: 1940–1944* (Pittsburgh: University of Pittsburgh Press, 1972), p. 12.

and exports rose to about 40 percent, and for the other four countries mentioned above, imports fell to about a quarter in 1933 and a fifth in 1934. Exports to those four fell to about 15 percent by 1934 (see Table 6.1).

We see that even before the Balkan economy became a key tool for the political foreign policy of the Third *Reich*, Bulgarian trade was centered on the two German states. In 1934, Sofia and Berlin signed a treaty similar to others Germany was making with Eastern European countries, putting trade on the barter and credit system indicated above.

Bulgarian imports from German immediately jumped to more than half of the total and remained there for the rest of the decade, in some years topping 60 percent. While exports to Germany remained 40 to 50 percent from 1935 to 1937, in 1938 they reached 59 percent and in 1939, 68. Bulgarian foreign trade with Germany in the second half of the 1930s was more than with the rest of the world combined. No other country in Eastern Europe had that much of its trade with Germany. On the other hand, Bulgarian trade with Germany only amounted to 2 percent of the German total. Thus we see the exchange was highly one sided.

By the end of the decade, Bulgaria also began buying arms from Germany, although it was negotiating with France as well. Nevertheless, in 1938, in a secret arrangement, Berlin agreed to supply Sofia with 30 million marks' worth of armaments, to be paid for over five years beginning in 1942. (This was about a third of the amount Boris had requested.) By the time World War II began, Boris, despite his avowed neutrality, already had one foot in the Axis camp.

NOTE

1. *Time*, Vol. XXIII, no. 22 (May 28, 1934).

7

Royal Dictatorship
and World War II (1935–1944)

KING BORIS, THE ROYAL DICTATOR

After Boris attained full control of his country, he first tried to revise Bulgarian borders through rapprochement, seeking a revision of the Treaty of Neuilly by working with his neighbors and the League of Nations. Although the Balkan Entente countries offered Sofia an opportunity to join the Balkan Pact, Boris could not accept because it would mean total rejection of border revision. Of the Bulgarian desires to regain territory in Macedonia, Thrace, and Dobrudja, the last seemed the most possible. During this period, Bulgaria supported the League of Nations' economic sanctions on Italy in the Abyssinian (Ethiopian) crisis of 1935, when Mussolini invaded and took over that country. Boris also supported the ban on foreign volunteers joining the Spanish Civil War. However, in the latter crisis, many Bulgarian Communists and others joined the Georgi Dimitrov Brigade, which fought for the republican side in Spain. Bulgaria also took part in the 1936 Montreux conference, which adjusted the administration of the Turkish straits between the Aegean and Black Seas.

In 1937, the government restored elections at the local level and the following year permitted elections for the 24th *subranie*. Parties were still not allowed. Candidates ran as government supporters or in opposition. Nevertheless, most successful candidates were members of the old political parties. At the same time, the *Comintern* adopted the policy Popular Front from Above and began to work with other parties in coalitions against fascism. None other than Georgi Dimitrov, the new General Secretary of the organization, announced this at the Seventh *Comintern* Congress in 1935. The Bulgarian Workers Party, of course, enthusiastically adopted the policy and joined a coalition with BANU-Aleksandur Stamboliiski and with several liberal parties called the People's Constitutional Bloc.

The government enacted new restrictions for the elections of the assembly. Voters had to affirm in writing that they had never been Communists—a tactic that obviously did not work because Communists were elected. Literacy was required at the elementary level for rural voters and at the secondary level for the urban electorate. For

Georgi Mihailov Dimitrov. (Hulton Archive/ Getty Images)

the first time, women were permitted to vote, but only if they were married or widowed; however, voting was compulsory only for men. The age for serving in the *subranie* was raised from 25 to 30 years. The new election law reduced the number of seats in the assembly to 160 using single electoral districts rather than the older proportional system. Voting took place over three Sundays in February and March, thus allowing for crowd control should demonstrations erupt. The government hoped that by applying the usual bullying tactics, they would ensure a large, favorable majority. While government supporters could campaign freely, speeches from their opponents were stopped by the administration, which used the ban on political parties as an excuse. The government also employed voter fraud, blocking opposition supporters from the polls, and police pressure. As it turned out, their measures were only partially successful. One third of the representatives stated that they supported the opposition, and they were strong enough to cause problems. In reality, the real strength of the *subranie* was not in an ability to halt the government programs, which the opposition accomplished in less than a handful of occasions over the next decade, but in its ability to make its voice heard and cause scandals. Furthermore, individual members were able to raise protests on behalf of their constituents. With only one representative per district, this ability was magnified and often effective.

BULGARIA MOVES TOWARD GERMANY

Bulgaria faced new foreign policy issues as Germany began its expansion policy in 1938. One of Hitler's goals on coming to power was the unification of all German territory, thus nullifying the Treaty of Versailles. When he attempted to do this in 1934, trying to annex his homeland, Austria, Mussolini, of all people, stopped him. However, Hitler judged that France and England were now too weak to stand in his way. He began to rearm, ignoring the restrictions of Versailles. In 1938, the international situation changed. Mussolini and Hitler were now allies supporting the rebelling troops under Francisco Franco in the Spanish Civil War. Furthermore, in 1937, Italy had joined the Anti-*Comintern* Pact with Germany and Japan. Later in May 1939, Berlin and Rome signed the Pact of Steel, nicknamed the Rome-Berlin Axis. This occurred as Boris was moving further away from Italy and closer to Yugoslavia.

In March 1938, Hitler, now with Italy his ally, absorbed Austria, arguing that it was justified on the basis of national self-determination. He then demanded that the German-populated area of Czechoslovakia, the *Sudetenland*, be added to the Reich as well. Mussolini arranged a meeting in Munich in September with the leaders of Germany, Italy, France, and England where the western countries agreed to "appease" Hitler by granting his request. The meeting drastically changed the world situation and made both the words *Munich* and *appeasement* synonyms for *cowardly retreat*. This was quickly followed by the First Vienna Award granting Hungary territory from Czechoslovakia also. These diplomatic settlements destroyed the security system of the little Entente and led to a need in Yugoslavia for an even closer relationship between Sofia and Belgrade. The Yugoslav government proposed a customs union and military alliance with Bulgaria and also some changes in the frontier if Sofia renounced all claims to Macedonia. Although the offer was tempting, Boris was not yet ready to reject Macedonia. He did not want to go to war for it, but with the other revisionist countries gaining territory, he thought some adjustments might be in the offing for Bulgaria. The two countries signed a minor treaty in April removing the barbed-wire fences on their border. Throughout the spring and summer, Bulgaria agreed to a series of nonaggression treaties with the countries of the Balkan Entente, who in turn agreed not to object to Bulgarian rearmament beyond the limitations imposed by Neuilly.

Bulgaria also sought new loans from the European countries. To further this and to reaffirm his country's international position, Boris made a trip to the various capitals in August and September. He was unable to get a British loan, but the French gave the country credits for buying arms and railroad equipment in that country.

Meanwhile, domestic crises once again disturbed the peace of Sofia. After an anti-Semitic riot by the *Ratnitsi* in the spring, the government banned the organization. In the autumn, new agitation for revision of the Treaty of Neuilly spread to the streets. Macedonians assassinated General Ivan Peev, a member of *Zveno*, and riots rocked the capital on several occasions. The government placed Sofia under martial law and ordered a curfew. Then a parliamentary crisis further disrupted Boris' political situation.

Two ambitious politicians with ties to the court moved to limit the king's power. One was Ivan Bagrianov (1891–1945), a wealthy tobacco farmer, the leader of a right-wing agrarian group, who had won an opposition seat in the *subranie*. Bagrianov had personal—and perhaps intimate—contacts with the royal court. Bagrianov's partner in the move on Boris was Purvan Draganov (1890–1945), the Bulgarian ambassador to Berlin. Both were close friends of Boris and his family. Secret German documents claimed that Bagrianov was the lover of

Princess Eudoxia, the king's sister and adviser, and that Draganov was Boris's half-brother, the illegitimate son of Ferdinand.[1]

Once in parliament, Bagrianov tried to win support for his group away from the BANU factions by promising benefits to the poor and middle farmers. In October 1938, he led a strong opposition movement in the *subranie* against a government bill that would appropriate funds for a semiofficial newspaper. K'oseivanov made the vote a measure of confidence and lost when it failed. Boris asked his trusted prime minister to form yet another cabinet that would include some of the members of parliament in order to gain that body's stronger support. He added Bagrianov as minister of agriculture.

The new minister of finance, Dobri Bozhilov (1884–1945), went to London to renew the loan request. He was unsuccessful, but Germany, in fear of losing a potential client state, leant Sofia an additional 22 million marks. K'oseivanov meanwhile met with the Yugoslav prime minister in October and then addressed the *subranie* in November, stating quite clearly that Sofia would continue to develop friendly relations with Belgrade and Ankara and push for territorial revision both with Athens in Thrace and with Bucharest in Dobrudja.

If the Munich agreement really meant peace in Europe, as the naïve and anxious wanted to believe, then Bulgaria would not have to choose sides in a European conflict. Because both the Western democracies and the fascist dictatorships signed the treaty, the government faction and the Western-oriented opposition in the *subranie* sent congratulatory messages to the signatories of the pact. If the pact meant the increased aggressiveness of Germany in Eastern Europe, as events would later prove, Bulgaria would have to move closer to Berlin.

The Munich accord collapsed in March 1939 when Germany seized the rest of Czechoslovakia and immediately began to demand Polish territory. Britain and France responded by guaranteeing to protect Poland and also Romania and Greece. Italy also took the opportunity to absorb Albania into its kingdom. Once again, as in 1914, Europe was divided into two camps of Great Powers and war seemed inevitable. Boris tried to keep Bulgaria neutral. In the spring of 1939, he banned fascist organizations, including Tsankov's National Socialist Organization. In the summer of 1939, K'oseivanov journeyed to Berlin, returning a diplomatic visit the German foreign minister had earlier made to Sofia. Both countries had requests. Germany wanted Bulgaria to join the anti-*Comintern* Pact, which Boris and K'oseivanov were not ready to do. It would soon be a moot point, for in August, Moscow and Berlin stunned the world by signing a mutual nonaggression treaty. Obviously this abrogated the anti-*Comintern* nature of the Axis alliance, although Germany, Italy, and Japan rejoined in 1940 in the Three Power Pact. K'oseivanov wanted a bigger loan and support for Bulgaria's irredenta but assured Germany that Sofia would concentrate on territorial adjustments from Greece and Romania because Berlin was also wooing Yugoslavia. Berlin sent an official of the economic division of the foreign office to discuss further aid. Britain's guarantee to Bucharest forced Bulgaria further toward Germany if it wanted an adjustment in Dobrudja, although London told Sofia it would try to help.

Shortly after K'oseivanov returned from Berlin, Stoicho Moshanov (1892–1975), the nephew of the Democrat leader Mushanov, and, like him, a party leader, went to Paris and London. The Democrats were well known as being pro-Western. Moshanov told the press that his trip was a private matter, but the king approved it. The situation embarrassed K'oseivanov, who had learned of Moshanov's travel plans while he was in Berlin and asked the German press to ignore them. He also tried in vain to persuade Moshanov to cancel his trip. Moshanov's journey was barely mentioned in the Bulgarian newspapers, which gave full coverage to K'oseivanov's visit to Germany.

From an ideological point of view, the Soviet-German pact seemed inconceivable, but from a geopolitical point of view, it made perfect sense. Russia's and Germany's division of Eastern Europe between them was the final reversal of the 1919 Paris territorial settlement. In fact, it was another reoccurrence of what the two powers had done both in the eighteenth century when they had divided Poland and in the nineteenth century when Russia and Germany had joined with Austria in the Three Emperors League. Hitler and Stalin were acting not as the leaders of Nazism and Communism but in the manner in which the tsars and kaisers had acted in the past. That their alliance would sooner or later collapse and lead to conflict was not only inevitable but also what lay in the back of the minds of the leaders of both countries.

WORLD WAR II

The Berlin-Moscow pact pushed Bulgaria closer to Germany and away from the West, but it had some advantages as well because Russia was still popular in Bulgaria. The kingdom exchanged cultural and sporting events with the Soviet Union. Furthermore, Sofia never broke relations with Moscow during World War II. The two countries signed new trade and communication treaties. The new atmosphere helped the Bulgarian Communists. They enjoyed a freedom unknown for years. Their press published without censorship and police surveillance, widespread just a few weeks before, relaxed.

However, Sofia feared new pressure from Turkey and Romania to join the Balkan Pact and asked Berlin for help in resisting it. Germany, unwilling to upset its relations with the Soviet Union, hesitated in intervening in areas of the Balkans not included in the Moscow-Berlin agreement. The Reich's foreign office instructed its military attaché in Sofia not to promise anything except that K'oseivanov might invite a German general as an advisor.

On September 1, 1939, Germany invaded Poland, and France and England declared war on the Reich two days later. World War II in Europe began. K'oseivanov immediately declared that Bulgaria would follow a policy of peace and neutrality. Boris repeated this a month later in his speech from the throne at the opening of the *subranie*. However, K'oseivanov assured Berlin that although unwilling to join the war, they still favored Berlin rather than London and Paris. At the same time, Moscow persistently demanded that Sofia sign a friendship and nonaggression pact with the USSR just as Germany had. The Bulgarian government rejected the proposal, saying it would not agree to a treaty with the USSR without German consent.

K'oseivanov, however, was somewhat dismayed over the direction the country was taking. He preferred England and France to Germany. More than that, he felt insulted over the affair with Moshanov's visit to the West just after he had been in Berlin. In addition, he could not get along with some of his own cabinet members, particularly Bagrianov. He also was disgruntled that the king and not he himself ran his government. He resigned toward the end of October 1939. King Boris asked him to remain as an interim prime minister until he could find a new government leader.

The minor changes in the cabinet had no apparent significance, but one new minister was of more than passing interest. K'oseivanov appointed Petur Grabovski, the fascist *Ratnik* lawyer, minister of telephones, posts, and railroads. He resigned from the illegal organization upon joining the government. The day after forming the new cabinet, K'oseivanov dissolved the *subranie* and called for new elections. Although the government had controlled the assembly, its sizable opposition had at times been an embarrassment, especially when Bagrianov had been able to bring down the council of ministers.

Elections for the new *subranie*, the 25th ordinary national assembly in Bulgaria's history, took place in December and January. The order of voting was changed so that the districts most likely to side with the opposition voted last. The government maintained a tighter grasp on the polls than it had in 1938. Dimo Kazasov, in his memoir of the era, reports that the government won 121 out of 160 seats. It is hard to say exactly what the split was because parties were not recorded, but Kazasov based his estimate on the vote for the *subranie* president, Nikola Logofetov (1880–1945). The government claimed 140 supporters, but on many issues they had considerably fewer, although they rarely lost a vote.

BOGDAN FILOV

Speculation was widespread that after the election, Bagrianov would replace K'oseivanov as prime minister, but Boris would not have it. In fact, he chose that relatively unknown minister of education Bogdan Filov (1883–1945), a German-educated art historian who had been appointed to the cabinet in 1938. Rumors persisted, however, that Bagrianov would soon take over the premiership. In fact, he was eased out of the cabinet a year later. Draganov, the other threat to the king's power, was removed from his important post in Berlin and dispatched to a less influential mission in Lisbon.

The cabinet needed a new foreign minister because K'oseivanov had held that post and a new minister of interior, the department that dealt with police matters, because the previous minister had been embarrassed by election irregularities. The new foreign minister, Ivan Popov (1890–1944), was the ambassador to Yugoslavia and a friend of K'oseivanov. More significantly, Gabrovski, the ex-*Ratnik*, moved from posts and railroads to minister of interior. Despite Popov's pro-Western leanings, the new government on the whole had a definite pro-German cast. King Boris continued to control affairs and met regularly with the key members of the cabinet—"the four"—Filov, Popov, Gabrovski, and minister of war General Teodosi Daskalov (1888–1945) to discuss the country's policies.

Bulgaria's hope for neutrality was wrecked on the course the war played out. After the quick German victory in Poland in September 1939, action stalled for the winter. In the spring of 1940, the Reich's steamrolling *blitzkrieg* began again. The *Reichswehr* conquered Denmark, Luxembourg, Holland, and Norway in rapid succession from April to June. The greatest blow was the fall of France on June 25, 1940. Britain now faced Germany alone. The Soviet Union now put pressure on its western neighbors in order to strengthen its borders. The incorporation of the Baltic states and part of Finland into the USSR had been sanctioned by the pact with Germany, but the Soviet Union also forced

Romania to give up Bessarabia (today Moldova) and continued to hound Sofia to sign a treaty with Moscow. Hitler decided in the summer of 1940 that Germany must attack the Soviet Union.

Mussolini, who had left his alliance with Hitler when the latter signed the pact with the USSR, now rejoined him and attacked France in June. Furthermore, *il duce* wanted glory of his own and decided he would invade and conquer Greece. All these events made neutrality virtually impossible for the states of southeast Europe. Neutrality in wartime was much more difficult to maintain than it had been during the days of peacetime diplomacy in the 1930s. Boris felt himself being pulled into the Axis camp, and as he moved more to one side, his government requested more favors from the Reich, blocking any retreat.

Bulgarian hopes for Greek and Romanian border revision grew stronger. The war seemed to encourage the readjusting of frontiers not only for Germany but also for the Soviet Union. Sofia hoped for similar retrieval. The cry for Dobrudja and the promised Aegean port resounded in the press, the *subranie*, and the streets. Of these claims, the government pursued Dobrudja with the greatest ardor. Moscow, after gaining Bessarabia, publicly supported Sofia's claim for southern Dobrudja and offered to help, suggesting the Soviet Union and Bulgaria occupy the region together, which would have formed a common border. Many in the country approved of such an agreement, and the Communists, whose press had been unfettered since the Berlin-Moscow pact, actively agitated for it.

Boris feared he would not be able to resist the Soviet demands for a treaty if they were coupled to a restoration of Dobrudja. He urged Berlin to bail him out of this difficult situation. Under these circumstances, the Germans decided to act and arrange the cession of southern Dobrudja to the Bulgarians themselves. Hungary, another revisionist ally of the Reich, also wanted a piece of Romanian Transylvania that it had lost in the 1919 Peace of Paris. Furthermore, Romania, which also wanted aid from Berlin, in the summer of 1940 was in worse shape than Bulgaria because of the struggle between King Carol II and the fascist Iron Guard, which was disrupting the peace of the country. In fact, Carol would be forced to abdicate in September 1940. Germany decided to satisfy both Sofia and Budapest with territorial revisions. Talks between Sofia and Bucharest took place at Craiova, Romania. The final awards were made under German auspices on September 7, 1940. The same day, ironically, King Carol and his mistress Elena Lupescu left Romania for good, pursued by Iron Guard thugs who were shooting at the king's train from their automobile.

In Bulgaria there was national jubilation. Streets in Dobrich, Dobrudja's provincial center, and Sofia were renamed after Hitler, Mussolini, and Victor Emmanuel III. Now Bulgaria was irrevocably tied to the Reich. When Hitler asked for favors, Boris had to accede. In October, Hitler's plans for a Soviet invasion moved a step forward. He used the excuse of unrest in Romania to send in German troops. Berlin also sent advisers to Bulgaria in order to discuss military matters there.

Inside the kingdom, the alignment with the Axis was reflected in the change in attitude toward the country's small Jewish population. There were only about 48,000 Jews, mainly of the Sephardic rite, living in Bulgaria—less than 1 percent of the population. The largest minority—about 10.5 percent—was still the Turks. Greeks, Armenians, and Roma were each more or less similar in number to the Jews. Virtually all the Jews lived in the cities, almost half in Sofia. Extreme anti-Semitism of the kind found in Russia or Romania was rare if not unknown in Bulgaria. The country had experienced, as we have seen, many different ethnicities and religions throughout the ages. However, Nazis forced measures and laws against the Jews on Berlin's allies.

In 1938, the government press as well as leading citizens (even Aleksandur Tsankov) proudly proclaimed the absence of anti-Semitism and racism in their country. However, late in 1939 a change occurred. For the first time, government officials made public anti-Semitic statements. The profascist police chief ordered foreign Jews expelled from the country, and even Jews with Bulgarian citizenship suffered abuse in the process. The most significant event determining the introduction of anti-Semitism into the country was the elevation of Gabrovski to the ministry of interior. He brought with him a number of *Ratnitsi*, in particular an anti-Semitic lawyer, Aleksandur Belev (d. 1944), to deal with the new "Jewish problem" in Bulgaria. Throughout 1940, Belev prepared a Bulgarian version of the German anti-Semitic Nuremberg laws. The government introduced a Law for the Defense of the Nation into the *subranie* in the fall of 1940. Large segments of the public denounced the bill and prestigious deputies articulately argued against it in the assembly. In spite of this, the anti-Semitic law was adopted and went into effect in January 1941. The king, embarrassed by the law, waited for the Christmas holiday to pass before signing it.

The law had gone through the assembly rather quickly. Very few of the speeches in favor of it were made by the more established Bulgarian politicians. There were, however, two incidents of special note. In addition to the anti-Semitic passages in the law, there was also an anti-Masonic section. Most members of the assembly and the government, including Gabrovski, had been members of the Bulgarian Masonic lodge. Rumors had it that King Boris himself was a member. They resigned only when the bill had been proposed. The most heated outburst on the floor of chamber during the debate on the bill was between an anti-Semitic member and the ex-prime minister and ex-Mason (and German favorite, we may add) Aleksandur Tsankov over the anti-Masonic passages. Another representative from the pro-Nazi fringe of Bulgarian politics proposed an amendment that all ex-Masons be registered for government sanctions. The whole chamber of ex-Masons roared with laughter. The amendment of course was not considered.

The other incident involved the Democrat leader and ex-prime minister Nikola Mushanov and the ex-minister of justice Dimitur Peshev. Mushanov, who was opposed to the anti-Semitic legislation, was giving a speech against the law while Peshev, who was a vice president of the *subranie*, sat in the speaker's chair. Peshev called time. Mushanov turned, asking him for time to finish, and prophetically said he, Peshev, would regret the passage of the law. Later Peshev would indeed regret his country's anti-Semitism and aid the Jews. In an ironic twist of fate, the issue would bring him into the pantheon of heroes of Bulgarian history.

Meanwhile, Hitler began to firm up his plans to invade the Soviet Union, finally issuing the directive Operation Barbarossa in December. Germany did not need the Balkan countries to join in the war. Having them friendly but neutral on the sidelines would have been sufficient. It was, in fact, England that wanted those countries to come in on its side. British Foreign Secretary Anthony Eden looked for help there. So did Franklin Roosevelt's special envoy Colonel William J. "Wild Bill" Donavan, later head of the Office of Strategic Services (OSS), the predecessor of the Central Intelligence Agency (CIA). Even though the United States was not yet in the war, Roosevelt wanted to keep the Balkans out of the German camp, and in January 1941, Donovan strong-armed Popov, urging the Bulgarians to defy Berlin. However, even Turkey, the country most likely to support Britain, assured Germany of its neutrality. Boris went to Berlin in November 1940 and assured Hitler of his cooperation, if needed.

BULGARIA ENTERS THE WAR

It was not Germany that brought the war to the Balkans, but Italy. Mussolini had suggested to Hitler that they invade the Balkans together, but the Führer refused. The Italian leader suggested the same to Boris, who also put him off. Mussolini then decided to invade Greece whether Hitler liked it or not and attacked at the end of October 1940. The invasion was a disaster and embarrassment for Mussolini and a crisis for Hitler. The Greeks stemmed the Italian advance and pushed them back into Albania. Hitler now had to bail his ally out.

Hitler ordered Operation *Marița*, the conquest of Greece, a few days even before Operation Barbarossa. Concerned about events in the Balkans, Moscow now also renewed its pressure on Sofia to sign a mutual defense treaty. Stalin sent to Sofia the secretary general of the Soviet Commissariat of Foreign Affairs with an offer to defend Bulgaria from Turkey and also to help get territory in Turkish Thrace. The Bulgarian Communists agitated publicly for the treaty (which was supposed to be secret). Popov refused the offer but assured Moscow that Sofia's negotiations with Germany, which were also going on at the same time, were not a threat to the USSR. Moscow was also in negotiations with Germany, which cynically suggested that the Soviet Union join the Three Power Pact.

For Operation *Marița*, Berlin needed cooperation from both Sofia and Belgrade. The plan called for German troops to march through Bulgaria while Yugoslavia remained neutral. It was for precisely this change in German plans that King Boris now had to pay the debt he owed Berlin for the return of Dobrudja. He agreed to new talks with Germany.

In January 1941, Prime Minister Filov went to Vienna for an unpublicized meeting with Hitler and German Foreign Minister Joachim von Ribbentrop to discuss an alliance. Filov prophetically recorded in his diary, "War is unavoidable. If, however, we realize this, it is best we follow it under conditions that are the least complicated for us. If we allow the Germans simply to pass through our country, they will treat us as an occupied land, like Romania, and this will be much worse than if we ally with them. We cannot gain anything from an English victory, for failure of German arms means we shall be Bolshevized."[2]

On January 20, the cabinet approved the German army entering the country. Filov recorded in his diary, "This was without doubt the most important meeting we have had to date."[3] The alliance with Germany put the king and government in a difficult international situation. Sofia was concerned about repercussions from Moscow and possible negative reaction from Turkey. Berlin wanted the Bulgarians to sign a friendship treaty with the Turks and in fact was able to persuade Ankara to agree. As for the Soviets, Ribbentrop told the Bulgarian prime minister that the "Russians [would] . . . put up with the situation and not react."[4] Filov was also concerned that the Yugoslav government leaders were showing some hesitation in agreeing to their treaty, which simply required them to remain neutral while the Germans went through Bulgaria. The German foreign minister reassured Filov that Belgrade would agree. Back in Sofia, some of the leaders of the opposition, namely Mushanov, Burov, and Gichev, also had inquiries. They requested a meeting to find out about the rumors of the German treaty. Filov put them off by saying that he could not meet with them because they had inquired as party leaders, and political parties were now illegal in Bulgaria.

In February 1941, the German preparations in Bulgaria became obvious. New bridges were built across the Danube, and a sudden influx of German "tourists" invaded Sofia. Indeed, Germans could be found in all the strategic Bulgarian cities wearing trench coats with their military boots showing underneath. The world press also suddenly showed interest in the country. As we have seen by the activity of Eden and Donovan, the British and American diplomats pressured foreign minister Popov about the German activity. The foreign minister became very anxious about his government's plans to join the war. The American minister plenipotentiary in Sofia, the former Pennsylvania governor George Earle, habitually went to cafés filled with German officers and tipped the orchestra to play "It's a Long Way to Tipperary." On one occasion he got into a fight, creating a scandal.

The government suppressed anti-German propaganda and arrested several outspoken critics of the Third Reich. In addition to the military technicians, Berlin sent economic experts to Sofia. On February 1, Dobri Bozhilov, the Bulgarian minister of finance, and Hermann Neubacher of the German foreign office signed a preliminary economic agreement for the expenses connected with the German passage through the country. The Bulgarian general staff arranged the military details with the Reich's Field Marshal Siegmund List in Romania. The main economic and political arrangements were worked out in Berlin. The final arrangements called for Bulgaria to join the Three Power Pact precisely on the day the Germans entered the country.

On March 1, Filov traveled to Vienna to sign the Three Power Pact, and the Bulgarian press finally announced the German intention to march through their country the next day. German troops were stationed not in Sofia but in the suburbs. Bulgarian troops were stationed on the Turkish border despite the friendship treaty with Ankara.

Only German troops took part in the war operations against Greece and were prepared, if necessary, to fight against Turkey.

Sir George Rendel, the British plenipotentiary, left the country for Ankara. The king significantly told him in an audience before his departure, "I hope nothing will happen to the Jews."[5] This statement would echo through the decades in a debate about the king's role in the Holocaust, a debate that still goes on in the twenty-first century. The Bulgarian ambassador to London, Nikola Momchilov (b. 1891), resigned in protest and remained in London for the rest of his life. Filov remarked in his diary that the ambassador always felt more English than Bulgarian.[6]

When Filov had met Hitler in Vienna on March 1, they discussed the situation in the Balkans. The Bulgarian prime minister mentioned that the Yugoslav ambassador had suggested to him that Belgrade, Sofia, and Ankara form some sort of defensive alliance. Filov recorded in his diary that at this point Hitler "winced as if suddenly he [had] made a decision—just as when he made the decision on the Dobrudja question. He summoned the Hungarian plenipotentiary minister and Ribbentrop, who came quickly, and he declared that the Yugoslavs whatever they did would never be able to be our friends. At the settling of Balkan affairs revision must affect them. They must make concessions both to Bulgaria and to Hungary. When I began to speak to him some more about Yugoslavia, he thought that we should once again raise claims for Macedonia. Then he cut me off and began to propose again what he told me at Berghof in January [i.e., not to expect revision in Macedonia]. I told him that on this problem we have already come to a decision and that now we are interested only in the behavior of Yugoslavia in connection with the military operations."[7]

Berlin finally persuaded Yugoslavia to join the Three Power Pact and agree to remain neutral in the German invasion of Greece. The Yugoslav prime minister and foreign minister made their journey to Vienna on March 25 and signed the treaty. However, the very next day a group of military officers overthrew the Yugoslav government. They deposed the regent, Prince Paul, and declared that Peter II, the son of Alexander Karadjordjević, had reached his majority and now ruled the country. The people of Belgrade celebrated in raucous glee at what to them seemed a courageous defiance of the Nazi juggernaut.

Hitler was furious, even though the new government said it would remain neutral in the conflict. The Führer regarded the coup as a personal insult and vowed to destroy Yugoslavia. Bulgaria's role in the campaign now changed, although it would still not fight on the battlefront. Instead, the Bulgarian military and government would occupy Macedonia along with Greek Thrace and a small territory around Pirot in Serbia some 50 miles west of Sofia.

Operation *Mariţa* began on April 6, and within a few weeks, both Yugoslavia and Greece fell to the German troops. The Bulgarian army and civilian authorities followed and occupied the designated areas— Macedonia, Thrace, and Pirot. The areas that Bulgaria occupied were those that had been designated to Bulgaria according to the agreement with Serbia before the First Balkan War, plus the unresolved central zone and then some. Thessaloniki and the surrounding area remained in Greek hands under German occupation. Bulgaria now occupied Skolpje, Shtip, and Bitolia in Macedonia and Dedeagach, Giumiurdzhina, Kavala, Ksanti, Seres, and Ziliahovo in Thrace. It even occupied the famous ancient islands of Thasos and Samothrace. The latter's name they changed to Paisii in honor of the first Bulgarian historian.

Bulgaria's goal of attaining the San Stefano borders assigned them in 1878 at long last had been reached. However, although Bulgaria now administered these areas, which they called the newly occupied territories, Germany did not yet give them to Sofia. The settlement, Berlin said, would wait until after the war, much to the chagrin of the Bulgarian public and press. The Axis powers broke up Yugoslavia completely. They established a Croatian monarchy under an Italian prince but controlled by the *Ustaše*. In addition to the territory they gave to Bulgaria, they gave portions of Yugoslavia to Hungary and Italy. In fact, Sofia and Rome disputed the border between Bulgarian-occupied Macedonia and the portion added to Italy's province Albania. The region was rich in silver and lead, and actual armed conflict between the two nations occurred until the Reich stepped in and halted it.

Operation *Mariţa* forced Germany to delay Operation Barbarossa until June. Although a minority of scholars believe the *Wehrmacht* would not have been able to move until then in any case, the consensus is that the invasion of the Balkans delayed the Reich's move against the Soviet Union long enough to stop Germany from taking Moscow and Leningrad before the winter and ultimately helping to cause the victory of the United Nations, the antifascist side in the war.

When the German army invaded the Soviet Union on June 22, 1941, Sofia did not declare war on Moscow but retained relations. Boris argued that Bulgaria could act as a liaison for Berlin with the Soviet state. Although some in Germany wanted the Bulgarians to join in, Hitler, in fact, agreed to let Boris remain out of the conflict. Tensions, of course, between Moscow and Sofia increased. The government expelled the Communist deputies from the *subranie*.

THE PARTISANS

The Communists now organized a resistance to fight against the government. In actuality, the Agrarians of BANU-Aleksandur Stamboliiski had already been carrying out acts of sabotage and resistance before the Soviet invasion, but they did not have the tradition that the Communists could now bring. In 1942, BANU-Aleksandur Stamboliiski joined with the Communists in a resistance movement called the Fatherland Front (*Otechestven Front*). Others, including members of Zveno and the Socialists, joined as well. The Front had both a political and military wing. The Communist Tsola Dragoicheva (1900–1993) led the former.

The military wing of the Front carried out sabotage and assassinations. All things considered, the resistance had more support than one would think, but not as much as in Bulgaria's occupied neighbors Yugoslavia and Greece. The strength of both the Agrarians and Communists in the country and the prestige of their leaders bolstered support. Inspiration came from both Georgi Dimitrovs and Nikola Petkov as well as from Zvenarists like Kimon Georgiev, Dimo Kazasov, and Damian Velchev. Other respected leaders like the head of BANU-*Vrabcha 1*, Dimitur Gichev, the Democrat leader Nikola Mushanov, and the jurist Petko Stainov (1890–1972), a member of the conservative National Party, were all pro-Western and opposed the Nazis as part of the legal opposition. The Fatherland Front attempted to get them to join and was successful at least in Stainov's case, who would serve in the postwar governments. He eventually earned the distinction of being the longest-serving member of the *subranie*, having served in assemblies from the 1920s to the 1970s.

Most of the members of the resistance, called *partisans* as in Yugoslavia, were young men and women. Because of the Nazi ideology and the anti-Semitic legislation in the country, a great number of young Jews joined the partisans, about 400 out of 10,000 total active fighters. Their membership was at rate four times greater than the population as a whole. The government publicized this as a justification for its laws and measures against the Jews, which increased after the Law for the Defense of the Nation was enacted. In fact, one of the first major acts of the resistance was carried out by a Jew, Leon Tadzher, who blew up a fuel depot in Ruse. Another, Ana Ventura, the daughter of a wealthy industrialist from Ruse, joined the Communists and became a partisan leader in her own group. The small partisan group, the Dark Angels that operated in Sofia, had two prominent Jewish members. One Violeta Iakova became one of the most celebrated partisans in postwar

Communist Bulgaria; Iakova assassinated General Lukov, the former minister of war and leader of the anti-Semitic fascist Legionnaires. Another partisan, Menachem Papo, assassinated a German agent in 1943 and was caught by the police. His trial and execution were major propaganda coups for the government both against the partisans and the Jews.

Although the Soviet Union and Bulgaria were not at war, Moscow sent aid to the partisans. Georgi Dimitrov, living in the USSR was still the head of the Bulgarian Communist Party. The Soviets set up a radio station called Radio Hristo Botev, named after the famed poet. It broadcast propaganda against the fascists and the Bulgarian government into the country. Bulgarian Communist leaders and political commissars were spirited into the country by submarine or dropped by parachute to lead the partisans. However, the Bulgarian Communists were at a disadvantage compared to their comrades in Greece and Yugoslavia. Josef Broz-Tito, the leader of the Yugoslav partisans, emerged as the most powerful of the Balkan Communists, although his differences with Stalin were developing even during the war. The advantage that the Bulgarians had because of Dimitrov's status in the *Comintern* was diminished when Stalin disbanded the organization in 1943 because of the difficulties it caused with his Allies. The Allies sent officers to fight with the partisans. Major Frank Thompson, the brother of the famous British Labor historian E. P. Thompson, was one. When he was caught with his detachment, the Bulgarians offered to put him in a prisoner-of-war camp, but he chose to die with his comrades. In September 1941, the Bulgarian and Greek partisans cooperated in a large-scale uprising in Thrace centering in Drama, Kavala, and Seres. German records indicated that 2,000 insurgents carried out the raids.

The relative strength of the Balkan Communist parties was an important issue for the Macedonian question and the future of the region in the postwar world. Greece, Yugoslavia, and Bulgaria all viewed the Slavs that inhabited the region differently. The Greeks, or more properly the Greek government, regarded them as Slavophone Greeks, that is, persons of Greek nationality because their grandparents had belonged to the Greek Orthodox Church even though they spoke a Slavic language. The Yugoslav government, run by Serbs, regarded them as South Serbs. The Bulgarians regarded them as Bulgarians. As we have seen above, the Macedonian Slavs themselves were divided, but the Bulgarian schools under the Ottoman Empire had for more than 70 years taught the children in their schools that they were Bulgarians.

Of course, there were also other religious and ethnic groups in the region—Vlachs, Greeks, Turks, Albanians, Jews, and others.

Macedonia's fate was in part determined by the partisans fighting there and by the various national Communist parties. The Bulgarian Communist Party assigned Metodi "Sharlo" Shatarov (1897–1944), a Bulgarian from Macedonia, to lead the resistance there. Tito wanted the partisans in Macedonia, be they Yugoslav, Greek, or Bulgarian, to fall under his command. Tito himself, the son of a Croatian father and Slovene mother, viewed Macedonia as a separate province in what he hoped would be a postwar Balkan, Communist federation like the Soviet Union. While many Bulgarians including the Communists and even IMRO had no objection to a separate Macedonia as a practical solution to the problem, they still regarded the Macedonians as Bulgarians.

Another factor that affected the resistance in the Balkan countries was the political differences among the various groups. In Bulgaria, differences had been resolved by the establishment of the Fatherland Front, which had brought together the partisan movement. Those like Mushanov and Gichev who did not wish to join the Communists opposed the government through legal means. However, in Yugoslavia and Greece, there were many different partisan groups. Not only did they not operate together, but they also often fought each other as well as their foreign occupiers with their fascist or *Quisling* governments. In Yugoslavia, the Communists' main rivals were the *Chetniks* led by Draža Mihailović. The *Chetniks* fought mainly on the side of the Serbian monarchists. Because of this, Tito was able to win over not only the other ethnic groups but also the backing of the Allies. In Greece, the political landscape was much more diverse. Separate resistance armies were formed by Communists, monarchists, republicans, and regionally based factions. Greek Communists, though strong, were not as strong as Tito's partisans.

In May 1941, Tito had sent Lazar Kolishevski, a Macedonian, to organize the fight in Macedonia even before the Germans had invaded the Soviet Union. Later in the year, the *Comintern* decided that Kolishevski, not Sharlo, should organize the Macedonian resistance. The Bulgarian Communists acquiesced and recalled Sharlo to Bulgaria.

In July the Reich recalled from Sofia their ambassador, the veteran diplomat Herbert von Richthofen, a cousin of the famous Red Baron— the German World War I flying ace. The new ambassador was a hard-line Nazi, Adolf-Heinz Beckerle, a member of the *Stürm Abteilungen* (SA), the paramilitary Brown Shirts.

Although Bulgaria retained relations with the USSR throughout the war, tension between the countries grew. In 1942, Sofia closed the Soviet consulate in Varna, keeping only the embassy open. The consulate had been an espionage center for Moscow, as was the embassy. In December 1941, the United States entered the war and the Bulgarian government declared what they called "symbolic" war on the United States. In World War I, Bulgaria was at war with Russia but not the United States; now Sofia was at war with Washington but not Moscow. In the United States, Bulgarian diplomats were interned at Biltmore, the Vanderbilt estate in Asheville, North Carolina, until they could be returned home.

February 1942 brought additional problems for the country because the Danube flooded, especially near Vidin. In March, Boris visited Hitler again while Ribbentrop came to Sofia to talk with Filov. The Germans did not ask the Bulgarians to participate in the war against Russia, which was going worse than they expected because of the winter. Instead they told them that they might have to send more troops to Serbia. Sofia wanted to concentrate their forces in Macedonia. For fear that Ankara might join the Allies, Hitler also asked Boris to "be more amicable toward the Turks."[8]

At about the same time, the Bulgarians were uncovering a conspiracy against the government involving a former artillery general, Vladimir Zaimov (1888–1942). Zaimov had been involved in the 1934 coup as an associate of Velchev. Like Velchev, he was part of the republican wing of the Military League. He was arrested at that time but acquitted for lack of evidence. However, he was dismissed from the army. He maintained contacts with the Communists and had a friendly relationship with the Soviet military attaché. The 1942 conspiracy involved some 40 people, and Zaimov was arrested again. This time he was convicted and executed. The case was a sensation in the country. Zaimov became a Communist martyr and hero and received both Bulgarian and Soviet decorations posthumously after the war. His story also became a major Bulgarian film in 1966, *Tsar i General* (*Tsar and General*).

There were known to be Communist and Russophile elements in the army, but Zaimov's rank made this case unique. The minister of war, Daskalov, who had assured Filov and the king of the military's loyalty, now had to leave the cabinet. Filov wanted to get rid of the pro-Western Popov as well, and a new government was installed in April.

A NEW GOVERNMENT

Beckerle, in fact, suggested to Boris that he revise the cabinet in a more pro-German direction. The king waited until he returned from Germany before making the change. Filov remained as prime minister.

Besides getting rid of Popov and Daskalov, Filov dismissed four other of the 10 cabinet members. Only Gabrovski (interior), Bozhilov (finance), and Dimitur Vasilev (public works) remained. Filov took over the ministry of foreign affairs. For war, he chose General Nikola Mihov (1891–1945), commander of the first army in charge of the Sofia garrison.

Filov's account of the event in his diary gives a clear indication how little power he actually had and that the real authority and decision making rested with the king. He entered in his journal for April 8, 1942:

> Around noon Sevov came and informed me that the king had decided to reconstruct the cabinet immediately, and only I, Gabrovski, Bozhilov, and Vasilev shall remain. He told me to come to Vrania [one of the king's residences] at 4:30. The king was very amicable to me. He told me that he decided to make the reconstruction immediately as a result of the discovery of the barracks conspiracy which disgraced not only the general [Daskalov] but also himself, as he had assured Hitler during the visit to Germany that there are no Communists in our army.[9]

Another problem Filov had to deal with was the *subranie*. The government had an overwhelming majority and the opposition, especially after the cashiering of the Communists, was reduced to a handful of individuals. However, some of these individuals like Mushanov and Stainov had outstanding reputations and could cause embarrassment to the government through their speeches. Serious problems for the government could only come from its supporters. This rarely happened, but one time occurred in March 1942 in what seemed like an innocuous environmental issue. In an attempt to protect the mountain and forest resources, the ministry of agriculture introduced a bill to limit the number of goats farmers could own. The representatives reacted with a storm of protest and insisted that the goats were more important than the trees and plants they destroyed. The government withdrew the bill. The king sent Sevov to Filov, suggesting that the agriculture minister be removed—another reason for the cabinet change.

Individual representatives could and did intercede on behalf of their constituents. For example, if a young partisan, many of whom were teenagers, were caught by the police, his or her parents would ask the representative to get the offender out of jail, and it often worked. Another issue with the *subranie* was corruption rampant not only in the assembly but in the government bureaucracy as well. The extent of the corruption would truly become evident to Filov later upon the death of King Boris when he became regent for the young Simeon. In 1942, he suspected that there was something suspicious about the agriculture minister involving the Agricultural and Cooperative Bank. He had long distrusted BANU's influence in the ministry and the bank's executive board, but in any case, self-serving graft was another reason for the cabinet shake-up. Filov also insisted on the revocation of the elections of several representatives because of their corrupt practices.

Filov and Boris also were worried that Berlin might force a more pro-Nazi government in Sofia—one led by the Legionnaires. Although the prime minister and the king believed that Gabrovski, the ex-*Ratnik*, also posed a danger, his ties with the extremists were already cut and the *Ratnitisi* regarded him as a renegade. In fact, while Generals Lukov and Geshov, the Legion's leaders, continually hoped that the *Reich* would reduce Boris to a figurehead and give the government to them, the Germans looked to Aleksandur Tsankov as a possible alternative if needed. Berlin never seriously considered deposing Boris or forcing Filov from power as long as Bulgaria remained an ally.

BULGARIA AND THE HOLOCAUST

The most crucial year of the war for both the Axis and Bulgaria was 1943. One issue that would have lasting repercussions into the twenty-first century was the fate of Bulgaria's small Jewish community. As indicated above, fewer than 50,000 Jews lived in the kingdom. These were mainly of the Sephardic rite, descendents of Jews who had been expelled from Spain in the fifteenth and sixteenth centuries. There had been a Jewish presence in Bulgarian lands even before the Slavs and Bulgars came there. In the Middle Ages, there was a lively community in Turnovo and, in fact, the wife of Tsar Ivan Alexander had been a converted Jew.

In the twentieth century, most of Bulgaria's Jews lived in modest circumstances and very few took part in Bulgaria's social and political life. There was also very little anti-Semitism in the country, although it was not unknown. Bulgarians were used to peoples of different religions and ethnicities living among them. They may have had their prejudices, but they saw no need to rid their country of the few Jews among them.

Nevertheless, the Germans put the Bulgarian Jews on the list of those to be exterminated in the death camps of Poland. In February 1943, the infamous Adolf Eichmann was in charge of what the Germans called "the final solution of the Jewish problem," today known as the Holocaust. He sent to Bulgaria Theodor Dannecker, who had worked on the deportation of the French Jews.

By that time, the Bulgarian government had enacted new laws and decrees much more damaging to the Jews than even the Law for the Protection of the Nation. In the summer of 1941, the *subranie* enacted a law that placed a special tax of 20 to 25 percent on the property of Jews above 200,000 leva (about $2,500). However, the major legislation that put Bulgaria in line for the German measures against the Jews was enacted in June 1942. It charged "the Council of Ministers to take all measures for solving the Jewish question and matters connected with it." This gave the cabinet authority to take action against the Jews without consulting the *subranie* in advance. The government thought the new law would squelch any protests against anti-Semitic legislation, which the opposition and even some government supporters had expressed in the past. Significantly, it removed the king from having to deal with the embarrassing problem of new measures against the Jews. There were some objections in the *subranie* against the measure, but it was not unprecedented; in 1941, a similar law gave power to the cabinet to handle the new territories Bulgaria administered in Greece and Yugoslavia. The law passed, and the cabinet used its authority to issue a decree on August 26 establishing a Commissariat for Jewish Questions. It gave great power to the Commissar in charge of the new bureau. Charged with the decision, cabinet member Gabrovski naturally chose as the Commissar the *Ratnik*, Aleksandur Belev. The decree also stated that the Jews of Sofia (half the country's Jewish population) could be expelled from the city or even the country.

Belev began to harden the policies against the Jews. Some of the measures that were included in the Law for the Defense of the Nation had not been strictly followed. Belev tried to make sure they now were. Some Jews such as those who converted to Christianity (and a number did in order to escape the restrictions) or those in mixed marriages were exempt under the Defense of the Nation law. Now the new decree included them in the community, and Belev strove to make sure they were subject to his harsh measures. The Jews were herded into ghettoes. In Sofia, Belev confined them to the Iuch Bunar section of the city, the poorest quarter. Living space was restricted and several families had to share cramped apartments. The Jews' movements were limited. They could only appear in the streets at certain times. In some cities, only children could shop for the family. Jews could not attend movies or go to parks and many other public places. Jews could not own radios or automobiles or even bicycles. Belev confiscated Jewish property that was already registered and froze accounts. He liquidated real estate and tangible assets.

Belev made the Jewish consistories, which under Bulgarian law had semilegal functions going back to the Ottoman Empire, responsible for the implementation of his decrees. He also assigned representatives of the Commissariat, usually civil functionaries or police officials, to all Bulgarian provinces. Unlike elsewhere, Bulgaria did not for the most part include the significant Roma population of the country in these restrictions or deport any to Nazi killing centers.

Belev's main task was to prepare with Dannecker for the deportation of the Jews to Poland. The Nazis did not expect any problems from Bulgaria, which up to this time had acceded to their requests concerning the Jews by passing legislation and surrendering the rights of Jews who were in German-occupied lands. The only question was when Bulgaria, with its small number of Jews, fit into the timetable of deportations. Many more Jews lived in the other countries of the Balkans—Yugoslavia, Romania, and Greece, with its large population in Thessaloniki. The plans called for the deportation of the Jews from Bulgaria and the Bulgarian-occupied lands to occur in the spring of 1943. The total Jewish population including the areas Bulgaria held in Greece and Yugoslavia was about 60,000, so Belev and Dannecker planned to deport the Jews in three stages of 20,000 each. The first group would include all the Jews of the occupied territories, between 11,000 and 12,000 persons. The rest, the remaining 8,500, would come from elsewhere in Bulgaria.

To fill out the quota, Belev order the Commissariat representatives to send him a list of the Jewish leaders and "supporters of antigovernment ideas or feelings." All of the Jews of southwest Bulgaria, where trains carrying Jews from Greece to the Danube River would pass, were to be included in the first transport. Belev and Dannecker signed the final agreement for deportation of the first Jews on February 22, 1943. The Commissariat agents and police began arresting the Jews from Greek Thrace on March 4 and sent them to holding centers in southwestern Bulgaria. Beginning on March 7, the authorities started to arrest the Jews from Bulgaria proper.

Immediately there were protests from some Bulgarians. One of the most prominent was from Metropolitan Kiril (1901–1971), the Orthodox bishop of Plovdiv, who, upon learning that the Jews of his city were to be deported, wired the king. The religious leader threatened to lie on the tracks before the trains that would be deporting the Jews. The most significant, however, occurred in the city of Kiustendil in the southwest, where all the Jews were to be gathered. The Jewish leaders of Sofia had learned of the secret plans for the deportations from Belev's secretary who had several Jewish friends. Word got through to Kiustendil. Since it was difficult for Jews to travel, a group of their Bulgarian friends went to Sofia, where they met with Jewish leaders there. The group decided to ask the *subranie* representative from Kiustendil to intervene on behalf of the Jews and stop the deportations. The representative was the vice president of the *subranie*, Dimitur Peshev.

Peshev confronted Gabrovski about the deportations, who, after consulting with Filov, agreed to delay the deportations of Bulgarian citizens. The deportation of the Greek and Yugoslav Jews, however, would continue. Throughout the month of March, the Bulgarians deported the Jews of the occupied territories to the death camps in Poland. Peshev continued to work to prevent the same fate for the Bulgarian Jews. He got 43 representatives of the *subranie*, almost all of them from the government faction, to sign a protest against the action. Petko Stainov signed an attachment of support but claimed that since he was in the opposition, he should not sign the document directly. Since there were "officially" no political parties, the distinction between opposition and government supporters was hazy. One member of the declared opposition who signed the document was, surprisingly, the German favorite, Aleksandur Tsankov. This caused a scandal in Berlin.

Boris, who on all other issues maintained control over government policies, shied away from the issue of the deportations, leaving it in Filov's hands. Filov forced most of the signatories to withdraw their names and the *subranie* voted to remove Peshev from his post as vice president of the body. For the second time in his life, Peshev made a moral decision at the expense of his political career—a decision, however, that not only would later save his life, but also would enroll him as one the greatest heroes of twentieth-century Bulgaria.

Filov tried to arrange that the *subranie* take the measures against Peshev without debate. Later in the same session, however, a policy issue came up about Bulgaria's forced deportation of Greeks from Macedonia (a policy of which the Germans did not approve). Stainov brought up the question of the deportation of the Jews, emphasizing that it would put a black mark on the pages of Bulgarian history.

In April after the disaster of Stalingrad, Boris became convinced Germany would lose the war. He told Filov that the United States and the Soviet Union would be the ultimate victors and that both countries were in Boris's words "too young to deal with it."

In mid-April Boris finally told Filov to find some way to prevent further deportation of the Jews. Belev, however, unaware of the king's message to the prime minister, continued to work on a plan to deport the Jews.

Believing that the large concentration of Jews in Sofia was the reason that deportations failed in March, he proposed that as a first step the Jews of Sofia be sent into the provinces, preferably near the Danube where they could be sent to Poland on ships. Gabrovski discussed the plan with German officials and decided to offer the king two proposals: one, that the Jews be sent to Poland as a measure of state security, or if Boris rejected that, then another as Belev proposed, that the Jews of Sofia be sent into the provinces. Boris accepted the second proposal, but not the first.

The expulsion of the Jews began on May 24, Sts. Cyril and Methodius Day, an important Bulgarian holiday. A number of Jews organized a demonstration in the ghetto to protest the expulsions. Two rabbis addressed the crowd: Asher Hananel (1895–1964), the chief rabbi, who had served in Boris's cavalry detachment in World War I, and Rabbi Daniel Tsion (1881–1976), who became a legend to both the Bulgarians and the Jews. The Jewish leaders did not appreciate Tsion because they believed that he was a member of a Bulgarian Christian sect called Dunovists. The Dunovists, or White Brotherhood, founded by Peter Dunov (1864–1944), were a sect of religious mystics who incorporated worship of the rising sun in their Christian beliefs. Members of the royal court, including Princess Eudoxia and some of Boris's advisors, were members of the sect. Even Boris himself may have been a member. Tsion was not, but as a scholar he was interested in their theology and was well known to the sect. The Jewish consistory, however, disapproved of his activity and was convinced that he indeed held their beliefs. They therefore removed him from his post on the Jewish religious court. In the critical days of 1943, the rabbi was able to get his friends among the Dunovists to intervene on behalf of the Jews. He was even able to deliver a letter to the king with what he claimed was a message from God warning against the Jewish persecutions.

On May 24, Nikola Mushanov advised both rabbis (Tsion and Hananel) that they should ask Metropolitan Stephan of Sofia (1878–1957), the head of Bulgaria's Holy Synod, to intervene on the community's behalf. Stephan was a staunch opponent of the anti-Semitic legislation and indeed had at times expressed anti-Axis sentiments. The rabbis and a few others went to see the Metropolitan, who told them that the king and Filov had assured Stephan that the Jews would not be deported from Bulgaria. He advised Hananel to go directly to the court.

In the meantime, Belev, officials from the Commissariat, and police-men were in the ghetto preventing Jews from entering the center of the city where the festivities were taking place. Stefan, however, addressed the crowd in front of Alexander Nevsky Cathedral. He pointedly remarked about the absence of Jewish students in the schoolchildren's parade, which celebrated the creation of the Cyrillic alphabet. He openly stated that the persecutions in the Jewish quarter marred the celebration.

Rabbi Hananel, following the Metropolitan's advice, went to see Ekaterina Karavelova, the widow of the late leader of the Democrat Party and Queen Ioanna's chief lady-in waiting.

Under her instructions, the rabbi wrote a petition to Boris stating that the Jews were willing to sacrifice for Bulgaria but that they wanted to do it in Bulgaria. King Boris, despite the holiday, had left the city. Others at the court, however, including the king's sister Eudoxia and Boris's advisors, interceded on the Jews' behalf. When the day ended, Belev's plans were frustrated. He arrested Hananel and threatened him, but the Jews no longer needed to fear deportation. The Jews would have to leave the city. However, in a few weeks Allied bombing turned Sofia into rubble, and very few people of any religion remained in the capital.

As the war progressed and the Allies appeared headed for victory, there were no more efforts to deport the Jews from the country. The Germans blamed the failure of the deportations on the Bulgarians, who having lived with Roma, Turks, and other races, did not under-stand the "Jewish Problem." Karl Hoffman, the German attaché of the RSHA, the SS agency that handled security issues including the Holocaust, cryptically told Berlin that the deportations were stopped when Gabrovski received "a nod of approval from the highest place."[10]

In September when the government changed and a new minister replaced Gabrovski, a great deal of corruption was discovered in the Commissariat, and a new commissar, who was not an anti-Semite, replaced Belev. Thus the entire Bulgarian Jewish community survived the war.

DEATH OF KING BORIS

Hitler summoned Boris twice during 1943. His first trip was in March. Filov recorded in his diary, "The trip does not please the king; he is going without heart; he considers that in the last analysis the

German cause is already lost."[11] Boris was disturbed because Hitler asked the Bulgarian chief of staff to accompany him. He feared that the Führer would ask Bulgarian troops be sent to the Soviet front, and he and Filov prepared a number of reasons why this was not tenable. Boris also wanted a free Bulgarian port in Thessaloniki under German protection and that Sofia be allowed to deport Greeks from Macedonia south to Greece. We have seen that the Germans did not approve of this. In fact, however, the Germans' main purpose of the meeting was to ask the Bulgarians to participate more against the partisans in Bosnia and Greece. Boris resisted, insisting that his army had enough to do in Macedonia and was needed to make sure that Turkey did not enter the war by invading Bulgaria.

Boris's next visit was in mid-August. By this time, the war had gone even worse for the Germans. The Italian government had replaced Mussolini a few weeks earlier and soon would capitulate to the Allies. Boris feared that Hitler would once again demand that Bulgaria take a more expanded role in the war. The meeting between the king and Hitler lasted only a few hours, and he returned the next day, August 15.

Filov reports that Boris was "not very satisfied" with the meeting. The prime minister recorded in his diary, "on the return he even had wished that the airplane would meet with some misfortune so that it all be over with."[12] Hitler had asked Boris to commit an army corps to fight in Greece and Albania. The king had offered the same objections he had in March, but in the end agreed to send the troops if the Germans provided more armament.

Boris then took a brief holiday in the Rila Mountains and even climbed the high peak of Mousalla. On August 23, the king suffered a heart attack and died five days later. Rumors immediately spread around the world that he was assassinated. The *New York Times* even reported that he was shot by a Bulgarian police inspector in the train station upon his return from Germany. Of course, he had been flown both ways by Hans Bauer, Hitler's personal pilot. These assassination stories continued to circulate at the time and even into the twenty-first century. Perpetrators of every kind have been said to have committed the act—Nazis, Communists, even his own advisor Sevov. The German physicians sent to care for Boris in his last days told the German ambassador that it was possible he was poisoned, but that they could not definitely say so. The most persistent story is that Bauer gave him poison through his oxygen mask on the return trip because he either refused to send troops to the Soviet front or to deport the Jews to Poland. We know, however, from Filov's account and the German documents that neither of these issues was part of the talks the king had with Hitler. Bauer in his memoir denies the story of his involvement.

Some Germans in the SS believed that the Bulgarian government, just like Italy's, might change to one less friendly to Berlin, one perhaps headed by K'oseivanov. However, the king most likely died as reported from a heart attack. In any case, the Germans were unprepared for his death and, to ensure a friendly government remained in power, interfered in Bulgaria's politics. The Bulgarian constitution required a meeting of a grand national assembly to appoint a three-person regency council for the young King Simeon. The constitution also required that former ministers and judges serve as regents, and by strong implication relatives of the royal family were ineligible. The Germans, however, wanted both the late king's brother, Prince Kiril (1895–1945), and Filov on the regency council. Furthermore, they did not want a grand national assembly, which might cause embarrassment. Thus the new regency council included Kiril, Filov, and minister of war Mihov.

Filov now led the regency council and was in charge of Bulgarian policy. Kiril was not interested in the affairs of government and Mihov depended on Filov. Gabrovski was prime minister for a few days. However, the new chief regent feared him as a rival and dropped him from the cabinet. The finance minister, Dobri Bozhilov, then became prime minister. A number of *subranie* representatives were included, making the cabinet more politically moderate.

BULGARIA SEEKS TO LEAVE THE WAR

The following months saw more German retreats and an intensified Allied bombing of Bulgaria. In November, more than a hundred planes attacked Sofia, destroying the main railroad station and part of the track to Plovdiv. The bombers hit private homes, leaving more than 150 casualties. More planes followed in the weeks and months to come.

In September, Filov had discussed with Mihov an exit strategy should Germany lose the war and ways to deal with growing antiwar sentiments within Bulgaria. They decided to publicize that they only went to war to regain lost territory and that they would crack down on war profiteers.

The regency also sent secret emissaries to the Allies seeking a way out of the war. In fact, K'oseivanov, who was the Bulgarian ambassador to Switzerland after he left the prime minister's post, had learned through third channels that the Allies might let Bulgaria keep Dobrudja but not the rest of the territories they occupied. In October, a Bulgarian industrialist met in Istanbul with Floyd Black, the former president of the American College in Sofia who was with the OSS. Filov was encouraged that the United States might look favorably upon Bulgaria as a bulwark against Communism but wanted to get word to the Allies that the bombings were driving the Bulgarian people into the Soviets' arms. In February 1944, Sevov went to Turkey on the pretext of building a pavilion for the Izmir market. He really wanted to contact the western agents and diplomats. However, he was not well received.

Filov did not want to break off from Germany unless the Allies were near enough to Bulgaria to prevent German forces from taking reprisals. The Allies, for their part, wanted the German army to withdraw troops from other fronts into the Balkans. From December 1943 onward, Sofia kept in contact with Allied diplomats in Turkey and Switzerland, looking for a way out of the war. When Sevov arrived in Istanbul, serious negotiations began. The Bulgarian ambassador to Turkey, Nikola Balabanov (1886-), informed the American embassy that Bulgaria was ready to negotiate an exit from the war without territorial demands. He asked only that the 1939 borders be preserved and that the bombing be stopped. On January 11, 1944, another heavy raid on the capital hit the parliament building while the *subranie* was in session. A number of representatives, including Petko Stainov, were injured. The evacuation of Sofia began. The *subranie* met in secret, and the ministries moved outside the city.

The OSS believed the offer to negotiate to be genuine and recommended a halt to the bombing, which was then temporarily suspended. President Roosevelt agreed that the bombing of the kingdom be eased. The Allies, including the Soviet Union, further investigated the offer for an armistice even though Moscow and Sofia were not at war. British Prime Minister Winston Churchill, however, responded about the bombing, "If the medicine has done good, let them have more of it."[13]

Roosevelt and the military chiefs came around, and the bombing continued.

Churchill also rejected holding informal talks in Istanbul as Filov wanted. Rather, he insisted on a "fully qualified mission" with representatives of the three major allies to be held in Cairo or Cyprus. After some hesitation, the Soviets agreed to participate but wanted nothing to do with the question of continued bombings. Bombs fell on Plovdiv, Pleven, Varna, Burgas, and other cities as well as on Sofia. The OSS informed the Bulgarians in Istanbul that they would hear their proposals in Cairo. The talks did not get under way until August, and by that time Bulgaria was on the verge of collapse.

The Fatherland Front grew in strength and partisan activity increased correspondingly. The government created a special police force, the gendarmerie, to deal with the guerillas. The harsh and brutal methods of the gendarmerie were not enough to stem the movement. The government also used the Bulgarian army and asked for weapons and soldiers from the Germans to fight the partisans. However, Communists also had infiltrated the army, causing the minister of war to overhaul the general staff in May 1944.

In order to deal with partisan actions in Macedonia, the Germans considered establishing the province as a territory separate from Bulgaria, under either IMRO leader Ivan Mihailov or Serbian administration. The Bulgarian government feared Mihailov even though he always claimed Bulgarian nationality. They knew he saw an independent Macedonia as a more realistic alternative to union with Sofia. Filov told the Germans that if the choice became necessary, they would prefer the Serbian option.

The Soviets also put pressure on the Bulgarians. They told Sofia to stop German ship construction in Varna. Bozhilov denied that such construction was occurring although, in fact, it was. Berlin advised the Bulgarian government to continue to deny the allegations and ignore Moscow's protests. In May, the Soviets increased their demands. While still insisting on a halt to German ship construction in Varna, Moscow demanded that its consulate in the port be reopened and that new Soviet consulates be established in Burgas and Ruse. Berlin advised Bozhilov to break off relations with Moscow if the Soviets persisted. However, by this time the Red Army had cleared the Germans out of Soviet territory and was inexorably moving westward. Bozhilov could barely deny Moscow the consulates.

In May, the Bulgarian government collapsed. Berlin tried to find someone friendly to them to replace Bozhilov, but no one on the extreme right was strong enough: not Mihailov, Zhekov, or Tsankov. Nor could Filov find a candidate he could dominate. In the end, the regents turned to Ivan Bagrianov, who brought in as his foreign minister his ally Purvan Draganov. Both were close to the court and did not heed Filov. The cabinet, in fact, was basically pro-German in sentiment, although not of the extreme right. The minister of internal affairs, Aleksandur Stanishev (d. 1945), a physician, was a personal friend of German ambassador Beckerle, who regarded him the strongest man in the cabinet. Stanishev continued the campaign against the partisans more ruthlessly than ever.

However, with the Red Army approaching and with the Allies tacitly agreeing that Bulgaria lay in the Soviet sphere of influence, there was little that the new government could do. Bagrianov's chief goal became the preservation of the monarchy and the prevention of a Communist takeover of the government. In his first address to the nation by radio, he hinted at conciliatory measures toward the Allies. Later on, his appeals to the West became more obvious. By the end of July, Bagrianov was forced to reopen Moscow's consulate in Varna and to extend its jurisdiction over Burgas and Ruse. He asked the Germans to move out of Varna beforehand. The government toned down its anti-Soviet propaganda and even attempted to stop the German embassy from publishing news unfavorable to the USSR. Moscow pressured Sofia to release the Soviet prisoners of war the Germans were keeping in Bulgaria. Bagrianov asked the Germans to make sure that no such prisoners were kept in the kingdom and Berlin agreed.

Beckerle considered forming a new government from the extreme fascist groups. He even considered a German takeover in Bulgaria as the Reich had done in Hungary the previous March. The German foreign office decided on Tsankov as the best choice to continue German interests.

On August 17, Bagrianov addressed the *subranie* and stated, "The government declares that it understands the will of the Bulgarian people and fiercely resolves to eliminate everything which impedes the devotion to peace of this nation including even the army of occupation [in Serbia] and the Jewish problem."[14] The representatives greeted his speech with prolonged applause. Earlier he and the minister of war met with Jewish leaders and assured them of a new, milder policy. On August 31, the government overturned the laws against the Jews, both the Law for the Defense of the Nation and the Decree-Law of August 26, 1942.

Bulgaria's German alliance was for all intents and purposes over. Stoicho Moshanov was in Cairo negotiating with the Allies. Initially, the Bulgarians requested to retain Macedonia and Thrace, but the Allies absolutely refused this, although they permitted Sofia to keep southern Dobrudja. The Allies demanded a withdrawal of the declaration of war, the right of the Allies including the Soviet Union to march through the country, the expulsion of the Germans, and a new cabinet. The latter would exclude the most pro-German and fascist ministers and include pro-Allied members.

The German embassy began a general evacuation. Beginning August 31, the Bulgarian and German armies actually engaged in battle. Berlin tried to establish a pro-German government in Skolpje under Mihailov, but it had no chance for success. In a few weeks, the Reich established a Bulgarian government-in-exile under Alexander Tsankov.

THE FATHERLAND FRONT TRIUMPHS

On September 2, Filov replaced Bagrianov with a pro-Western cabinet led by Stamboliiski's nephew Konstantin Muraviev (1893–1965). Other members of the legal pro-Western opposition joined the new government. The Agrarian Virgil Dimov (1901–1979) became minister of internal affairs. Dimitur Gichev, Nikola Mushanov, and Atanas Burov all joined without portfolio. Muavriev, in addition to his prime minister post, took over the ministry of foreign affairs.

Moscow, however, was not satisfied with the new government and wanted one led by the Fatherland Front containing Communists and members of BANU-Alexander Stamboliiski, not Muraviev's coalition of Democrats, Nationalists, and BANU-*Vrabcha 1*. Muraviev was in a no-win situation. The Germans still had not completely left the country and were fighting Bulgarian troops on the way out. However, the royalist officers and soldiers still in the army were fighting the partisans as well. Moshanov continued to negotiate with the Allies, hoping that Bulgaria could be part of the Western camp rather than that of the Soviets. The Allies, however, would not commit themselves, all but acknowledging that in the postwar world, Bulgaria would be in Moscow's sphere of influence. Indeed, later in October, Churchill met with Stalin and agreed to give the Soviets 75 percent interest in Bulgaria.

On September 5, the regents and the cabinet met to discuss their precarious situation and debated if and when they should sever their ties with Berlin. The minister of war, General Ivan Marinov (1896–1979), was secretly working with the Fatherland Front. He advised the cabinet to delay the declaration of war for a few days in order to allow the Bulgarian troops in Macedonia to withdraw without interference from the Germans. In fact, the real reason was to give Moscow an opportunity to declare war on Sofia before the latter declared war on Berlin. The Soviets did so on the 5th while the cabinet and the regents were still arguing. On learning of Moscow's declaration, Sofia broke off relations with Berlin. Filov resigned from the regency. On September 8, Muraviev finally declared war on Germany. Bulgaria, which in 1939 had hoped to remain neutral, found itself at war, if only for a day, with Germany, the Soviet Union, Great Britain, and the United States.

Strikes and demonstrations in favor of the Fatherland Front had been going on for several days, and Fatherland Front forces seized several cities in the provinces. On September 8, the Red Army crossed into Bulgaria and met little opposition to its advance. The Front carried out its coup d'etat in Sofia on the 9th. In the succeeding Communist period, the Ninth of September would replace March 3, the date of the signing of the Treaty of San Stefano in 1878, as Bulgaria's national day. Many officers and soldiers, as well as members of the police force, had gone over to the Fatherland Front. Most of the rest remained neutral. The revolutionary army arrested the Muraviev cabinet and reinstalled Kimon Georgiev, who had been prime minister after the 1934 coup, as head of the government once more. The new cabinet had 15 members. Four were Communists, the most important being Anton Iugov (1904–1991), minister of internal affairs, and Mincho Neichev (1897–1956), minister of justice. Four members came from BANU-Aleksandur Stamboliiski, including Nikola Petkov, who served without portfolio. Four came from *Zveno*. They included Georgiev, Damian Velchev as minister of war, Petko Stainov as minister of foreign affairs, and Stanko Cholakov (1900–1981) as minister of education. There were two Socialists in the ministries of trade and social welfare. Two independents served: one in the ministry of finance and one, Dimo Kazasov, as minister of propaganda.

The new leaders also replaced the regency council with the Marxist philosopher Todor Pavlov (1890–1977) from the Communist Party, Tsvetko Boboshevski (1884–1952), a lawyer and former minister from Zveno, and Venelin Ganev (1880–1966), a former minister of justice from the Radical Party.

The Allies recognized the new government immediately. Moscow signed an armistice with it, and Bulgaria joined the United Nations in the war against Germany. Bulgarian troops who had been occupying Yugoslavia now joined the Red Army and Tito's partisans in driving their former allies out of the Balkans. They chased them into Austria. For the only time in the war, Bulgarian troops saw front-line action. The Bulgarian Fatherland Front commanders allegedly ordered the most aggressive tactics, hoping that high casualty rates would impress their new allies.

Georgiev agreed without hesitation to the armistice terms the Allies presented even though the Fatherland Front government had vainly

asked for part of the Thracian coast. The armistice was signed in
Moscow on October 28, 1944. The Bulgarians agreed to put their forces
under Soviet command. Furthermore, an Allied Control Commission
was placed over the kingdom. However, Soviet officials administered
Bulgarian industry, transportation, utilities, fuel, the press, radio,
theatre, and other economic and social institutions on behalf of the
Allies. The armistice also specified that Bulgaria would dissolve all
fascist organizations, release persons who were imprisoned because of
pro-Allied sentiments, end discriminatory legislation, and cooperate in
war-crime tribunals.

In the meantime, until the war ended, the regency and the
government dissolved the *subranie*. Indeed, virtually all the government
supporters in the body as well as cabinet members were put on trial
in the following months. The new cabinet ruled by decree until new
elections were held in 1945. In the meantime, parties that were not
part of the Fatherland Front were outlawed, although opposition parties
reemerged after the war. In the remaining months of the war, the
Fatherland Front began its consolidation of power in the kingdom,
and the Bulgarian Communist Party, under the protection of Soviet
administrators and Soviet arms, strengthened its position within the
Fatherland Front.

(ABC-CLIO)

NOTES

1. These rumors are from reports by the German ambassador in Sofia on May 31 and June 1, 1944.

2. Bogdan Filov, *Diary*, entry for Tuesday, January 7, 1941. An English translation can be found in "The diary of Bogdan Filov" in *Southeastern Europe*, Vol. I, no. 1 (1974), p. 60.

3. Ibid., entry for Monday, January 20, 1941, p. 63.

4. Ibid., entry for Saturday, March 1, 1941, Vol. II, no. 1 (1975), p. 72.

5. Interview with Sir George Rendel conducted by the author in October 1965 in London.

6. Filov, *Diary*, entry for Monday, March 3, 1941, p. 76.

7. Ibid., entry for Saturday, March 1, 1941, p. 73

8. Ibid., entry for Friday, April 3, 1942, Vol. 2, no. 2 (1975), p. 172.

9. Ibid., entry for Wednesday, April 8, p. 173.

10. Report of the German embassy, April 5, 1943.

11. Filov, *Diary*, entry for Monday, March 27, 1943, Vol. III, no. 1, p. 57.

12. Ibid., entry for Sunday, August 15, 1943, p. 69.

13. Francis L. Lowenheim, Harold D. Langley, and Manfred Jonas, eds. *Roosevelt and Churchill: Their Secret Wartime Correspondence* (New York: Saturday Review Press, 1975), 434.

14. Bagrianov's speech is found in the *subranie* minutes for August 1944.

8

The Communist Era (1944–1953)

THE LAST MONTHS OF WAR

The Fatherland Front government, more specifically the Communists in the government, enthusiastically fulfilled their pledge to prosecute war criminals. The trials and punishments had an aura of revenge rather than justice. The courts found guilty and executed the regents Filov, Prince Kiril, and General Mihov. They meted out the same sentence to the ex-prime ministers Bagrianov and Bozhilov. K'oseivanov escaped trial by not returning to Bulgaria from his post in Switzerland. All of the ministers of Filov's and Bozhilov's cabinets were sentenced to death, as were six of the 10 members of Bagrianov's cabinet. Boris's advisors and staff were also sentenced to death. The members of Muraviev's cabinet were spared the death sentence but received prison terms ranging from six months to life. Only General Marinov, Muraviev's minister of war, who cooperated with the Fatherland Front, was not tried.

One hundred and thirty members of the *subranie* were put on trial and 68 were sentenced to death. There was one notable exception:

Dimitur Peshev. As a fascist sympathizer and important government leader, the former vice president of the chamber was tried on the same war crime charges as his colleagues. However, an attorney, Joseph Yasharoff (1898–1971), who the Jewish community hired on his behalf, successfully had his sentence reduced to a prison term. Yasharoff did not argue that Peshev helped the Jews by his daring petition, as this would have not impressed the court. The justices gave the capital sentence to another representative who was more outspoken against the anti-Semitic laws than was Peshev. Yasharoff won his case by pointing out that Peshev's 1943 action was his second moral decision. His first was refusing to sign the death warrant of Damian Velchev in 1935. Damian Velchev was, at the time of Peshev's trial, the Fatherland Front's minister of war.

Noteworthy too, was Aleksandur Tsankov's escape to Argentina. A boyhood friend of Boris, the son of King Ferdinand's secretary, believed he was saved because he was a 33-degree Mason[1], and the Allies allowed him to escape. A Jewish partisan caught and assassinated the escaping Aleksandur Belev, who had been sentenced to death *in absentia*.

The top leaders of the government were not the only ones hauled before the courts. People's tribunals operated throughout the country and tried more than 11,000 persons accused of working for the old regime. More than 2,500 were sentenced to death and more than 1,000 executions were carried out. However, the records were not carefully kept, and scanty information indicates that a minimum of 3,000 were executed, murdered, or had "disappeared." Perhaps there were thousands more.

In addition to the courts, the government instituted workers' councils that investigated businesses that collaborated with the government during the war. The charges could have been leveled against almost anybody, and thousands of entrepreneurs lost their companies. By the time the war was over, only the parties and factions of the Fatherland Front remained as forces in Bulgarian politics.

THE COMMUNISTS MOVE FOR POWER

The goal of the Communists in Bulgaria was to obtain mastery of the state and put the Marxist ideology in practice or, as they stated it, to build Socialism. This put them in some conflict with their partners in the Fatherland Front, particularly the Agrarians, whose goal always was to work for independent farmers. These, at best, had worked together in Raiffeisen cooperatives. The Communists had a vision for agriculture along the lines of the cooperative farms that Stalin had introduced in the Soviet Union.

In addition, the Bulgarian Communists, like the others of Europe and around the world, had the problem of solidifying their own ranks. The fight against fascism that went back to the 1930s and culminated in World War II swelled the ranks of Communist movements nominally led by the Soviet Party. However, Stalin had two chief items on his international agenda. First, he wished to ensure that the Soviet Union would survive another attack, which he believed would come from his former allies in the West. Second, he wanted to make sure that the international Communist movement was loyal to him and would serve Soviet interests rather than the interests of a worldwide Communist revolution.

His first goal led him and his successors to concentrate Soviet troops in the northern tier of East European States: Poland, Hungary, Czechoslovakia, and East Germany. This protected the invaders' route to Russia, which Charles XII of Sweden, Napoleon, and Hitler had followed in ages past. It was on these countries that Moscow put the most pressure to be submissive. Stalin's second goal of favoring only those most loyal to him led to another round of purges in the world Communist movement.

The postwar world witnessed a number of civil wars between Communists and their opponents for control of the states emerging from the disasters of war. These included China and the Balkan states of Yugoslavia, Albania, and Greece. There were also political struggles in France and Italy, where strong Communist movements existed. Both the decisions made by the Allies at the end of World War II and the force of Stalin's objectives would shape the outcome of these wars and struggles. Communists won in China, Yugoslavia, and Albania, where their own leaders were not dependent on Stalin. Communists lost in other countries whose parties were not of Stalin's immediate concerns.

From another point of view, because the Soviet Union concentrated on the northern tier of Eastern Europe, the countries of the Balkans, being in the southern tier, had more leeway to go their own way. In Greece, the Communists lost the civil war. In Yugoslavia, Tito broke with Stalin in 1949. In the next decade, the Albanian Communist leader Enver Hoxha broke with Stalin's successor Nikita Khrushchev. In Romania, the Communist leadership fell not to those closest to Stalin but to more independent cadres. However, the leading Bulgarian Communists were the two who had established dominance in the 1920s and 1930s as leaders of the *Comintern*: Dimitrov and Kolarov. From then on, Sofia carved out its own unique position in the Balkans as the most loyal of Moscow's allies in the region. Some even joked of it as the 16th Soviet republic.

GEMETO DIMITROV AND NIKOLA PETKOV

The first task of the Communists was to win control of the Fatherland Front from their partners in the coalition. The main challenge was from the Agrarians. The Communists put pressure on and threatened the BANU leader Gemeto Dimitrov, singling him out as anti-Russian because of his ties to Britain, an old enemy of Bulgaria since the nineteenth century. The Communists launched a strong propaganda campaign against him, accusing him of trying to destroy the Fatherland Front coalition and establish a dictatorship. Gemeto, because of ill health, turned the leadership of BANU over to Nikola Petkov, but the accusations against Gemeto continued. The government placed him under house arrest in April. Later he managed to escape with the help of the American ambassador and find refuge in the United States, where he led one of the Bulgarian émigré factions against the Communist government. Oddly enough, members of the fascist Legionnaires, including Ivan Dochev, also came to the United States and led another anti-Communist faction. The Bulgarian government tried Gemeto *in absentia*, sentencing him to life imprisonment.

Although the Agrarians were disappointed in losing Gemeto as their leader, they rallied around Petkov, a charismatic speaker from a well-known and respected political family. He rapidly became the most popular figure on the Bulgarian political scene. The Communists could not take him on directly with a propaganda campaign as they did Gemeto for fear of alienating the farmers. Instead, they formed a rival BANU under one of Stamboliiski's cabinet ministers, Aleksandur Obbov (1887–1975). Obbov had a somewhat shady reputation, but he had left-wing Agrarian credentials and was willing to work with the Communists. The ministry of justice declared him the rightful leader of the Agrarian Union and handed him BANU's property and publications. Petkov set up his own party, BANU-Nikola Petkov. The Communists were able to split the Socialists in the same way, but they were less a threat to them than the Agrarians.

In August 1945, a national election was to be held. Under Communist direction, the Fatherland Front ran a single slate with the Communists and BANU each having 95 candidates. Petkov objected, claiming that the Agrarians had greater support in the country than the Communists and the slate was unfair. He appealed to the American and British members of the Allied Control Commission, who took up his cause.

The Communists, of course, had the backing of Moscow. Petkov asked that the single slate be abandoned in favor of multiparty elections and that the vote be postponed. He obtained the latter objective and elections were delayed until November. However, the single slate remained. Petkov's stand earned him even more popularity, and his BANU party grew in membership. However, against the advice of Washington and London, he unwisely ordered his followers to boycott the election.

The Fatherland Front slate won, and Georgi Dimitrov, the Communist leader, returned from the Soviet Union to assume the premiership in a new government. Petkov, who had the backing of the West, demanded that he be given the premiership and new elections for the *subranie* be held. The Communists, backed by Moscow, refused.

Besides Petkov, their last obstacle among the parties, the Communists had to fear the military, which, through *Zveno*, had been another rival within the Fatherland Front. After the 9th of September (1944), the Front government had ordered the army to join Soviet forces fighting abroad, thus removing the military from the country. Over Velchev's objections and with the support of the Soviet military administration, the Fatherland Front government had replaced officers who were unsympathetic to its politics. The new chief of staff was a Bulgarian who had served in the Soviet Red Army. The Communists still feared that when the war ended and the army returned to Bulgaria, Velchev and Georgiev would be able to thwart Communist political objectives, especially if they linked up with Petkov.

In February 1946, after Dimitrov replaced Georgiev as prime minister, the government warned of an alleged military plot by antigovernment forces. The government transferred power over the military from Velchev's ministry to the entire cabinet and purged 2,000 more suspected officers. Velchev resigned and became ambassador to Switzerland, where he subsequently left his government's service and remained abroad.

THE DIMITROV CONSTITUTION

In September 1946, a plebiscite showed that most Bulgarians agreed to change the monarchy to a republic. Since in Marxist ideology Bulgaria had not yet achieved the stage of history termed "Socialism," the government used Stalin's terminology, designating Bulgaria a "People's Republic." In October, an election for a grand national assembly took place to change the constitution. Contemporaneously, the final peace with Bulgaria was being drawn up in Paris. To avoid friction with the West, the Front allowed the opposition to field candidates. Petkov consolidated other opposition parties in a rival group to the Fatherland Front called the Federation of Urban and Rural Labor. The Federation complained of voter fraud and threats to its supporters, and its Western sponsors agreed that the elections were less than fair. In any case, the Front won by a three-to-one margin and was given 366 seats to the Federation's 99. The Communists took the lion's share (275) of the Front's seats.

The Communists restructured the government as well with Front members. Dimitrov remained as prime minister. Kimon Gerogiev, unlike Velchev, remained in the Front and continued as foreign minister. The cabinet also included a number of Agrarians from Obbov's group. BANU would remain a part of the Fatherland Front for the remainder of the Communist period and its representatives would serve in the cabinet, the *subranie*, and other government positions including, at times, the honorary title of head of state. Official histories in Bulgaria began recognizing and honoring the contributions of Aleksandur Stamboliiski. The narratives emphasized, however, the times he cooperated with the Narrow wing of the Social Democrats and its successor, the Communist Party. Approved accounts also stressed his opposition to the monarchy but rarely mentioned the conflicts he had with Marxists. One of the major thoroughfares of Sofia bore his name. A huge statue of him stood before the old BANU headquarters, whose auditorium became the city's opera theater.

Political influence of the Agrarians in Communist Bulgaria was minimal at best. Membership in the Union was a sinecure and limited to the children and grandchildren of members of the Union. Stamboliskii's children were representatives in the *subranie*. Raicho Daskalov's daughter served as the country's minister of justice in the 1970s.

Even though the Fatherland Front won an overwhelming victory and the Communists received the bulk of the seats in the *subranie*, their control in the country was not firm. The other parties, including those in the Federation and in the Front itself, had won about half the electorate. Many members and cells in Obbov's BANU switched their allegiance to Petkov's Party. The non-Communist parties in the Fatherland Front considered dissolving the coalition.

Furthermore, the economic situation in the country was chaotic. The destruction caused by the bombings at the end of the war and the dislocation of the Bulgarian economy by the German loans and trading system had brought disaster. The government restructured currency to deal with inflation, froze accounts, and introduced high taxes. This furthered the Marxist move to Socialism but prevented economic recovery. Sofia could also not get new loans and trading partners because a final peace had not been signed. Furthermore, aid would have to come from the West, particularly the United States, which would save Western Europe through the Marshall plan in the following years. Bulgaria's sponsor, the Soviet Union, wanted to divert resources from Eastern Europe, including from Bulgaria, to help its own recovery, not give sustenance to its new clients. The demands that Moscow made on Bulgaria in the immediate postwar both for exports to the Soviet Union and the cost of maintaining Soviet soldiers and civilian administrators in the country cost the Soviets much of the goodwill that Russia traditionally had. Shortages even provoked food riots.

In addition, the Communists slowly began to introduce measures and policies imposing the Soviet style of collective farming. The Bulgarian farmers were wary and suspicious of this activity and looked to Petkov further. The urban workers, too, began to question the government because of the growing unemployment caused by the economic situation and compounded by the return of Bulgarians who had been working in Germany and the demobilization of the army. By 1947, tens of thousands were without jobs, about 20 percent of the work force. The tobacco industry a Communist stronghold, was especially affected.

The final peace treaty with the Allies was signed in February 1947. Bulgaria lost all the occupied territories but kept Southern Dobrudja. This was somewhat of a disappointment because to the last moment, many Bulgarians believed that they would receive additional territory in the south. Sofia also had to pay additional reparations to Greece and Yugoslavia, and as after World War I, the Bulgarian military forces were limited.

The treaty also called for the Red Army to leave Bulgaria. Petkov hoped that the Soviet retreat, along with the new American policy toward curbing the advance of Communism in the Balkans, the Truman Doctrine, would strengthen his position. He began once more to aggressively attack the Fatherland Front government. The Communists counterattacked, and help for him from Washington did not come because the Truman Doctrine was meant for Turkey and Greece, not Bulgaria. Not only did the Red Army leave Bulgaria, but so did the Allied Control Commission, which had been a check on the Front government in 1945 and 1946.

Against all tradition and law, the police arrested Petkov in the *subranie* chamber while the parliament was in session. He was charged with conspiring with the army and the Greeks to break the bond of friendship between Bulgaria and the Soviet Union. He was also charged with dividing the workers from the peasants inside the state and with attempting a coup d'état.

The government then carried out a judicial lynching of Petkov. Together with four others, three soldiers and a farmer, he was tried without counsel or witnesses on his behalf. He was sentenced to death and executed. Thus the Agrarian leader met the same fate as his father and brother as part of one of the most tragic families in twentieth-century Bulgarian history. The government then disbanded BANU-Nikola Petkov.

In the next weeks following the execution, the Communists, now in complete control of the Fatherland Front, dissolved the remaining parties except for Obbov's BANU. They also purged the military of officers who had the power to oppose them. In December, the Grand National Assembly adopted the new constitution. It incorporated the Communists' draft, which was modeled on Soviet suggestions for Eastern European countries in Moscow's sphere of influence. The country became more centralized as local autonomy weakened. A *subranie* remained, but it was reduced to an almost meaningless body as the Fatherland Front handpicked candidates who ran in "elections" without opposition. The *subranie* chose the executive praesidium, acting as head of state, and the praesidium chose the council of ministers. The Communists also introduced economic planning on the Soviet model with five-year cycles. One of the flaws of the plans was the emphasis on heavy industry, which was consistent with Marxist theory but unsuitable for Bulgaria.

THE PURGE OF TRAICHO KOSTEV

The Communists were now in complete control of the country. They changed their name back from the Bulgarian Workers' Party to the Bulgarian Communist Party. Following the system established by Stalin in the Soviet Union, the first secretary was the party leader. For the first years of Communist control in Bulgaria, the first secretary also served as chairman of the council of ministers or what in other countries would be prime minister. By 1951, the government and *subranie* approved new rules and legislation that repealed all laws passed before the Communists came to power.

Until the death of Josef Stalin in 1953, the Bulgarian party closely followed Moscow's model. So closely were they linked to the Soviet leader that they renamed the great port of Varna Stalin. Sofia's adherence to Moscow's practices resulted in a new purge of the party to rid it of more independent members. This is the stage of revolution when the victors "eat their own children." It occurred in the French Revolution of the 1790s under the Jacobins and in the Russian Revolution in the 1920s and 1930s when Stalin turned on his colleagues. In the 1940s and early 1950s it was the fulfillment of Stalin's goal to make sure that the international Communist movement was loyal to him and served the purposes of the Soviet Union.

In Bulgaria, the Communist Party turned on Triacho Kostov (Dzhunov; 1897–1949). Kostov was a leading member of the party who had been part of the Communist delegation in the *subranie* before the war. He had been arrested in the 1920s during the Tsankov period. While being tortured, Kostov tried to commit suicide by leaping from the fourth floor of the police building but survived. Later, he was in Moscow when Dimitrov arrived there after the Leipzig trial. Kostov became part of his coterie. He was also a member of the party's Central Committee. He returned to Bulgaria during the war and fought with the resistance. After the war, he filled important posts in the party and the government, including the secretary of the party and president of the council of ministers. However, he was too popular for Dimitrov's and Kolarov's tastes and too independent for Stalin's. Kostov even dared to question the unfair bilateral trade agreements that Sofia was forced to sign with Moscow.

The government tried Kostov in December 1949 with 10 other prominent party leaders and government officials. This was a "show" trial in the manner that Stalin ordered in the Soviet Union in the 1930s. The defendants were tortured to make them confess their crimes. All but Kostov did so. Kostov was the only one sentenced to death and executed. The others received long prison terms, as did those in several other trials. However, in 1956, totalitarianism in Eastern Europe ameliorated after Khrushchev admitted the crimes of Stalin. The Soviet Bloc entered the era known as "The Thaw." The Bulgarian Communist Party and government exonerated those charged in the trials of Communists and released them from prison. Kostov was posthumously rehabilitated and, in 1963, ironically was awarded the esteemed Order of Georgi Dimitrov.

The purges of the 1940s and 1950s in Bulgaria and elsewhere in the Communist movement were linked to the unexpected split between Tito and Stalin. During the war, Stalin and Dimitrov had given complete backing to Tito, and he emerged after the war as the leading Communist in the Balkans. Not only could he demonstrate his independence from Stalin, but he had his own ideas for Yugoslavia and Communism in the Balkans. Stalin had tried to weaken Tito's power by planting his own agents in Yugoslavia, but Tito was able to ferret them out.

In the late 1940s, Tito was hampering Stalin's goal of complete mastery over the international Communist movement. He also posed a threat to Soviet foreign policy by trying to extend his control over the Balkans. After the war, Tito restructured Yugoslavia into a federation of republics similar to the Soviet Union's. The new Yugoslavia included Serbia, Croatia, Slovenia, Macedonia, Montenegro, and Bosnia. Tito discussed with Dimitrov a plan for Macedonia that would include the Bulgarian districts and put the remainder of Bulgaria into the Yugoslavian federation of South Slavs. If the Greek Communists should win the civil war then raging, another section of Macedonia could also be added. Perhaps Albania could be added as well, Tito thought.

Dimitrov supported the idea of having Bulgarian and Serbian Macedonia united, but others, including Kostov, did not want to give up Bulgarian territory. However, in 1946 Dimitrov prevailed. He went even further than Tito in suggesting that all of the Eastern European countries with Communist governments form a federation. Then Stalin stepped in. He invited Dimitrov and Tito to come to Moscow

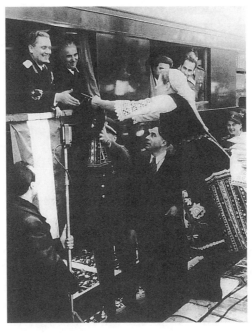

Josef Broz-Tito visiting Bulgaria. (AP/Wide World Photos)

to discuss the plans. Dimitrov promptly went. Tito refused. Dimitrov agreed to follow Stalin's lead on foreign policy. Yugoslavia was shortly expelled from the *Cominform*, the organization of Communist parties that Stalin established to replace the old *Comintern*. Dimitrov's health deteriorated in the succeeding months, and he returned to Moscow in 1949 for medical care. He died in July 1949. An apocryphal story claims that if Tito had gone to Moscow as Stalin demanded, he, too, would have had a heart attack. The implication that Stalin had Dimitrov murdered was a rumor that circulated after the Bulgarian leader died, but there was no reason for the Soviet leader to do so. Dimitrov had no problem adhering to Stalin's wishes. In any case, Bulgaria did not join the Yugoslav federation, and Bulgarian Macedonia remained part of the state. Sofia would now and until the end of the century claim that the Macedonians, wherever they lived, were in fact Bulgarians. The body of Dimitrov, like Lenin's in Moscow, was embalmed for public viewing and placed in a mausoleum across the street from the former royal palace, which had been converted into a museum.

KOLAROV AND CHERVENKOV

Vasil Kolarov replaced Dimitrov as party leader and chairman of the council of ministers after Dimitrov died, but Kolarov only lived until January 1950. Next in line was Dimitrov's brother-in-law Vulko Chervenkov (1900–1980), who kept the Stalinist practices of Dimitrov and Kolarov. In the period between 1947 and 1953, Bulgaria underwent a thorough change in society and in the economy as it modeled the country on the Soviet system of building socialism. Collective farms were introduced to replace the independent farms. The party established economic planning on the Soviet model. Youth and civic organizations were subjected to control of the Communist Party. The Young Pioneers and *Komsomol* now replaced groups like Boy Scouts and Girl Scouts.

The Party also subrogated the churches to the state even though the constitution had established the separation of church and state. Metropolitan Stephan was removed from his post in Sofia and retired to a monastery. In 1951 the government declared the Bulgarian church to be a patriarchate, thus breaking its connection with the head of the Orthodox Church in Istanbul—a connection that had only been established six years prior after more than 70 years of schism. In 1953, Kiril, the metropolitan of Plovdiv, became patriarch. The government made the church subordinate to the state but recognized it as the leading religious body of the Bulgarian nation. The Catholic Church continued to exist, but its independence was also severely limited. Sofia severed relations with the Vatican and rejected the Papal See's nominees for clerical office in the country.

The government also brought the few but influential protestant churches under control and took over their charitable and educational institutions. Among these was the American College in Sofia. Priests and ministers were dismissed for suspicious behavior. A number were put on public trial to get the message across that religious institutions and clergy must adhere to the new Marxist conditions. Four Catholic priests were executed.

Mosques and synagogues remained open, too, but all religious attendance was strongly discouraged even in later years when there was a lessening of the strict Stalinist totalitarianism of the postwar decade. The government would carry out petty, annoying acts to make religious observance difficult. In some years, the red dye popular with Bulgarians for dying eggs at Easter could not be found. At Easter and Christmas, the trams in Sofia would stop running earlier than usual, which made the trip to Alexander Nevsky Cathedral for midnight mass difficult.

In accord with Marxist internationalist ideology, there was some reluctance among the Bulgarian Communists to stress their nationalism. As we have seen above, Dimitrov had been willing to give away Bulgarian Macedonia and have Bulgaria itself become part of a larger federation in the Balkans or even Eastern Europe. September 9, the victory of the Fatherland Front, replaced March 3, the liberation from the Ottoman Empire, as Bulgaria's national day. However, as it proved to be in Soviet Russia, nationalism was an important tool for bringing the people of the state together. There was a special emphasis, of course, on the Slavic kinship between Bulgarians and Russians. Even the symbols of tsarist Russia remained. Alexander Nevsky Cathedral remained the chief landmark of Sofia, and the great statue of Tsar Alexander II still stood in Parliamentary Square. Even during the years of the resistance, Bulgarian heroes were celebrated. Streets, towns, and other geographic features were named after heroes of the Bulgarian past as well heroes of Marxism. The recognition that the Bulgarian Orthodox church was the traditional religious institution of the Bulgarian nation was certainly not a Marxist one. As the years passed, nationalism grew stronger.

One of the more peculiar linkings of nationalism, Marxism, and Orthodoxy involved the two great May celebrations in the Bulgarian calendar. Great parades in downtown Sofia occurred on May Day and on May 24. The former celebrated world labor, the latter, Sts. Cyril and Methodius. On May Day, citizens, soldiers, and civilians paraded before Dimtrov's mausoleum on the gilded bricks of the avenue. Military ordinance, emblematic of Moscow's May Day parade, was lacking because the street tiles could not tolerate it. The placards at the front of the parade showed the heroes of Bulgarian and international Marxism—Karl Marx, Friedrich Engles, Vladimir Lenin, Dimitur Blagoev, Georgi Dimitrov and, in the early years, Josef Stalin. The May 24th parade stressed the saints' creation of the Bulgarian alphabet, not their religious activity. Some western observers noted that the placards of Cyril and Methodius looked a lot like Blagoev and Dimitrov in clerical robes.

One advantage that Bulgaria had in promoting nationalism was the relative homogeneity of the population. More than 86 percent of the population was Bulgarian if it included Macedonians, recognized as a separate nationality only in early postwar censuses. Ten percent of the population was ethnic Turks. In the first decade of Communist rule, all minorities, including the Turks, had cultural autonomy. They had schools taught in their own languages, theatres, and other institutions. However, assimilation soon became a government goal that took different forms at different times. The state took over the non-Bulgarian schools, and Bulgarian became the primary language. In 1950, the government announced that it would "permit" a quarter million Turks, more than a third of the Turkish population, to emigrate to Turkey. Most of them came from the northeast, where the new collective farms were to be started. The émigrés included Roma as well as Turks. A number were expelled even though they wanted to remain in Bulgaria. Ankara objected to the influx. In the end, only one 160,000 left. The Turkish population, which increased at a higher rate than the Bulgarian, would remain between 8 and 9 percent of the total.

The few remaining minorities were permitted or encouraged to leave. The Greek population dwindled to insignificance. Armenians had the option of moving to Soviet Armenia. Most of these preferred to remain in Bulgaria, but some emigrated not only to the USSR but also to the United States. The Roma, who at about 2.5 percent, were the largest minority after the Turks, remained. The government tolerated and generally ignored them, although Sofia's Gypsy Theater, supported by the state, gained some international renown. The government was only partially successful in having them settle in one place. Their birth rate was higher than even the Turks'. By the end of the Communist, period their percentage of the population rose to 4.5 percent as the Bulgarian percentage declined. As in other nations, the Bulgarian people harbored great prejudices against the Roma.

The Jews were a special case. The entire community survived, and according to the postwar census, its population increased over the pre-war period. As we noted above, many Jews fought with the partisans and now enjoyed special privileges in Bulgaria. There was a Jewish section of the Fatherland Front. Many Jews wanted to emigrate to Palestine, but before 1948 this was not easy, although a few had been able to obtain the difficult visas even during the war. The Communists initially wanted the Jews to remain in Bulgaria.

The Agrarians, sympathizing with those who wished to leave, even helped the urban Jews become accustomed to the farming life they would need in Palestine.

However, a number of circumstances convinced the Communists that Jewish emigration would be a good idea. First of all, the terms of the peace treaty with the Allies required the Bulgarians to restore Jewish property. Much of this had been destroyed in the Allied bombings or had evaporated in the blocked accounts with the collapse of the Bulgarian economy at the end of the war. Another reason was the growing confrontation between Moscow and London in 1946 and 1947. In those years, before the Truman Doctrine, England, rather than United States, was the chief rival of the Soviet Union. A large Jewish emigration from Europe to Palestine would cause problems for Britain. Furthermore, there was a belief that the Zionist movement, which had a significant socialist agenda, might lead a new Jewish state into the Soviet Bloc. As it turned out, Moscow was mistaken on that score.

Thus the Fatherland Front advocated for the departure of the Bulgarian Jews to Palestine—illegal before the creation of Israel in May 1948 and then legal afterward, when most of the community left. The Jewish population in Bulgaria dropped to about 5,000 in 1956 and rose to 6,000 a decade later. Those who remained were the elderly, Communist Jews, or former partisans. Many assimilated. The former partisans and their children enjoyed privileges, especially access to higher education. Although few in number, many Jews were prominent in academia and the arts. Very few reached the highest ranks of the Communist Party, but a number served in government and diplomatic posts. The majority of Jews were employed in management, the economy, science and the arts. The Jewish emigration to Israel made that community of some 45,000 one of the largest groups of Bulgarian speakers outside of the Balkans. Since most families had money in the soft currency of the Communist era in Bulgarian banks, as part of the reparations required under the peace treaties, visits back to Bulgaria from Israel were not uncommon. Some even occurred in the years when there were no diplomatic relations.

Initially after the war, Sofia attempted to win favor with the Allies by touting the survival of the Jews during the war. The government appointed General Vladimir Stoichev (1892–1990), a member of *Zveno* and a renowned Olympic equestrian, as special emissary to Washington. He told the press the Bulgarian people "forced the government to abandon its contract with the Germans for . . . export to Poland [of Jews]."[2] Then not much was said of the survival until the 1960s, when the Society of Bulgarian Jews began to publish its yearbook and established a permanent exhibit in Sofia on the events of World War II.

Meanwhile, Bulgaria under Chervenkov followed the same strict, authoritarian regime that Dimitrov and Kolarov initiated. In fact, Chervenkov wanted to align the policies and practices of Bulgarian institutions even closer to those of the Soviet Union. The military, the educational system, art, science, and culture were all now ordered to follow the Soviet paradigm. Two letters used in Bulgaria Cyrillic were even eliminated to make the alphabet identical to the Cyrillic used in the USSR. Pure research in science was neglected in favor of applied science and technology. Russian language and Marxist-Leninist science were required at all levels of education. Political and socioeconomic class criteria were applied for entry into the university. The Soviet grading system was used for students, and in some courses, Soviet textbooks were used.

In the economy, collectivization, and Soviet-style economic planning took their toll. Workers were required to perform extra work without pay. More than 90 percent of Bulgarian trade was now with countries of the Socialist Bloc. While the government could claim that the first five-year plan in industry met its goal before the target date, the forced collectivization of agriculture led to a great loss in production, the destruction of livestock and crops, and even large-scale riots. Ties with the countries not in Moscow's orbit were eliminated. Westerners in the country were routinely characterized as foreign agents. Diplomatic relations with the United States were severed, and ties to other countries in the West were severely limited. Relations were also cut with Greece, Turkey, and Yugoslavia. The harshness of the regime, however, changed in Bulgaria, as it did in Eastern Europe and the USSR, with the death of Stalin in March 1953.

NOTES

1. Interview with Dmitrii Stancioff, son of King Ferdinand's secretary and friend of Boris, conducted by the author July 1965 in Frederick, Maryland.

2. *New York Times*, March 30, 1946, p. 6, and May 12, 1946, p. 29.

9

The Zhivkov Years
(1953–1990)

When Josef Stalin died, there was an immediate expectation in the East Bloc that changes would be made, easing life for the population and lessening the totalitarian control. While the Communist Parties in those countries still maintained their political monopoly, daily living became easier as the Bloc moved into what is called "The Thaw." Taking their lead and direction from Moscow, the countries in the Soviet orbit established governments with shared leadership rather than the rule of one man. They committed the economy to more production for consumer needs, lessened the demands on the workers, and made overtures to ease relations with countries not in the Bloc.

Bulgaria began an almost immediate move toward moderation. In fact, even in 1951, the publication of the controversial novel *Tiutiun* (*Tobacco*) by Dimitur Dimov (1909–1966) showed signs of a modest return to freedom of thought. In 1953, with the new post-Stalin conditions, Chervenkov made overtures to the non-Communist world. He resumed relations with Greece, which had been broken since 1941, and approached Washington, which later exchanged missions in 1959.

Chervenkov followed the new course laid down in Moscow in domestic matters as well. The new plans emphasized more consumer goods. Concessions were made in agriculture, but only on collective farms. Most of the political prisoners were freed and the detention camps closed.

In Moscow, after Stalin died, there was another power struggle with considerably less bloodshed. In the end, Nikita Khrushchev and Nikolai Bulganin emerged as the new Soviet leaders. The Kremlin ordered their Eastern European allies to likewise separate the party and state leaders. In 1954, Chervenkov reluctantly agreed. He remained head of the council of ministers and chose a three-man secretariat to lead the party. For first secretary, he nominated a minor party official, Todor Zhivkov. Through Zhivkov, Chervenkov hoped to remain in control of both the government and the party. However, two years later, the wily Zhivkov outmaneuvered his boss and became the leader of Bulgaria for the next 33 years. Zhivkov's opportunity came in 1956, after Khrushchev denounced the crimes of Stalin. Chervenkov, whose power depended on Stalin, would lose his position as head of government. However, Dimitrov, who had been more dependent on Stalin than even his brother-in-law, remained a Bulgarian hero and was not disturbed in his tomb.

Zhivkov, like most Bulgarians, came from a peasant background. As a teenager, he went to Sofia and, like Georgi Dimitrov, became a printer. He

Todor Zhivkov. (Chris Niedenthal/TIME &
LIFE Images/Getty Images)

became involved in the Printers' Union and then joined the Communist Party. During the war, he was in a party cell in the Iuch Bunar section of the city and acted as a liaison with partisans in the area. His connection with Iuch Bunar later would allow him to make an exaggerated claim of responsibility for saving the Bulgarian Jews. In 1945, he was elected to the Communist Party's Central Committee and the head of the Sofia cell. In 1951, he was promoted to the Politburo, the leading section of the Communist Party, specializing in agriculture.

THE APRIL PLENUM

At the beginning of April 1956, a special plenum, or full meeting, of the Central Committee met to discuss the implications of Khrushchev's speech for Bulgaria. Henceforth, this meeting, known as the April Plenum, would be noted as a major step in the development of Bulgaria under Communist rule, perhaps second only to the 9th of September. The main victim of this party shake-up was Chervenkov himself, who was seen as Bulgaria's Stalin. Chervenkov resigned as premier.

As the changes wrought by the April Plenum were explained to the public, questions, complaints, and accusations rained down on party members. Many of the persons purged from the party or put in prison or labor camps for political crimes were freed and rehabilitated. Although the full details of the April decisions were never made public, the obvious changes ameliorated the atmosphere of totalitarianism in Bulgaria. Artists and academic researchers had more freedom of expression and inquiry, even though some limits still persisted. For example, no Bulgarian historian dared question that the Nazis deliberately burned down the *Reichstag* building in 1933, even though research in the West showed that it was the act of Van der Lubbe himself. After uprisings in Poland and Hungary later in 1956, there was a renewed crackdown, and Chervenkov rejoined the cabinet as minister of education.

Zhivkov now moved to gain complete control of the party, removing potential rivals and opponents from key positions. He also increased his personal relations with Khrushchev. His main rival was the new premier, Anton Iugov. In the next few years, Zhivkov's ambitious plans for economic restructuring and increased production based on Soviet practices failed, and in the early 1960s the country suffered a food shortage that brought about considerable unrest. In 1962, Iugov and Chervenkov challenged Zhivkov for the country's leadership. They mocked his economic program as a "great leap forward," referring to the policies in vogue in China at that time. Zhivkov, with his supporters in control of the party and Khrushchev's backing, was able to win the power struggle. Iugov and Chervenkov were forced out of their posts. They were not executed but retired into obscurity, which was the new method of dealing with Communist opponents in Bulgaria as in the Soviet Union. Chervenkov, in fact, resided the rest of his life in a comfortable apartment in the center of Sofia. This was a rare commodity in postwar Bulgaria, where the city, with its antiquated infrastructure, grew into a huge metropolis. There living space was harder and harder to find. Iugov reemerged in the party ranks in the 1980s while Zhivkov was still in charge.

When the Soviet party removed Khrushchev from power in 1964, some military officers thought they could also remove Zhivkov, but the state security foiled the plot. Zhivkov's control of Bulgaria remained unchallenged from then on until 1989, regardless of who ruled in Moscow.

Beginning in the 1960s, Bulgaria's economy slowly began to improve. The censorship and controls on art and academic research also lessened again. The country became less isolated as Zhivkov forged relationships with the non-Communist world. Bulgaria hosted all varieties of international conferences. The country's engineers and specialists helped develop the Third World. They exported its products: high-quality feta cheese made from sheep's milk, award-winning wine, high-grade tobacco, and its famous rose oil. Gradually Bulgaria even exported industrial products: Balkancar forklifts and computer components.

The country developed a tourist industry that eventually brought more than a million people annually to mountain ski resorts and Black Sea beaches. Not only East Europeans but Westerners came as well. Foreign companies built hotels and restaurants—Novotel from France, Otani from Japan, and, in the 1980s, even Sheraton from the United States. The latter remodeled Sofia's stodgy, Stalinist-style Hotel Balkan in Lenin Square.

One of the most ambitious enterprises was Teksim, an import-export company that brought products from the West into Bulgaria and made them available for leva, the local currency. In 1966, the company arranged for Coca-Cola to be bottled in Varna. It later sold Gucci products in its shop in Sofia. However, the company got too big for its britches. When it offered to purchase a transport ship that even the Soviets refused because of the cost, Moscow ordered Zhivkov to pull in the reins. The most obvious failure in the Bulgarian economy under Zhivkov was the grandiose plan to build the Kremikovtsi iron and steel works outside Sofia. In the wrong area for such an enterprise and needing to import raw materials Bulgaria lacked, the plant never produced more than it cost to run.

In addition to tourists, Bulgaria welcomed foreign academics, scientists, and artists to participate in educational and cultural exchanges. After tentative beginnings in the 1960s, these exchanges grew. Sofia University hosted a summer seminar for studying Bulgarian language. Students and professors from the non-Socialist world participated along with those from Eastern Europe. English and American lecturers came regularly to both Sofia University and the University of Veliko Turnovo to teach their specialties to Bulgarian students. Bulgarian professors and students went to Western European, Japanese, and North American universities to study and lecture there. By the 1970s, even private citizens were able take tours outside the Soviet Bloc.

Under these circumstances, many Bulgarians were able to obtain hard currency—dollars, pounds, German marks, and so forth—either from relatives or by earning it abroad. If the money were registered, Bulgarians could use it to buy foreign goods in shops run by the Corecom company. *Corecom*, the natives joked, stood for Correction of Communism.

SOCIALIST BULGARIA

In 1971, Zhivkov declared that Bulgaria had reached the Marxist stage of historical development called Socialism and was ready to proceed toward the final stage: Communism. Zhivkov ordered a new Constitution that declared the country a Socialist Republic and emphasized the leading rule of the Communist Party following the principles as set forth in the April Plenum. To move toward Communism, Zhivkov said, the country must intensify its efforts as a "scientific-technological state." The president of the Bulgarian Academy of Sciences and the Agricultural Academy entered the cabinet.

The Constitution also reversed the policy adopted by Khrushchev of separating state and party functions. The Constitution provided for a state council that would act as the executive in the country. As Zhivkov became the head of the state council, he effectively was both head of the party and head of state.

Zhivkov, like his predecessors, remained stalwartly loyal to the USSR. As the other countries of the Balkans moved more or less on independent roads, Sofia proved to be the country in the region that Moscow could depend on the most. Furthermore, Zhivkov benefited from his loyalty. While under Stalin, Bulgaria, like the other countries, had to give more than it received from Moscow; now the Soviet Union was willing to supply Sofia with raw materials, including precious oil, at bargain rates.

Zhivkov maintained his position by regularly changing ministers and party officials. He brought up younger cadres from the ranks. Only a few of the most loyal comrades like Milko Balev (1920–2002) and Dobri Djurov (1916–2002) remained with him throughout his tenure. While expelling members from the party when he felt it necessary, there were only two mass purges. One occurred in 1977 when the pace of liberalization—although improving—was too slow for the public, and unrest threatened his position. Boris Velchev (b. 1914), a Politburo member who advocated more rapid changes, was purged along with 38,500 other party members. Zhivkov carried out another mass purge in 1988, just months before his fall. Zhivkov often would make unilateral decisions. At most he would privately consult a few close friends or colleagues and not the cabinet or other state and government bodies or even the Politburo. One example was his decision to have the Bulgarian military join the Soviet armed forces in the crackdown on Czechoslovakia in 1968 in quelling Alexander Dubĉek's Prague Spring.

Zhivkov's plan to move Bulgaria along the path to Communism depended on the successful improvement of the country's economy. He tried all sorts of new ideas, but none of them achieved the desired results. He borrowed from the Soviet system of long-range planning and then from the Yugoslav method of factory control. He tried centralization of economic units and then decentralization. In the 1960s and 1970s, he introduced profit incentives as they did in the USSR, the policy known as Libermanism. He tried bailing out farms and factories that fell short of their production quotas and then refused to bail them out if the incentives the government decreed did not work. He invented new economic forms like the agricultural-industrial complexes (ACIs), which were supposed to allow manufacturing of agricultural products in the same location. He switched from plans that emphasized quantity (always a problem in economic planning) to emphasis on quality by using incentives. Nothing he tried, however, reached the goals he hoped for.

While Zhivkov provided an unquestioned loyalty to the Soviet Union in Bulgaria, he also, as we have seen, succeeded in developing better relations with the West. He visited France and even the United States, if only to attend United Nations meetings. He opened trade with Western nations. In 1975, he met with Pope Paul VI, and Catholic bishops were once more appointed for Bulgaria. Most important for Sofia was its relation with the Third World. Students from Africa, Asia, and Latin America came to Bulgaria to study. Zhivkov visited many countries on those continents and Bulgaria exported many of its manufactured goods there.

With the era of détente in the 1960s and 1970s, Bulgaria's relations with its non-Communist neighbors improved as well. Oddly enough, it had the most difficulty with Communist Yugoslavia over, of course, Macedonia. With Greece and Turkey, both members of NATO, Bulgaria hoped to work toward making the Balkans a nuclear-free zone. The two issues, the nuclear-free zone and Macedonia, were areas in which Sofia differed from Moscow.

There had been, as we have learned, much conflict between Bulgaria and Greece throughout the ages. In the twentieth century they fought wars and skirmishes. They argued over borders and political ideologies. The Bulgarian Communist Party supported the Greek Communists in the Civil War the latter lost. Many Greeks who supported the Communists fled to Bulgaria. In a controversial action, tens of thousands of Greek children were taken to Eastern European Communist countries, including Bulgaria. The Greek government claimed they were kidnapped. The Communists said they were taken to move them out of the war zone.

Greece itself had a tortured history in the twentieth century with thrice-repeating cycles of monarchy, republic, and dictatorship. The last dictatorship occurred in 1967 when a military junta overthrew the monarchy and Prime Minister George Papandreou. Oddly enough, although the junta claimed to have acted because of the Communist influence in Greece, the junta leaders were ostracized by the West and only the Soviet Bloc would completely deal with them. Moscow told the world that no nation had the right to interfere in the policies of another. Relations between Greece and Bulgaria improved during the junta's rule. Once relations were restored, Greek tourists regularly made their way to Bulgaria to take advantage of cheap medical services and also to find bargains on Bulgarian wares, which were cheaper than in Greece, even with hefty export tariffs.

In the 1960s and 1970s, Zhivkov also maintained correct if less-than-friendly relations with Turkey and Yugoslavia. He visited Ankara and allowed more Turks to emigrate from Bulgaria to Turkey. While Macedonia was an issue that flared up from time to time, the question never led to the canceling of relations with Belgrade. However, the Bulgarians were outraged in 1971 when Skopje published a Macedonian edition of Nikola Vaptsarov's (1909–1942) poetry. Vaptsarov, a Bulgarian poet born in Bansko, part of Bulgarian Macedonia, was a Communist partisan executed in World War II. What outraged the Bulgarians was the Macedonian advertisement for their edition of his works, which loudly proclaimed, "At last we can read Vaptsarov in his native language!" The Macedonian issues continued to simmer between the countries. Once, in 1982, they even led to a fistfight between scholars at an academic Slavic conference in Washington, D.C.

LIUDMILA ZHIVKOVA

Much of Zhivkov's softening of totalitarianism in Bulgaria can be traced to his devotion to his colorful daughter, Liudmila (1942–1981).[1] Liudmila studied history and art history at the Sofia and Moscow universities and British-Turkish relations at Oxford in Great Britain. She became a force in Bulgarian cultural and intellectual circles, holding a regular salon in her apartments. She was a representative in the *subranie* and served as the head of the Committee for Art and Culture, a cabinet post. She also, shortly before her death, was a member of the Politburo. She had in the 1970s control over the media—press, radio, and television.

Zhivkova was a patron of Bulgarian nationalism, especially of Bulgarian art and historical memory. She ordered theaters and opera troupes opened throughout the country. She saw the Bulgarian

Liudmila Zhivkova with Secretary-General Kurt Waldheim at the United Nations in 1979. (UN Photo by Saw Lwin)

Orthodox Church as part of the country's identity, culture, and history and supervised the restoration of churches and monasteries. She also advocated that the history and art of Bulgaria be known abroad. She arranged to have the Thracian gold, those artifacts and jewelry discovered near Panigiurishte, sent to a number of countries for display. She believed eventually Bulgaria would become the cultural center of the world.

One of her achievements was the great 1981 celebration of the 1,300th anniversary of the founding of the Bulgarian state. International statesmen, artists, academics, and other persons associated with Bulgaria in some way were invited to the country, partially at state expense, to take part in the conferences, performances, and other festivities. In connection with the anniversary, the government constructed the huge and expensive National House of Culture near the center of Sofia, which later was named after Liudmila Zhivkova.

Zhivkova's pro-Bulgarian views, which put a degree of separation between her attitudes and the obsequious homage the country's leaders paid to the Soviet Union, proved to be very popular. Her efforts also showed the world a positive image of the country in contrast to the often negative reputation it had in the West because of its alliances to Germany during the World Wars, its dependence on Moscow, and several notorious scandals with which Sofia was associated. The latter included the murder of Georgi Markov (1929–1978) and the country's alleged involvement with the 1981 assassination attempt on Pope John Paul II. In 1979, Zhivkova started the Banner of Peace movement for the care and education of children in Bulgaria and around the world, especially in the developing countries.

If her interest in religion and unbridled nationalism were not enough, in the mid-'70s Zhivkova exhibited even more un-Marxist behavior. She became obsessed with mysticism and the occult. In 1978, she went to the Himalayan country of Nepal, where she claimed to have learned the mysteries of the East. She practiced meditation, asceticism, and even self-mortification. She claimed she had met "otherworldly people" and had learned to levitate.

Zhivkova did not need to go all the way to Nepal to find mysticism. She found it also right in Bulgaria and often went to see the famous Old Witch of Petrich—Baba (grandmother) Vanga. Vangelia Gushterova (1911–1996) was a renowned blind Bulgarian soothsayer. Her predictions were so astonishing that her reputation spread around the world. Even Communist officials would go meet with her, but before Liudmila, they did not publicize their consultations. Since Vanga lived in Petrich on the Greek border, government permission was needed to approach the area. As her reputation spread abroad, the government charged foreigners for consultations. When Zhivkova became one her visitors, Liudmila's father permitted more publicity about Baba Vanga. Bulgarian television even made a documentary about her. In 2008, after the Communist period, the government turned her house into a museum.

Zhivkova's mysticism increased. She believed that she could improve her inspiration if she contacted the "enlightened" from the past through séances. She sought aid from Alexander the Great, Napoleon Bonaparte, and even Jesus Christ himself.

Zhivkova even privately criticized the Communist Party and the Soviet Union, although never in public. Nevertheless, her attitudes emboldened some authors to be more objective when writing about Bulgaria's relations with Russia and the USSR. Although popular with the public, there were murmurings against her within the party. Furthermore, some of her associates, whom she protected, took advantage of their connection to her by embezzling funds earmarked for the 1,300th anniversary celebrations.

As the anniversary approached, Zhivkova was in poor health. She had been in a serious automobile accident in 1973, and her ascetic diets and mortifications did not help her condition. She relied on homeopathic remedies rather than standard medical treatments. In the midst of celebrations in July 1981, she died. The official cause of death was a cerebral hemorrhage. Although there is no evidence to the contrary, given the circumstances of her life, rumors of foul play spread immediately. Some said she was murdered by either her Bulgarian foes or Soviet agents. Others said that medical help was delayed in saving her life. Still other rumors claimed that she died as a result of a drug overdose. In any case, a popular, influential figure was removed from the scene. Tens of thousands mourned her passing.

HARD TIMES IN THE 1980S

After the 1,300th anniversary and Liudmila Zhivkova's death, a decade of hard times hit Bulgaria. Zhivkov cancelled many of his daughter's projects and removed many of her friends from their positions. Some of them deserved to be punished for corruption. Her children's project, the Banner for Peace Movement, remained. In the early years of the 1980s, things appeared to be going well for Bulgaria. It had one of the best consumer economies in the Soviet Bloc. Compared to neighboring Romania, it was almost a paradise. However, Bulgaria was soon hit with a series of bad harvests and other disasters that sent the economy into a downspin.

By the 1980s, Bulgaria had transformed from a rural, agricultural country to an urban one as population shifted to the cities. While agriculture was still an important section of the economy, industrial output was now a major factor as well. Unfortunately, the country could not compete on a global scale. Furthermore, since much of its trade was still with the Soviet Bloc, it lacked the hard currency needed to buy necessary parts and technology from the West and Far East, especially from Japan, with whom it had built up a dependency in the 1970s. American restrictions on exporting software and computer components to Communist countries also hindered Bulgaria's industry. Bulgaria's foreign debt mounted. By 1989, it reached $15 billion. Many of the best-quality products were also sold abroad just to pay the interest on the loans.

Another issue that brought difficulty to Zhivkov's government was his changed policy toward the Turks. In the past there had been policies dealing with minority populations trying to make Bulgaria even more nationally homogenous than it was. Turks had been expelled in the early 1950s. Their separate schools were eliminated and their press gradually disappeared. The government in the 1950s and 1960s put pressure on Roma and some Moslems, including the Pomaks, to add "ev" or "ov" to their family names, making them more Bulgarian. The reaction against this by the Pomaks, however, was so strong that the government halted the policy. In the 1970s the campaign to force the Pomaks to change their names began again, and the Pomaks resisted just as before. This time the government did not back down and imprisoned those who did not comply.

Part of the reason for the name changes was the belief that the Pomaks were ethnically Bulgarian and the Communists had thought when they took power that the Pomaks would reassimilate back into the national community. When this did not happen, the pressure was applied. Bulgarian governments going back to 1878 had all tried to bring the Pomaks back into the nation, so the Communist efforts were not new. Yet the problem for Bulgaria was not the relatively small number of Pomaks (about 3 percent of the population), but the more numerous Turks.

The Turkish population was officially about 10 percent. The Turks were concentrated in specific areas. If other Moslems joined them, some officials believed they could demand autonomous status. Zhivkov allegedly feared that the Turks could create another area in Bulgaria like they had in Northern Cyprus, perhaps demanding incorporation into Turkey. Zhivkov had other reasons to fear the Turks and Moslems. The rise of fundamental Islam in the world had reached the Balkans in Yugoslav's Kosovo province. The Bulgarians feared it might break out in their country. Another concern was the difference in birth rates between Bulgarians and Turks. While the Turkish rate was increasing, that of the Bulgarians was slowing down. The government tried to encourage Bulgarians to increase their families with monetary and other incentives, but the Bulgarians wished only one or two children. With abortion on demand a right in the country, this was easy to accomplish. Some scholars argued that the refusal of the Bulgarians to procreate was a sign of their discontent with the regime. However, this argument would mean that the Turks and Roma were the most contented people in the country. Obviously, this was not true. More likely, the small families were a sign of a society modernizing as it was elsewhere. The difficulty of finding living space in Bulgarian cities was another disincentive to large families.

In 1969, the government signed a treaty with Ankara permitting the emigration of Turks to Turkey. In the 1970s, 130,000 took advantage of the offer, but this did not answer Zhivkov's problem. In 1983, the government turned toward forced assimilation—a program called the *revival* or *regenerative process*.

In the revival process, the government forced Turks in Bulgaria to adopt Bulgarian names—the controversial policy they had early tried to force on the Roma and Pomaks. To justify it, Bulgarian historians and ethnographers argued with dubious evidence that the Turks among them were really descendants of Bulgarians who were forcibly converted to Islam in the Ottoman period. The government also outlawed certain Moslem religious customs. The Communists accompanied the revival process with demonstrations of extreme Bulgarian nationalism in its propaganda, festivals, and ceremonies.

The revival process brought international condemnation on Bulgaria, which was already suffering negative publicity for its involvement in the assassination of Georgi Markov and its alleged complicity on the attack of Pope John Paul II (see below). For historical and political reasons, the United States was particularly strident in its attacks on Sofia. Bulgaria was already a whipping boy in America because of its association with Germany in the two World Wars and its closeness to Moscow in the Cold War. In addition, there were fewer Bulgarian immigrants in the United States than its Balkan rivals, Serbia and Greece. This made influence in Washington small indeed. Furthermore, it has been a peculiar fact of American relations with the Balkans that ever since the Greek War of Independence in the 1820s, the American Congress tended to be pro-Greek for political reasons and the executive branch pro-Turkish for economic and military ones. When an opportunity to engage in "Bulgarian bashing" arose, both branches of the government could weigh in.

The Turks reacted, too. Many of them worked on Bulgarian construction sites and had access to explosives. On August 30, 1984, with the 40th anniversary of the Ninth of September less than two weeks away, explosions rocked Varna and Plovdiv, two cities where Zhivkov was scheduled to make appearances. The philosopher Ahmed Dogan (b. 1954) founded the illegal Turkish National Liberation Movement, which organized resistance and carried out sabotage. Flyers promised 40 bombs for 40 years. The government reacted with massive force. Elite military troops zeroed in on the Turkish areas, particularly the towns near the border with Turkey. Dozens were killed and hundreds arrested. Cities were put on alert, with soldiers guarding important buildings, making sure that citizens did not approach them. The international community increased its condemnation of Sofia. The United Nations, the European Economic Community, the European Council of Justice, and the Organization of the Islamic Conference all censured Bulgaria. The division between the Turkish and Bulgarian citizens in the country carried over into the post-Communist era.

As indicated above, two other scandals put Bulgaria on the front pages of the world press. One was the assassination of Georgi Markov. Markov was an accomplished author and playwright who enjoyed some freedom of expression in The Thaw of the 1960s. However, some of his writing went too far and ran afoul of the Bulgarian censorship. In 1969, he defected to the West, where he continued his career as a successful writer. He also made broadcasts to Bulgaria on America's Radio Free Europe, the British Broadcasting Company, and West Germany's *Deutschewelle* Radio. He criticized the Communist government and attacked Zhivkov personally. The latter, perhaps, most raised the ire of the Bulgarian leader. The Soviets offered to get rid of him, most likely as repayment to a loyal ally, although some have speculated that Moscow just wanted to try out a new weapon in its counterespionage arsenal. The weapon, an umbrella, gave the story a bizarre cloak-and-dagger twist that caught the world's attention. The umbrella was designed to inject a ricin-laced pellet when brushed against the victim. It was first tried on another Bulgarian defector in Paris but failed to kill the victim. Then on September 7, 1978, Todor Zhivkov's 67th birthday, an agent brushed by Markov as he was walking on Waterloo Bridge in London. The umbrella's pellet entered Markov's leg, and four days later, he was dead. After the fall of the Communist government in Bulgaria, Sofia admitted to the crime, but no one was charged because of lack of evidence. Investigations into the incident, however, continue.

The second scandal was Bulgaria's alleged involvement in the Mehmet Ali Ağca's attempt to assassinate Pope John Paul II on May 13, 1981. Ağca, under interrogation, confessed to having committed the act for Bulgarian agents acting on behalf of Moscow. Later the Italian secret service, backed up by the American CIA, claimed that the assassination was directed against the Solidarity movement. The Bulgarians denied any involvement. Later the CIA admitted that the agency had no proof of Bulgarian involvement, and a State Department official has said that the idea that Moscow would employ the Bulgarian secret service for such as task was improbable. The Italian courts acquitted the alleged Bulgarian agent accused of involvement in the crime. Even after the fall of Communism, Bulgaria still adamantly continued to deny any culpability. Is seems unlikely that Sofia was involved. Even John Paul himself, when he visited Bulgaria in 2002, stated that he believed the Bulgarians were not involved in the assassination attempt. In any case, both scandals, along with the revival process, damaged Bulgaria's international reputation and that of Zhivkov in his last decade of rule.

THE FALL OF ZHIVKOV

By the mid 1980s, the Communist Party had lost the trust of the majority of the population. Bulgarians were dissatisfied with the poor economy, government corruption, and the obvious differences between life in the Socialist Bloc and the West. When Mikhail Gorbachev assumed the leadership of the Soviet Union and introduced his policies of openness and restructuring (*glasnost* and *perestroika*), the Bulgarian government was unprepared to follow the rapid changes that were sweeping over Eastern Europe. The Bulgarian population had complete access to the Soviet situation because Russian newspapers and journals were sold in the country and Soviet television was one of the channels available to Bulgarians. Indeed, the problem now was finding a copy of *Izvestia* or *Pravda* before it was sold out. Bulgarians sent messages to the Soviet embassy saying, "You saved us two times before. Save us again."

Zhivkov tried to firm up his relationship with Gorbachev as he had with his predecessors, but the Soviet leader was cool to him. Gorbachev did not like the economic policies that Bulgaria had adopted. He told Zhivkov that the favorable trading relations that Sofia had enjoyed with Moscow were about to end. As a matter of fact, Gorbachev told all of the Eastern European countries that they would have to go their own way.

The inadequacies of restructuring and the 1986 Chernobyl nuclear disaster in the Soviet Union caused Gorbachev enough problems without having to worry about Eastern Europe. In any case, the rapid changes in the Soviet Bloc put the events in Bulgaria in context. Starting with the Polish Solidarity movement in the early '80s, the whole Communist system in the region began to unravel. In 1989, almost all the leaders of the Bloc fell from power and the remainder lost power shortly thereafter. The democratic revolution was complete. Bulgaria was just one of the countries where it occurred, and, in fact, not the most important or noted one.

In 1987, new economic reforms were introduced, and Zhivkov decided to allow a few private enterprises. Bulgarians were allowed to use their cars as taxis. Private restaurants, laundries, and repair shops were opened. The new establishments were better run and comparably priced to the state-owned enterprises. Still, the discontent among the population continued. It also grew within the party. Zhivkov purged a number of critics, but this did not stop the criticism. A popular saying of the time was "the fear is gone," meaning Zhivkov could no longer terrorize his comrades or the public into submission.

The attacks against Zhivkov, the Communist Party, and the government took a variety of forms, some of which had not been seen since the 1940s. Earlier in the decade, the philosopher Zheliu Zhelev (b. 1935), who had been purged from the Communist Party in 1960, published his 1982 book, *Fascism*, which was a veiled attack on Zhivkov. Zhelev was sent into the provinces and the historian who authorized its publication demoted. Another author, the popular poet and novelist Blaga Dimitrova (1922–2003), who had frequently run afoul of the authorities with her independent views, criticized the Communist government in her 1981 novel *Faces*. Zhelev and Dimitrova would serve as president and vice president of Bulgaria in the 1990s.

In 1987, Zhivkov ordered a closed economic discussion at Sofia University in which all proposals were permitted, the party leader said, without repercussions. However, when the criticism turned on him, he went back on his word and had a number of professors dismissed. At the celebration of the centennial of Sofia University in 1988 in which foreign academics from all over the world including the United States were invited, the mood among the Bulgarian professors was quite somber.

For the first time in decades, a member of the *subranie* spoke against a government proposal in open session. The delegate was Neshka Robeva (b. 1946), one of the founders of gymnastic dance. In a country where soccer is king of sport, when one spoke of "the coach," he or she meant Ms. Robeva. Furthermore, various types of opposition groups formed, literary and artistic, political, social, and especially environmental. One was the Club for Support of Restructuring and Openness formed by party members, ex-party members, former partisans, and others. Leading dissidents like Zhelev and Dimitrova joined. Another was the independent labor union, *Podkrepa* (Support). A third was the Committee for the Defense of Religious Rights. Even the old fascist Legionnaires came out of the woodwork to form an opposition organization.

In the spring of 1989, there was a revolt within the party as the professional organizations met to select their officers. One by one the members voted against the party slates. Writers, artists, journalists, and academics all turned against Zhivkov's candidates for office and chose people who would bring reform to their associations and Bulgaria.

However, the most critical associations at this time were the environmental groups. Robeva's protest in the *subranie* was over an environmental issue. Environmental concerns had long been rumbling under the surface in Bulgaria, as they did everywhere in Communist countries. Of course, it was not just in the Communist countries where degradation of the planet was an issue, but in open societies, it could at least be discussed and pressure brought to bear on the government policies. Since economic goals in a planned society took precedent, pollution concerns were unconscionably neglected. In Bulgaria, rivers and forests and even the Black Sea were affected.

The nuclear meltdown at Chernobyl in the Ukraine in 1986 brought the environmental issue to the forefront in Bulgaria. The country suffered much radioactive fallout from the disaster. Rumors spread that party members and other privileged members of society were receiving "safe" food from abroad. Futhermore, Bulgaria's own Koluzdoy nuclear power plant was among the most dangerous in Europe. Construction of the new plant at Belene, which had been planned for more than a decade, was just getting under way. Criticism of the government's handling of nuclear power was so pervasive that the government banned the playing of a popular military march that contained the lyrics "boom, boom, boom" because of a satirical parody of it relating to Koluzdoy.

More concern centered on the dangerous pollution of the Danube near the port of Ruse, Robeva's district. The culprit, actually, was not a Bulgarian enterprise, but a Romanian chemical plant across the river.

The sickness that the children of Ruse suffered spurred demonstrations by the mothers of Ruse beginning in 1987. At an art exhibition in the city, protesters put up a chart showing that the official rate of lung disease in Ruse had doubled in 10 years. More protesters joined the effort to clean up Ruse. A number of organizations joined together and sent out a national appeal. The documentary film *Breath* told the story, and its opening led to the formation of the Civil Committee for the Ecological Defense of Ruse. A number of prominent Bulgarians joined, including the journalist Sonia Bakish (b. 1925). Bakish was married to Stanko Todorov (1920–1996), who was a prominent member of the party, the chairman of the *subranie*, and a member of the Politburo. Bakish, a distinguished party member herself, had been a young partisan in World War II. The party expelled her, and the police harassed the members of the committee. However, the committee spurred the growth of a green movement in Bulgaria. In 1989, the organization Ekoglasnost picked up the cause, and the ecological movement grew larger. It drew up a petition against the government's polices, which collected thousands of signatures. The movement played a major role in the fall of Zhivkov, and the Green Party that emerged in the 1990s was a major factor in the change in Bulgarian politics. In October 1989, an international ecological conference ironically was held in Sofia. A huge protest demonstration by Ekoglasnost of perhaps 5,000 was broken up by the police.

Some of the dissidents now joined up with the Turks and encouraged their protests. The Turks went on hunger strikes. With the Commission of Security and Cooperation in Europe about to meet in May 1989, the Politburo felt pressure to act. Disturbances erupted in the Turkish areas. The Politburo decided that Zhivkov should publicly announce permission for Turks to emigrate to Turkey. Hundred of thousands (about half the community) did so before Ankara closed the borders in August. The Turks called it the Grand Excursion.[2] Some found life in Turkey for them was worse than Bulgaria, and more than 40 percent returned. Within several months, Zhivkov's regime began to collapse, and the revival process ended. Moreover, the international condemnation of Bulgaria, particularly by the United States, did not lessen with the Turkish exodus. In Bulgaria, sections of the agricultural economy suffered with the loss of the Turkish workers, and the government mobilized student brigades to take their place.

The Turkish and environmental demonstrations undid Zhivkov's rule. Of course, as mentioned above, the whole Communist system was collapsing in Eastern Europe, and this was the overriding factor. The party members who thought they could save Communist rule in

Bulgaria by replacing Zhivkov were sadly mistaken. It was doomed even in the Soviet Union. Zhivkov's colleagues deserted him. Stanko Todorov complained to the Central Committee of the party about Zhivkov's handling of the Turkish situation. In October, Foreign Minister Petur Mladenov (b. 1936) resigned. Two weeks later, Minister of Defense Dobri Djurov, Zhivkov's comrade in the World War II resistance, advised Zhivkov to step down. At a meeting of the Politburo on December 10, the party leader admitted his mistakes and resigned his post.

In January 1990, the former leader was expelled from the Communist Party. He was arrested and charged with embezzling public funds. Found guilty, he was sentenced for seven years, which the court allowed him to serve under house arrest because of his age and illness. He continued to justify his rule until his death in 1998. Indeed, he still retained some admirers, and many Bulgarians attended his funeral.

Zhivkov's 35-year tenure as leader of Bulgaria was the longest in its modern history—longer than any of its monarchs. He is not generally well regarded outside of his country, and he has also had many Bulgarian critics. This is somewhat unfair. Much of the criticism is simply raised because he was on the losing side of the Cold War. During his tenure, many of the commentators from outside the Communist world who did not pay attention to Bulgaria habitually described him as nondescript. Yet no one could last as the head of state in a nonhereditary position without some skills and accomplishments. Zhivkov, in fact, was a consummate politician who knew how to weave his way through Communist Party intrigues. Once he achieved power, he never let anyone who could replace him move into a position where they could do it. The few attempts to do so from the party or the military failed.

Critics have no trouble pointing to his failures, but what were his achievements? When he resigned in 1989 after 35 years in power, he left Bulgaria far behind the West in economic attainment. However, this really was no different than the rest of the Soviet Bloc. He did leave it more urban than rural and much more modern than it had been in 1954. The greatest success of his tenure was raising a generation of Bulgarians literate and well educated, ambitious and industrious, albeit much more cynical and opportunistic than their grandparents had been. (However, there were also idealistic Bulgarians such as those that led the organizations in the 1980s, which brought about the end of Zhivkov and Communist Party rule.)

In the economy, despite all the measures he tried, his achievements were far too modest for the twentieth century. Perhaps it was a fault of employing Marxist principles in a country where even Marxist theorists stated they were not yet ready. However, even the more industrialized countries in the East Bloc lagged behind the West. The greatest economic fiasco in Zhivkov's time undoubtedly was the Kremikovtsi steel works, which cost an immense amount of labor and money and did not produce nearly enough to warrant the expenditures. The forced collectivization, which started before his tenure, also was economically destructive. Some of his incentives after 1965, such as private plots, did bring about some improvement in agricultural output. The Bulgarian farmers were amenable to cooperative faming and would probably more readily have accepted that as a reasonable alternative. The most successful economic measure under Zhivkov may have been his opening of the country to international tourism where visitors from all over the world could enjoy the country's marvelous beaches, wonderful ski slopes, spectacular scenery, and historical monasteries, churches, ancient tombs, and other sights at unbelievably cheap rates. Bulgaria also exported technology, technicians, and engineers to the Third World.

Zhivkov could be vindictive, as we have seen in the case of Georgi Markov, but he was no mass murderer like Stalin or Cambodia's Pol Pot. He executed some of his enemies and imprisoned more, but a good many that ran afoul of him were purged from the party, were demoted, or lost their positions. Was there a better alternative than Zhivkov? What if Bulgaria remained a monarchy? No other kings from the Balkans survived into the 1970s, and when King Simeon returned to lead the country in the twenty-first century, he came back as prime minister, not king. What if Gemeto Dimitrov, Nikola Petkov, or Dimitur Gichev survived to serve as prime minister in a multiparty republic of Bulgaria or under King Simeon? It is difficult to imagine that BANU, even under the leadership of these popular figures, could have lead Bulgaria into the last decades of the twentieth century. The Union was divided and would have met stiff challenges from the other parties. Perhaps as in other European countries, several leaders of various parties would arise and change leadership back and forth, but would the country be any better off than Greece or Turkey, the two non-Communist countries of the Balkans in that period? Both of those certainly have had their share of problems in these years. Ironically, his fellow Balkan prime minister, Andreas Papandreou, with whom he got along reasonably well considering one was linked to NATO and the other to the Warsaw Pact, was tried also for corruption at the same time as Zhivkov. Pictures of the two in the press accompanying the accounts of the trials looked almost identical. In any case, the question of Bulgaria following a non-Communist path is moot. The victors at the end of World War II consigned Bulgaria to the Soviet sphere by the Churchill-Stalin agreement of 1944 and subsequently with the Truman Doctrine.

The question then becomes whether or not another Bulgarian Communist could have filled Zhivkov's role. Chervenkov or Iugov? The former was too rigid in his Stalinism to remain in power, and Zhivkov succeeded in removing the latter. It is doubtful if either would have been better for Bulgaria in the long run. Traicho Kostev was a more likely candidate, but he did not take the precaution of keeping silent during the Stalinist period as Khrushchev did in the Soviet Union. Zhivkov was more than silent; he was unknown. That is why Chervenkov chose him when Moscow ordered him to take a partner. The Bulgarians told a joke that during World War II, Zhivkov was in semi-hiding: he was hiding but no one was looking for him.

Zhivkov was less well known outside his country than either Tito or Ceausescu, his neighbors in the Balkans. He certainly lacked the daring, experience, and reputation of Tito. He did try some of the Yugoslav's policies in the 1980s with some success, but even Tito failed in the long run. Yugoslavia fell apart after his death. Ceausescu was able to con the West into thinking him an independent Communist while still maintaining ties to Moscow. He received awards from the Soviet Union, Great Britain, Japan, and even the United States. However, Romania was far worse off under his rule than Bulgaria was under Zhivkov's, and Ceausescu was the only East Bloc leader to be executed by his people after he fell from power.

The reasons for Zhivkov's long tenure include his decision to hitch his wagon to Moscow rather than show any independence like the other Balkan leaders. He was rewarded for this by favorable trade agreements and low prices for resources such as oil. Could he have received better deals? Perhaps. Janos Kadar had for Hungary by agreeing to cooperate with the Kremlin after 1956. Zhivkov also provided consumer goods for his people in the 1970s but bought them with high debts for the country.

In the final analysis, he was just an average Communist apparatchik fulfilling a role that many others could have but with whom the party was comfortable and whom the population tolerated. He survived until the revival process and the economic and environmental problems convinced the party and the population that he had outlived his usefulness.

Mladenov replaced him and immediately called a full meeting of the Central Committee to assess the situation. In great expectation, new organizations and clubs formed. Old political parties reemerged like BANU-Nikola Petkov and the Social Democrats. Ahmed Dogan's Turkish National Liberation Movement became the Movement for Rights and Freedoms (MRF). Ekoglasnost formed the Green Party. Several parties and organizations, including the Greens, Zheliu Zhelev's Club for the Support of Glasnost and Perestroika, and the independent labor union *Podkrepa* formed the *Suiuz na demokratichnite sili (SDS)*—Union of Democratic Forces (UDF). Mladenov and the Communist Party did not fight back. Given the events in the other countries of Eastern Europe, they had to accede to the demands of the dissidents. After the Central Committee meeting, Mladenov announced that there would be more democracy within the party and the revival process would end. He also apologized for the party's past mistakes and revealed that Bulgaria's international debt was five times higher than what was listed in the official reports— $15 billion American. He further stated that he foresaw changes in the constitution, implying that the Communist Party might give up its "leading role." Mladenov called for a constitutional commission that he would lead and that would make recommendations to parliament. Zhelev, speaking for UDF, told the Bulgarian press that the coalition demanded free elections with a multiparty political system and a free-market economy. The dissidents organized a large, religious demonstration in Sofia of several thousand persons carrying crosses, posters, and icons and asking that Christmas and Easter be recognized as national holidays. Then another demonstration of tens of thousands followed demanding a quicker route to democracy. There were still more demonstrations. The Turks marched asking for their names back and to have their religious rights and their property restored. Large counterdemonstrations against the Turks throughout the country took place in answer. In response to the demonstrations, the Central Committee purged more members of the party associated with the Zhivkov regime and agreed that a new constitution would be drafted by a grand national assembly. In the meantime, Mladenov planned to hold a round-table discussion, putting all items up for consideration. The era of post-Communist Bulgaria began.

NOTES

1. For a good account of Zhivkova's career, see R. J. Crampton, *Bulgaria* (London: Oxford University Press, 2007), 367–70.

2. Mary Neuburger, *The Orient Within: Muslim Minorities and the Negotiation of Nationhood in Modern Bulgaria* (Ithaca, NY: Cornell University Press, 2004), 82.

10

Post-Communist Bulgaria (1990–2010)

The Round Table lasted five months from January to May 1990. It included the Communists and the BANU organization that had been part of the Fatherland Front as well as representatives from UDF, MRF, the *Podkrepa* labor union, and other dissident groups, including some persons who returned from exile. Both Turkish and anti-Turkish Bulgarian nationalists took part as well. Events moved faster than the politicians could establish the rules for changing the constitution and the country. Many of the dissidents' complaints and suggestions were enacted by government fiat or by the people themselves while the Round Table was meeting.

THE NEW CONSTITUTION

The first question on the agenda was the role of the Communist Party. The 1972 constitution's first article called the party the leading institution in society, but now UDF and other dissidents wanted to remove the article and have all parties compete on an equal basis. The

Communists agreed and before the Round Table talks ended changed their name to the Bulgarian Socialist Party. Various institutions and societies ended their connection with the party as well. The labor unions, for example, formed the Confederation of Independent Trade Unions in Bulgaria (CIUIB), which now existed in competition with *Podkrepa*, although their goals were similar. The right to strike was granted, but only after compulsory arbitration failed. (This, however, was not extended to the police, military, health professions, power plants, or port facilities.) Communist Party cells ended in professional organizations, the university, and even the military. The Fatherland Front and the Komsomol became irrelevant. The State Security, the police department that spied on individual Bulgarians and carried out "dirty tricks" including murder, was dissolved. In March, the government enacted a law allowing citizens to choose any personal name they wished. More than a half million Turks applied for their old names back.

Interim Prime Minister Petur Mladenov fell into trouble by condemning the continued demonstrations and threatening police action. He resigned as party chief in February and as prime minister in July. Aleksandur Lilov (b. 1933), a protégée of Zhivkov, took his place as party leader, and the *subranie* appointed Andrei Lukanov (1938–1996) prime minister. Lukanov, a member of the reformist wing of the party, came from a well-established Communist family going back three generations. His father had been Zhivkov's foreign minister, and he himself served in the diplomatic corps and had been appointed minister of foreign economic affairs in 1987. Lukanov asked UDF to join his cabinet, but they refused. He, therefore, nominated only Communist ministers. The new government recognized Easter and Christmas as national holidays. It also removed the body of Georgi Dimitrov from the mausoleum; however, it did so with full public honors in recognition of his courageous stand against Hitler and Göring in 1933. The Round Table finished its business by calling for a grand national assembly to write a new constitution.

Economic reforms followed the political changes. The government ordered new policies based on market principles. Persons subsidized by the state lost their positions. Subsidies for goods also disappeared and inflation approached 1000 percent. Agriculture was privatized and businesses were allowed to expand by using hired labor, previously forbidden. The government floated the lev, which fell to one tenth the previously pegged official rate. Despite some aid from the West, store shelves emptied of their wares, and a resulting black market flourished. The country joined the International Monetary Fund (IMF) and also received most-favored-nation trading status from the United States. In foreign relations, Sofia's problems with Turkey eased somewhat as the revival process ended, but the continued confrontations between Turks and Bulgarians within the country left some coolness with Ankara. Sofia moved closer to Athens to face their common enemy. Bulgaria also resumed relations with Israel, which had been broken since the 1967 Six-Day War. The large community of Bulgarian Jews in Israel made this an advantageous connection.

The new freedom permitted the Bulgarians led to agitation for a whole gamut of solutions. Various parties and societies sprang up advocating everything from the return of the monarchy and free market capitalism through Scandinavian-style socialism to the continuation of orthodox Marxism. The constitution banned parties based on ethnicities, but the Turkish-dominated Movement for Rights and Freedoms continued because it successfully argued it was open to all Bulgarians. The new parties and organizations lobbied and obtained office space and access to the public media. However, the Socialist (formerly Communist Party) was able to keep its advantage for a while.

In the meantime, the demonstrations continued and became more violent. Acts of vandalism occurred throughout the capital, including the arson of the massive Communist Party headquarters in downtown Sofia, almost destroying the building.

Elections for the Grand National Assembly took place in June. More than 25 parties and coalitions took part. The fractious nature of the opposition helped the Socialists to win a slim majority of 211 of the 400 seats. BANU split between the party that had been in the Fatherland Front and the exiles of BANU-Nikola Petkov, which joined UDF. UDF came in second to the Socialists, winning 144 seats. MRF won 23, BANU won 16, and the six remaining seats went to smaller parties and independents. Some of the parties claimed that there were improprieties in the voting, but foreign observers disagreed on whether those claims were justified. However, most Bulgarians thought the election was fair. The Socialists may have been able to apply pressure in some areas, especially in the rural villages. The countryside was, in fact, a bastion of Socialist support. The Socialist leaders there had strong family and neighborhood connections. Furthermore, the economic reversals in the months following the upheaval, along with the rural conservative attitudes and their mistrust of Sofia (where the opposition had strength), may have also given the Socialists an advantage.

According to the new pre-Constitution electoral rule the Round Table had established, the Grand National Assembly chose the president. After Mladenov resigned, the Socialists, despite their majority, agreed to select Zhelev, the UDF leader, to replace him.

They did choose a Socialist as vice president. Petur Beron (b. 1940), an environmentalist, replaced Zhelev as head of UDF. A general strike by the unions in December brought about the resignation of Lukanov, and Dimitur Popov (b. 1927), a politically independent judge, replaced him. Popov formed a cabinet with Socialist, UDF, and BANU ministers. In UDF, Filip Dimitrov (b. 1955), the leader of the Green Party, replaced his colleague Beron, when it was revealed that the latter had been an informer for Zhivkov's secret police.

When the Grand National Assembly finished the constitution, the conservative elements of UDF objected that it gave the Socialists too much power and staged new demonstrations. Some even went on a hunger strike. There was also a debate whether Bulgaria should be a republic or a monarchy. Some wanted a referendum. Although the monarchists had some strength, the assembly decided to declare Bulgaria a democratic republic under the rule of law. The new constitution called for a *subranie* of 240 members and a president to be elected every five years with a two-term limit. It separated executive, legislative, and judicial powers and created an independent constitutional court. A restriction requiring the president to have resided in the country for at least five years was directed against King Simeon's running for the post. However, he returned to Bulgaria in 1996 and then took an active part in politics.

The constitution also stated that the term of the *subranie* be four years, a different length than the presidential term. The *subranie* also chose the prime minister. Although the *subranie* was primarily the legislative branch of government, both the president and prime minister had executive responsibilities. Inherent in this, obviously, was the same flaw that plagued the Turnovo Constitution, which arose if the two leaders were from different parties or had opposing programs.

THE UDF GOVERNMENT

Elections for a new *subranie* went ahead in October 1991. UDF, after settling its internal disputes, won 110 seats. The Socialists, running in a bloc with four other parties, won only 106. MRF, the only other party to garner the minimum 4 percent necessary to qualify, won 24 seats and held the balance of power. The dozens of other parties and blocs, running the whole political spectrum from monarchists to irreconcilable Marxists, gathered 25 percent of the votes, but none of them individually had enough for even one seat. Both BANU and BANU-Nikola Petkov, which left UDF, were among those groups shut out. Soon a half dozen BANU parties appeared on the scene. Zhelev remained as president, winning the election carried out several weeks after the *subranie* elections. However, he had more difficulties than expected. The Socialists and a populist candidate gained enough votes to force a second round. Blaga Dimitrova won on his ticket as vice president.

The assembly named the UDF leader, Filip Dimitrov, prime minister and endorsed his cabinet by a 128-to-90 majority. At 36, Filip Dimitrov became the youngest prime minister in Bulgaria's history and led the first non-Communist government since the 1940s. The *subranie*, in one of its first acts, transferred the property of the Socialist Party to the state. With the MRF in a position of power, the Turks were able to gain more rights. Turkish-language schools were reopened. Anti-Turkish attitudes among some Bulgarians continued, but they were considerably less than those that appeared in the first months of 1990.

With the economic situation in Bulgaria still severe, industrial, government, and union leaders agreed to cooperate in a transition to a market economy with as little hardship as possible on the population. The unions agreed to a 200-day moratorium on strikes. However, the economy suffered a blow when the government defaulted on its borrowings and could not receive additional loans, but some relief aid came from abroad. Energy was also in short supply. Four of five of the Koluzdoy nuclear reactors were shut down, and electricity was rationed.

The country's relations with countries outside the East Bloc continued to improve. Bulgaria joined the European Council. Sofia supported the United Nations in its resolutions against Iraq in the Persian Gulf War and sent a medical team to aid there. Relations with the Vatican were resumed after 40 years of separation. President Zhelev, Prime Minister Dimitrov, and other Bulgarian leaders made goodwill trips abroad. Dimitrov met with President George Bush. The University of Maine, with private funds, opened an American University in Blagoevgrad in Bulgarian Macedonia. Israeli Prime Minister Yitzhak Shamir, whose wife was born in Bulgaria, made a state visit to the country and gave Bulgaria $3 million to aid the transfer of Soviet Jews to Israel through Bulgaria. Zhelev said relations with the Arab States would not change, but material aid to the Palestinian Liberation Organization stopped.

The question of Macedonia once more sparked debate. With Yugoslavia on the verge of breaking up, Zhelev announced that Bulgaria was ready to recognize an independent Macedonia but would not yet recognize the Macedonians as a nationality separate from Bulgarian. Certainly, Bulgaria would not recognize the inhabitants of its section of Macedonia as anything other than Bulgarians. When Macedonia declared its independence in September 1991, Bulgaria was the first country to recognize it. The *subranie*, however, divided on almost every issue between the Socialists and the UDF, adopted a nearly unanimous resolution stating that there was no such thing as a Macedonian nationality. There was also some talk in Romania about reversing the Vienna award of 1940, which returned Southern Dobrudja to Bulgaria. Sofia sought help from the West and the countries of the former Soviet Bloc to prevent such an event.

Differences between Zhelev and Dimitrov disrupted UDF and the government, exposing the constitutional flaw mentioned above. Improvement of economic conditions stalled, and political unrest again shook the country. The Dimitrov faction within UDF wanted the privatization of the state enterprises and the farms. It wanted property seized by the Communists returned to the original owners. Members of the bureaucracy, particularly in the foreign office, who had worked for the Communist regime were replaced with younger functionaries. The upheaval impeded the work of the government. Furthermore, the new officials were not as enthusiastically anti-Communist as Dimitrov had hoped.

Moreover, Dimitrov also wanted to try Communists who were involved with the corruption and crimes of the Zhivkov regime. The accusations led to the *subranie*'s replacement of the Patriarch Maxim (Marin Naidenov Minkov, b. 1914) because of his cooperation with the Zhivkov regime. They replaced him with Pimen (d. 1999), the metropolitan of Nevrokop. The constitutional court, however, restored Maxim. The followers of Pimen formed an alternative synod that continued the conflict through the next two decades and divided the church into rival factions, each claiming to be legitimate. Several times the rivalry broke out into open, even fatal, battles, including a very public fracas between the various factions in front of the Alexander Nevsky Cathedral. Later in 2004, the government enforced the legitimacy of Maxim by evicting alternative priests from the churches they still occupied, but the alternative church continued the struggle.

In 1992, Zhelev and Dimitrov continued to disagree on solutions. Inflation and unemployment rose geometrically. The privatization of collective farms and the claims and counterclaims for compensation by families whose properties had been seized by the old regime added to the confusion. The unions reneged on their no-strike agreement. On the other hand, the government opened a stock exchange in Sofia and foreign investors bought shares in Bulgarian enterprises. Tourism revived in 1992. Foreign aid to the Koluzdoy nuclear power plant eased the energy shortage. The government also began repaying its foreign debt. In October, MRF withdrew its support from Dimitrov, and he lost a vote of confidence in the *subranie*. The respected economist Liuben Berov (1925–2006) replaced him in December and brought in a cabinet of experts.

Still, through 1993, the divisions in the *subranie* hampered economic reform and recovery.

Inflation abated a little from the 1992 high of 81 percent to less than 70. Unemployment was at 8 percent. Privatization insisted upon by the Dimitrov government slowed down. "Asset stripping," the transferring of funds from state enterprises to private companies, lessened the value of the former before they could be sold. The *subranie* also enacted an 18 percent value-added tax.

Furthermore, Berov's support faded quickly after his selection as prime minister. The austerity measures he advocated were unpopular with the Socialists and MRF, who had originally brought him to power. However, some of these measures were forced on the country by international creditors. Additionally, UDF was wracked by internal struggles and a faction split off as the New Union for Democracy. The other parties split as well, recalling the political fractionalization that plagued the country in the days before World War I. The parliament could not agree on a replacement for Berov. Much anger was directed at President Zhelev, who supported the prime minister. Vice president Dimitrova resigned over the government's policies and the limited role they allowed to her play. One UDF representative in the *subranie* went on a three-week hunger strike. While this gained some support for ousting Zhelev, the president and prime minister remained in office.

Ceremonies were held honoring Boris III on the 50th anniversary of his death in 1993. His widow, Queen Ioanna, visited the country for first time since her departure in 1946 and attended the reburial of her husband's heart at Rila Monastery.

Despite the government's success in renegotiating its foreign debt down by half and receiving loans from the IMF, Bulgaria's economy still remained stagnant in 1994. Corruption in the government and crime in the country rose to serious proportions. The minister of interior denounced the police as corrupt and incompetent and recommended that the *subranie* pass a law allowing citizens to arm themselves for protection. Berov did get a law through the *subranie* requiring judges to have five years of legal experience. The anti-Communist parties complained that this meant that only persons who were trained and served under the old regime could be appointed to the bench. Furthermore, Berov's serious illness forced his resignation in September. The *subranie* could not agree on a successor, so Zhelev used a constitutional provision to call for new elections. In the interim, he appointed as prime minister Renata Indzhova (b. 1953), another economist, the director of privatization. Even though her appointment was temporary, she entered the annals of Bulgarian history as Bulgaria's first woman prime minister.

THE SOCIALIST GOVERNMENT

In December 1994, the elections returned a slight majority for the Socialists, who won 125 of the 240 seats. UDF won 69 and the MRF 15. Two other parties—the People's Union and the Bulgarian Business Bloc—shared the remaining 31 seats. The Socialist leader Zhan Videnov (b. 1959) now formed a government that included Agrarians and Ekoglasnot members. The government confronted President Zhelev on a number of issues it supported: limiting the sale of land, restricting environmental protection measures, and restoring rights to Communists. When it tried to override the president's vetoes, the constitutional court backed Zhelev. The president criticized the Socialist government for its lack of progress on economic reform and controlling crime, even hinting that the Socialists were connected to the criminal gangs. Socialist accusations against both Zhelev and the courts continued. The Socialists also enacted measures reasserting Bulgaria's close relations with Russia. These included some economic transactions and the reintroduction of compulsory Russian language instruction in Bulgarian schools. However, as the months passed, relations between Sofia and Moscow cooled again when the Kremlin demanded that Bulgaria not move closer to the West.

After some initial, positive signs, such as the lowering of inflation, economic conditions in Bulgaria worsened under the Socialists. There were several reasons for the difficulties. International agreements required the repayment of Bulgarian debt. The government's inexperience with free-trade economic principles was exacerbated by the Socialists' interference in the market. However, one of the more serious problems was the export of Bulgarian grain, which was controlled by conglomerates formed by Communist officials in the last months of their regime. In January 1996, the Agricultural Bank Vitosha failed. In May, the Bulgarian National Bank could not make required payments on its foreign debts because of insufficient funds. President Zhelev announced that the financial system was on the brink of collapse. The lev had fallen by half in less than six months. The IMF demanded immediate action. Zhelev raised taxes and prices, closed state enterprises, and limited public credit. The IMF was unsatisfied and refused Bulgaria more money.

The crisis resulted in more disorder. Inflation began to spiral upward again. More than a million protesters took to the streets. The disputes and arguments between Zhelev and the *subranie* increased. Rumors of a military coup d'état spread through the capital. In October, former Prime Minister Lukanov was assassinated by an unknown assailant. Lukanov thus joined a numerous list of murdered Bulgarian prime ministers going back to Stambolov. Neither the murderer nor the motive was ever discovered. People speculated the assassin was either a personal or political rival, possibly a member of one of the criminal gangs.

Elections for president took place in October and November 1996. President Zhelev had lost a primary vote to run as the UDF candidate. The Socialists were going to slate Georgi Pirinski Jr. (b. 1948). Pirinski was the son of Georgi Pirinski Sr. (1901–1992), a prominent Communist who fled to the United States after the 1923 September Uprising. In America he became a member of the Communist Party USA and executive secretary of the American Slavic Committee. He also married his wife Pauline, who was from New York. Their son Georgi Jr. was born in the United States. The elder Pirinski was expelled from the USA in 1951, and the family moved to Bulgaria, where Pauline became a professor of English in Sofia University. As the younger Pirinski moved up the Communist ranks, he renounced his American citizenship. He served in Videnov's government but resigned over differences with the prime minister. His political opponents argued that his renunciation of his American citizenship was invalid and, in any case, he could not be president of Bulgaria because he was not born in the country. The courts agreed and the Socialists chose another candidate. The UDF candidate, Petur Stoianov (b. 1952), won in a landslide. Videnov resigned as prime minister, and Pirinski continued as a member of the *subranie* to play an important role in Bulgarian politics and even later to chair the assembly.

Videnov resigned as Socialist leader as well, and Georgi Parvanov (b. 1957) and Nikolai Dobrev (1947–1999) now headed the party. The public, particularly those in Sofia, did not care who was in charge. Demonstrators again demanded new elections to oust the Socialists, and once again the picketers and police clashed. The UDF representatives in the *subranie*, fed up with the economic situation, walked out of the chamber. Following the law, President Stoianov, who was not sworn in until January 19, 1997, asked Dobrev to establish a new government because the Socialists still had a majority in the assembly. However, Stoianov feared if a change of government did not occur, there might be civil war!

UDF BACK IN POWER

Dobrev got the message and refused to serve. Stoianov appointed his UDF colleague, the mayor of Sofia, Stefan Sofiianski (b. 1951), as interim prime minister until the 1997 elections for a new *subranie* took place. UDF then won 137 of the 240 seats. The Democratic Left, a bloc that included the Socialists, won 58. Three other parties split the remaining 55 seats. Ivan Kostov (b. 1949), the head of UDF and former finance minister in previous UDF governments, now became prime minister. UDF now held the presidency, the premiership, and a healthy majority in the *subranie*. The bickering that plagued and stifled the country under Zhelev and Videnov ended. New economic policies emerged: an independent currency board put the lev on a sound basis; subsidies to agriculture ended; and efforts in privatization resumed. The IMF extended more loans to the country. By the end of the century, 70 percent of the state enterprises were privatized. The Kremikovtsi works were sold to an Italian firm for $1 American, but the problems of disposing of it or finding some useful function continued. Bulgaria's trade with the European Union countries also doubled.

Kostov soon ordered investigation of public officials who served as State Security officers under Zhivkov. He succeeded in moving Bulgaria closer to joining NATO and the European Union, but admission into those organizations occurred only after he left office. However, he was not successful in fulfilling his pledge to curb the country's crime problem.

Although the political chaos had now quieted down somewhat, two new parties emerged—the Euroleft and the Liberal Democratic Alliance. The Euroleft had won 14 seats in the *subranie* elections. The Liberal Democratic Alliance was a coalition of liberal parties formed after the elections with ex-President Zhelev as honorary president. Stoianov ordered the retirement of a number of senior military officers after they complained about cuts in their budget. Turks received more rights. They could broadcast radio in Turkish and could perform ritual circumcision, which had been banned in 1959. However, the Turkish community still complained about the removal of memorial plaques set up for Turks executed for the bombings in the 1980s protests. Roma also demonstrated in the river port city of Lom because of employment discrimination and cessation of welfare.

In 1999, the Bulgarian government finally took the surprising step of acknowledging the existence of a Macedonian nation. In return, Skopje renounced any claims to Pirin, Bulgaria. Then the two countries signed a mutual defense treaty, and Sofia sent arms to Skopje. Sofia's recognition caused turmoil in the North American Macedonian Patriotic Organization, as mentioned above, an outgrowth of IMRO. The founders and older members of the organization believed that Macedonian Slavs were Bulgarians. The younger members increasingly thought of themselves as Macedonians and were interested in supporting the Republic of Macedonia. Many arguments, sometimes extremely hostile, ensued, and a rival organization broke off. The organization's newspaper still continued to publish in English and Bulgarian, but occasionally also in Macedonian.

In 2000, a corruption scandal rocked the government. Prime Minister Kostov denied the allegations against him, but a number of members of his government had to resign. The *subranie* enacted legislation mandating that all senior government officials reveal their income and expenditures. More scandals involved the discovery of clandestine microphones in the private home of an official of the ministry of justice. Kostov again denied any responsibility.

Relations between Russia and Bulgaria worsened when the country expelled Russian citizens it accused of involvement with the Bulgarian crime syndicate. Sofia also had a dispute with Moscow over a trade agreement involving the sale of Russian aircraft. However, Russia did come to Bulgaria's aid in an international incident involving the arrest of Bulgarian medical personnel in Libya. Kostov was committed to move Bulgaria closer to the West. His cooperation with NATO in the crisis in Kosovo in 1998 led to thanks from Washington. President Bill Clinton visited the country in 1999, the first sitting president to do so.

TSAR-PRIME MINISTER

As the millennium changed, UDF's problems resulted in a loss of popular support. Crime and corruption led the list of Stoianov's and Kostov's worries. Petty crimes had blighted Bulgaria since the fall of the Communist regime. In addition, large-scale smuggling and even forced prostitution plagued the country. Bulgarian criminals were linked to the Russian mobs. Corruption in the government involved even Kostov's wife and her charities. Reforms that Bulgaria underwent in preparing the country for entry into the European Union and NATO caused economic stress, too. The required agricultural reforms led to shortages, inflation, and unemployment. Furthermore, Sofia had to limit its use of its nuclear facility at Koluzdoy, which was considered the most dangerous in the Balkans. In the meantime, the Socialist Party rebuilt its strength, and the former king had returned from abroad to lead a new political party, the National Movement Simeon II (NMSS), with the intention of running for elected office. UDF lost some of its membership and did poorly in local elections in 1999.

Rumors in the country said the king was preparing to run for president in the fall, but he did not meet the constitutional resident requirement. The court also initially barred the NMSS from running for the *subranie* in the spring election of 2001, but by joining in coalition with other legal parties, Simeon's bloc won precisely half the seats (120). UDF won 51, the coalition that included the Socialists won 48, and MRF won 21.

With the votes of MRF, the *subranie* chose Simeon as prime minister. This was the reverse of a Balkan oddity of 1928 when Akhmed Zogu, the president of Albania, declared himself to be King Zog I. However, no country before this had ever chosen its monarch as premier. After his exile in 1946, Simeon and his family lived in Egypt with his grandfather, Victor Emmanuel III of Italy, who also had been exiled. In 1951, the family was given asylum in Spain. Simeon attended schools in Alexandria, Spain, and in 1958 and 1959 at the Valley Forge Military Academy outside Philadelphia, immortalized in J. D. Salinger's *Catcher in the Rye* as Pencey Prep. At university, he studied law and business administration and then worked as an international business consultant. He learned about a half dozen languages. He and his wife Margarita have five children, all with Bulgarian names. After the fall of Communism, he seriously observed and studied Bulgarian politics and did not hinder his supporters from mentioning his name as the country's leader either as king, president, or prime minister. From 1996 onward, he visited the county several times. In 2001, he settled there and went on to lead the government. To emphasize his civilian role, he now went by the name Simeon Saksekoburggotski (literally: "of the House of Saxe-Coburg-Gotha," his family's noble line).

In the presidential elections of November 2001, once again no one received the required majority in the first round. In the runoff between Stoianov and the Socialist candidate Parvanov, the later won by almost 10 percent. The flaw of Bulgarian constitutional government appeared in its most extreme example. A Marxist was elected president and the tsar was now prime minister. Fortunately, for the good of the country, they agreed to work together.

Simeon chose for his cabinet persons from various ethnic backgrounds and parties, including the Socialists. He appointed Western-trained officials to financial posts. He announced his economic plan was to attract foreign entrepreneurs, lower taxes on businesses, and increase privatization. Like his predecessor, Simeon vowed to deal with crime and corruption, but this was as difficult for him as it had

Simeon II, the royal prime minister, and Peter Stoianov, the Marxist president, in 2001. (AP/Wide World Photos)

been for Kostov. Furthermore, the privatization of the large Bulgarian tobacco monopoly seemed to be carried out in a less-than-fair manner. Also, a scandal arose over the reform of the customs authority, which apparently benefited certain smuggling rings.

Simeon's austerity regime and the European Union's requirements for Bulgarian admission caused dissention within the country. Roma near Plovdiv rioted for three days in February 2002 after power was cut off from their homes for nonpayment. Also, in continuing their cooperation with NATO, Bulgaria sent soldiers to fight in Iraq under Polish commanders. The deaths of some of the Bulgarian combatants led to more protests at home. The opposition Socialists gained strength in the local elections of 2003. Bulgaria, however, was admitted to NATO in 2004 and the European Union in 2007.

Integrating the Roma into Bulgaria was an important factor for Bulgarian entry into the EU, which had made a point of treatment of minorities as a precondition for admission. The Turks were no longer a major problem after the end of the revival process, and with the political clout of MRF, they found a place in Bulgarian society. However, the Roma were still outsiders and, as noted above, the conservative economic measures often hit them the hardest. Kostov had tried various measures to improve their lot. Simeon's government continued these with even more attention. The government launched an adult literacy campaign. In 2003, the *subranie* passed antidiscriminatory legislation that protected the rights of ethnic and religious minorities and outlawed bias on the basis of gender, race, age, education, property, and sexual orientation as well. The parliament established an independent office to handle all cases of violation of the law.

THE RISE OF THE RIGHT

By the middle of his term, the tsar-premier had lost much of the popular support that had swept him into power. While the international community praised Simeon and Bulgaria for its cooperation with NATO and the European Union, the people at home did not feel an economic recovery. Crime and corruption still seemed to rule Bulgarian politics and society. In 2004, there were bombings and assassinations laid at the feet of the criminal gangs. In fact, Simeon's government actually was making steady progress in both the economy and against the criminal element, but the battles he had to fight against those with entrenched power, particularly in the judicial branch, did not sit well with the public. In the economy, inflation and unemployment were down. Privatization and tourism continued to be successful. However, foreigners now were buying prime property in the country, particularly along the Black Sea coast, which had both positive and negative effects.

Nevertheless, given the public's skepticism, it is not surprising that NMSS did not do well in the parliamentary elections of 2005 despite its real progress in the economy. Seven parties earned enough votes to be seated. No one won a majority.

The Socialists running in the Coalition for Bulgaria joined other left-of-center parties to capture the lead with a third of the seats. Simeon's party came in second and MRF third. We see from the Table 10.1 that UDF fell behind among the other parties. One of them, Coalition Union Attack, advocated a program of extreme Bulgarian nationalism and directed some of its election slogans against the Roma. After a number of weeks of fruitless attempts to form a new government, the Socialist leader Sergei Stanishev (b. 1966) was able to put together a black-red coalition government consisting of his party with NMSS and MRF. The following year, with the opposition divided, Parvanov ran unopposed and was elected for a second term as president.

The government, however, continued to be plagued by corruption, and criminal gangs as well as petty crime remained uncontrolled. Despite foreign investment pouring into the country and foreigners buying prime real estate, the average Bulgarian citizen lived at a

Table 10.1.   2005 *subranie* elections[i]

Party	Percentage of Votes %	Number of Seats Won
Coalition for Bulgaria	34.17	82
NMSS	22.08	53
MRF	14.17	34
Coalition Union Attack	8.75	21
UDF	8.33	20
Democrats for a Strong Bulgaria	7.08	17
Bulgarian People's Union	5.43	13
Total	100	240

[i]"Bulgaria Sees Official Election Results" in *Sofia News*, June 29, 2005; Lyubka Savkova, "Election Briefing no. 21: Europe and the Parliamentary Election in Bulgaria, 25th June 2005," p. 7, in http://www.sussex.ac.uk/sei/documents/epern-eb-bulgaria_2005.pdf

lower standard of living than the rest of Europe. In 2007, school-teachers went on a hunger strike because of their low pay. The government agreed to modest pay raises. The divided opposition failed, however, in its attempts to remove Stanishev from power until the 2009 elections.

Since the 2005 elections, Bulgarian politics went through yet another major reformation of parties and coalitions. Simeon resigned as head of the NMSS, which changed its name to the National Movement for Stability and Progress, a centrist liberal party—liberal in the European sense, that is, more conservative than American liberalism. It in fact joined the Liberal International, headquartered in London. Another new party formed in 2005 was the conservative Order, Law, and Justice party, which pledged to fight against crime and corruption. The leaders associated their party with the British Conservative Party and other European parties of similar views. Furthermore, a new populist party emerged—Citizens for the European Development of Bulgaria (GERB) led by the mayor of Sofia Boiko Borisov (b. 1959), a former fireman and member of Zhivkov's State Security police. GERB was center right, and its nationalist and anticrime message had great appeal. The Socialists accused Borisov of promoting anti-Roma and anti-Turkish attitudes, which he denied. GERB certainly did not use the openly racist slogans of *Ataka*, the leading party of the Coalition Union Attack. UDF joined a new coalition, the Blue Coalition, composed of center and left-wing parties, including the Democrats for a Strong Bulgaria and one of the BANU factions, among others.

The elections of the summer of 2009 were closely watched at home and abroad. Again, no single party or coalition won a majority, but this time GERB won the most seats—116. The Socialists' coalition dropped to second with 40, and MRF gained four more representatives. We see from the table below that Order, Law, and Justice won a few seats while Simeon's party did not gain enough votes to be represented in the *subranie*.

Borisov, after gaining promises of support from Coalition Union Attack and Order, Law, and Justice, was able to form a government. The trend toward the right could already be seen in the elections for the Bulgarian representatives in the European Parliament in 2007 and 2009.

Bulgarian representation in the EU parliament dropped in the two years from 18 to 17. Clearly the right-wing parties, GERB and *Ataka*, were gaining support at the expense of the Socialists and especially the centrist parties. In European Parliament elections, voters all over the continent tend to vote along ideological lines more than they do in national elections. However, voting in the Bulgarian *subranie* elections showed the same trend shown in the EU voting, both tending toward the right (see Tables 10.2, 10.3, and 10.4).

As Bulgaria moved into the third decade after Communism, it faced the Herculean task of completing its change to a twenty-first century European country. The post-Communist generation was now moving into young adulthood, but the leadership still rested in the hands of those who grew up under Zhivkov. Bulgaria was now an open society. Cafés and casinos were seen everywhere in its major cities. The armed police overlooking the streets from their turrets were gone. The country was firmly committed to the West as a member of NATO

Table 10.2.   2009 *Subranie* Elections[i]

Party	Percentage of Votes %	Number of Seats Won
GERB	39.70	116
Coalition for Bulgaria	17.70	40
MRF	14.40	38
Coalition Union Attack	9.40	21
Blue Coalition	6.80	15
Order, Law, and Justice	4.10	10

[i]"Another Election, Another Government in Bulgaria" in *Sofia News*, July 17, 2009; Election Results on the Internet: Elections to the Bulgarian National Assembly [July 5, 2009] at http:// electionresources.org/bg/assembly.php?election=2009

Table 10.3.   2007 European Parliament Elections[i]

Party	Percentage of Votes %	Number of Seats Won
GERB	21.69	5
Socialist	21.41	5
MRF	20.26	4
Coalition Union Attack	14.20	3
NMSS	6.26	1

[i]"Bulgaria's central Electoral Commission Announces Final MEP Vote Results" and "Eight Bulgarian MPs Turn MEPs" in *Sofia News*, May 23, 2007.

and EU. However, its links to Russia were not forgotten. Its people were educated and ambitious. Many of the brightest left to seek their fortunes abroad whenever and wherever they could. A number of foreign companies were very willing to hire highly qualified Bulgarian engineers who were willing to work at technicians' salaries. At home, politics split between left and right. Governments controlled by different political parties alternated ever since the change in 1989. While the economic situation seemed to be leveling off, the country was still one of the poorest in Europe despite its resources. Foreigners were buying up its prime real estate. Crime and corruption still were not under control. Bulgaria's infrastructure needed a major overhaul. When Prime Minister Borisov was mayor of Sofia, his chief concern was rebuilding Sofia's antiquated sewer system. Construction projects filled the entire country. What will happen in the coming years, perhaps Baba Vanga could have told us; a historian cannot—although, as the saying goes, *ako bog e bulgarin* (if God is a Bulgarian), they will succeed and prosper.

Table 10.4.   2009 European Parliament Elections[i]

Party	Percentage of Votes %	Number of Seats Won
GERB	24.36	5
Coalition for Bulgaria	18.05	4
MRF	14.14	3
Coalition Union Attack	11.96	2
National Movement for Stability and Progress	7.96	2
Blue Coalition	7.95	1

[i]"MEP Elections 2009 Final Results Issued" in *ibid.*, June 10, 2009.

Notable People in the History of Bulgaria

Alexander of Battenberg (1857–1893): First prince of modern Bulgaria (1879–1886). His conservative policies led to tension with Bulgaria's liberal leaders. Tsar Alexander III of Russia also opposed him, and he abdicated in 1886.

Asparuch (circa 640–700): The third son of the Volga Bulgar leader Khan Kubrat. He was assigned to rule over the lands of the Ukraine. In the late seventh century (traditionally 681), he moved south of the Danube and united his Bulgar *boyars* with the eastern branch of the South Slavs living there. Thus he began the First Bulgarian Empire.

Todor (d. 1197) and Ivan Asen (d. 1196): Two brothers who raised a revolt against the Byzantine Empire in 1185 and started the Second Bulgarian Empire. They established their capital in the city of Turnovo.

Ivan Ivanov Bagrianov (1891–1945): Artillery officer and adjutant to King Ferdinand in the Balkan and First World wars; large landowner, lawyer, and politician; close to the royal court. Bagrianov served as minister of agriculture from 1938 to 1941 and attempted to become prime minister. King Boris III mistrusted him; however, after the king's death, he became prime minister and tried to make peace with the West to avoid having Bulgaria fall to the Soviet Union. The Fatherland Front government executed him.

Basil II (958–1025): Byzantine emperor from 976 to 1025. From 986 to 1018, he waged war against the Bulgarian Empire and conquered it. He was then given the title Boulgaroktonos—the Bulgarslayer.

Boris I (d. 907): Bulgarian khan (852 to 889). Converted Bulgaria to Christianity and built the second capital at Preslav. He also brought in missionaries, who developed the Bulgarian language into a liturgical tongue and created a new alphabet for it. After he abdicated and retired to a monastery, he returned on occasion to lead troops in battle.

Boris III (1894–1943): Bulgarian tsar (king) from 1918 to 1943. He tacitly approved the coup d'état against Alexander Stamboliiski. He began his personal rule in 1935 in the wake of the 1934 coup and led Bulgaria into an alliance with Axis powers in World War II. Controversy surrounds both his role in the survival of the Bulgarian Jewish community during the Holocaust and the circumstances of his death.

Hristo Botev (Petkov) (1848–1876): National Bulgarian poet and revolutionary. His patriotic poem, "The Ballad of Hadzhi Dimitur," is a popular Bulgarian folk song. He participated in the April Uprising in northern Bulgaria, where he fell in a skirmish. However, the circumstances of his death remain controversial, with some claiming he was killed by his own men.

Vulko Velev Chervenkov (1900–1980): Communist leader; brother-in-law of Georgi Dimitrov. He led the party from 1950 to 1954 after the death of Vasil Kolarov and was prime minister from 1950 to 1956. Todor Zhivkov succeeded him as party leader in 1954. He followed the strict policies of Josef Stalin and lost power after the post-Stalin reforms. After 1962, he was forced into retirement and left the party inner circles and public life.

Filip Dimitrov (b. 1955): Conservative Bulgarian politician; a leader of the Green Party (a conservative ecological party) and the Committee for Religious Rights. Led the Union of Democratic Forces from 1990 to 1994 and served as prime minister from December 1991 to November 1992. During his tenure, he quarreled over policies with President Zhelev and was discredited by a scandal involving illegal arms sales to Macedonia.

Georgi Dimitrov (Mihailov) (1882–1949): Communist Party leader. He joined the Bulgarian Social Democratic Party in 1902 and then joined the Narrows when the party split. He was a leader of the printers' union and the Communist labor union organization. He was also on the Executive Committee of the *Comintern*. In 1933, the Nazi government in Germany charged him with conspiring to burn down the *Reichstag* building. His trial was an international sensation and made him the most famous Bulgarian in the world. He was acquitted after a brilliant defense supported by worldwide public opinion. He then went to Moscow and became General Secretary of the *Comintern*, where he advocated a policy of cooperation with all parties opposed to fascism. After World War II, he was prime minister of Bulgaria from 1946 to 1949 and moved the country toward a Stalinist form of socialism.

Georgi M. Dimitrov (Gemeto) (1903–1972): A Bulgarian physician and politician; leader of BANU-Alexander Stamboliiski. He opposed the personal rule of King Boris III and the Axis alliance. He headed the Allied Bulgarian National Committee abroad during World War II. After the war, he opposed the Communists in the Fatherland Front. To avoid arrest, he escaped to the United States, where he continued to lead the Bulgarian National Committee opposed to the Communist regime. His daughter Anastasia Dimitrova-Moser, the wife of the American Bulgarian literature specialist Charles Moser, returned to Bulgaria after the fall of Communism to lead Gemeto's party.

Blaga Dimitrova (1922–2003): Popular Bulgarian poet and novelist. She was a critic of some of the policies of the Communist regime. In 1989, she was one the leaders of the movement against Zhivkov, and she help found the Club for Glasnost and Democracy. In 1992, she was elected vice president on Zhelev's ticket but resigned the next year after falling out with the UDF.

Aleksander Mihailovich Dondukov-Korsakov (1820–1893): Russian prince and general who was military governor of Bulgaria after the Russo-Turkish War of 1877–1878. He helped to establish the Turnovo Constitution and the election of Alexander of Battenberg as the first Bulgarian monarch.

Bogdan Filov (1883–1945): Art historian and academician. He served as minister of education from 1938 to 1940 and then was promoted to prime minister by King Boris, who controlled the government during World War II. In 1943, after the death of the king, he served as *de facto* chief regent for the young king Simeon II. He continued the pro-Axis policies and then reluctantly sought peace negotiations with the Allies. He was executed by the Fatherland Front government.

Ferdinand of Saxe-Coburg-Gotha (1861–1948): Second monarch of Bulgaria; prince 1887 to 1911; tsar (king) 1911 to 1918. His reign started with controversy because of some foreign opposition to his selection for the throne and difficulties with his Catholic religion. For almost a decade, he was under the thumb of Stefan Stambolov. Then in 1994, he began his personal rule. Dreaming of a greater Bulgaria, he broke from the Ottoman Empire in 1908 and raised his status to king. He led Bulgaria into the disastrous Balkan Wars and the wrong side in World War I. The victorious Allies forced him to abdicate and leave the country in 1918.

Kimon Georgiev (Stoianov) (1882–1969): Army colonel; member of the Military League, *Zveno*, and the Fatherland Front; prime minister 1934 to 1935 and 1944 to 1946. During the Communist period, he continued to serve in various government and *subranie* posts.

Dimitur Liubimirov Gichev (1893–1964): Leader of BANU-*Vrabcha 1*; minister of agriculture and then trade in the Popular Bloc government (1931 to 1934); joined in the "group of five" opposition parties; minister without portfolio in the September 1944 Muraviev government. He was sentenced to prison by the Fatherland Front government.

Anton Iugov (1904–1991): Joined the Communist Party in 1921; fought as a partisan in World War II. He held various high party and government positions, including prime minister (1956 to 1962). He was in disgrace from 1962 until 1989, when he was rehabilitated.

Ivan Alexander (d. 1371): Tsar of the Second Bulgarian Empire from 1331 to 1371. He ruled during the height and decline of the empire. Turnovo, during his reign, was a wealthy cosmopolitan commercial center. It was also a religious center. He divided his empire among his sons, but shortly after his death the empire fell to the Ottomans.

He is also remembered for the magnificent tetraevangelia created during his reign.

Kaloian (d. 1207): Tsar 1197 to 1207; younger brother of Todor and Ivan Asen; best known for his victory over Baldwin I (of Flanders) of the Latin Empire in 1205.

Liuben Stoichev Karavelov (ca. 1834–1879): Author, publicist, and folklorist; one of the major organizers of the Bulgarian independence movement. He was one of the founders of the Bulgarian Revolutionary Central Committee (BRCC).

Petko Stoichev Karavelov (1843–1903): Lawyer; brother of Liuben Karavelov; one of the leaders of the Liberal Party; later a founder of the Democrat Party. He served as prime minister four separate times between 1880 and 1902.

Dimo Kazasov (1886–1980): Author; journalist; politician. He was a member of the Social Democratic Party (broad) and a founder of *Zveno*. He, however, joined the Fatherland Front as an independent. He wrote important books and articles on Bulgarian social and political life in the twentieth century. He also held important ministerial posts and ambassadorships in various governments, including those of both the Democratic Alliance and the Fatherland Front.

Georgi Ivanov K'oseivanov (1884–1960): Lawyer and diplomat; court chamberlain of Boris III; prime minister from 1935 to 1940; later ambassador to Switzerland, where he remained after World War II.

Vasil Petrov Kolarov (1877–1950): A leader of the Bulgarian Social Democrats (Narrow) and the Bulgarian Communist Party; also a leading figure in the *Comintern*. He was Bulgarian prime minister from 1949 to 1950.

Ivan Iordanov Kostov (b. 1949): Professor of economics; conservative minister of finances 1990 to 1992; then leader of the UDF 1994 to 2001 and prime minister 1997 to 2001. His administration was marked by much corruption.

Triacho Kostov (Dzhunov) (1897–1949): Journalist; major Communist Party leader; helped organize partisan movement in World War II; served in various important party and government posts. After the war, he opposed many of the Soviets' and Dimitrov's policies applied to Bulgaria and was executed after a show trial. Posthumously rehabilitated in 1963.

Krum (d. 814): Khan of the First Bulgarian Empire from 803 to 814. He is celebrated as a great victorious warrior, remembered especially for his victory over the Byzantine emperor Nikephoros I in 811. Krum is still a popular Bulgarian name for boys.

Vasil Levski (ne Vasil Ivanov Kunchev, 1837–1873): Major, almost mythic, figure of the Bulgarian struggle for independence from the Ottomans. Levski served in the Bulgarian Legions formed in Belgrade in 1862 and with guerilla *chetas* in Bulgaria. He was one of the founders of the BRCC. He hoped to establish an Internal Revolutionary Organization inside Bulgaria; while organizing it, he was caught and hanged by the Turks. His grave has never been found.

Andrei Tasev Liapchev (1866–1933): Journalist; politician; member of the Democrat Party and Democratic Alliance. Liapchev served in various ministerial posts and was prime minister 1926 to 1931. He was from Macedonia and supported IMRO.

Aleksandur Pavlov Malinov (1867–1938): Lawyer and politician; one of the founders and leaders of the Democrat Party. He served three times as prime minister: 1908 to 1911, 1918, and 1931.

(Ahmed Sheflik) Midhat Pasha (1822–1884): Ottoman government official; reformer. As governor of Northern Bulgaria, he introduced major economic reforms, improving the lot of Bulgarian farmers. Later, as grand vizier, he helped author a constitution for the Ottoman Empire that granted equal rights to all citizens. It was rejected but served as a basis for the 1908 constitution. Midhat's goal was to create a single Ottoman nationality, and he opposed Bulgarian independence.

Ivan "Vancho" Mihailov (Gavrilov) (1896–1990): Leader of IMRO after 1924. Lived in exile, chiefly in Italy, after 1934. Mihailov used terror and assassination to obtain political aims. He believed Macedonian Slavs were Bulgarians but advocated a Macedonian state separate from Bulgaria as a political compromise. He allied himself to Croatian and Italian fascists in the interwar and World War II era. He was also instrumental in establishing the North American Macedonian Patriotic Organization.

Petur Toshev Mladenov (1936–2000): Leading Communist; foreign minister from 1971 to 1989. Mladenov succeeded Todor Zhivkov as leader of the Communist Party and head of state in November 1989. He was the first interim president before the 1990 constitution was written. Resigned after threatening the mass demonstrations of 1990.

Nikola Stoichev Mushanov (1872–1951): Lawyer and politician; a leader of the Democrat Party. Mushanov served in several ministerial posts. He served as prime minister from 1931 to 1934. He was opposed to the Axis alliance as part of the legal opposition in the *subraniia* during King Boris's personal rule. He served as minister without portfolio in the Muraviev government of September 1944. The Fatherland Front government sentenced him to a prison term.

Paisii Hilendarski (1722–ca. 1773): Monk of the Hilendar monastery on Mount Athos. He wrote the first important history of Bulgaria in the eighteenth century, leading to the Bulgarian national awakening.

Georgi Sedefchov Parvanov (b.1957): Historian. Parvanov joined the Communist Party in 1981 and remained after 1990 when the party changed its name to the Socialist Party. He was elected president of the republic in 2001 and reelected for a second term in 2006.

Peter I (d. 970): Bulgarian tsar of the First Bulgarian Empire from 927 to 969. Peter is a controversial ruler. Although Bulgaria enjoyed prosperity and relative peace during his reign, toward the end he lost much of the territory won by his father, Simeon I. The Bogomil heresy also flourished during his years. The church canonized him on his death.

Dimitur Iosifov Peshev (1894–1973): Lawyer; judge; minister of justice from 1935 to 1936; representative from Kiustendil; and vice president of the 25th regular *subranie* during World War II. Peshev is one of the most worldwide-honored Bulgarians of the twentieth century. He twice sacrificed his career for moral decisions. In 1936, he refused to sign the death warrant of Damian Velchev, and more importantly, in March 1943, he intervened to prevent the deportation of Bulgarian Jews to the killing centers of Poland during the Holocaust.

Nikola Dimitrov Petkov (1889–1947): Politician; member of BANU-Alexander Stamboliiski. Petkov joined the Fatherland Front in World War II and served in the first Fatherland Front government of 1944. Broke with the Communists and served as leader of BANU after Gemeto Dimitrov resigned. Formed BANU-Nikola Petkov. The Fatherland Front government executed him in 1947.

Georgi Stoikov Rakovski (1821–1867): Author; historian; folklorist. Rakovski was one the most important figures preparing the way for Bulgarian independence. He was the founder of the Bulgarian liberation movement. His books, poems, and articles promoted his ideas. He fought with *chetas* inside Bulgaria, worked for the establishment of an independent Bulgarian church, and laid plans for an armed uprising implemented by his successors.

Simeon I (ca. 863–927): One of the greatest tsars of the First Bulgarian Empire, he reigned 893 to 927. Simeon was the third son of Boris I. He conquered much of the European area of the Byzantine Empire up to the walls of Constantinople itself. He claimed for himself through marriage arrangements the title Emperor of the Romans (i.e., Byzantines).

Simeon II (b. 1937): King 1943 to 1947. Simeon, the son of Boris III, lived in exile from 1947 to 2001. He then ran and won a seat in the *subranie* as the head of his own party, the National Movement Simeon II, which won the plurality of votes. Simeon served as prime minister 2001 to 2005.

Sofronii Vrachanski (ne Stoiko Vladislavov, 1739–1813): Monk; disciple of Paiisi. Sofroni preached in Bulgarian about Bulgarian history using Paiisi's history. He spread Bulgarian nationalism among the population.

Petko Stoinov Stainov (1890–1973): Lawyer; professor; politician. Stainov was a *subranie* representative from the 1920s until his death in 1973. He originally was a member of the conservative National Party. During the personal rule of King Boris, he was an outspoken critic of the government's policies and opposed the Axis alliance. He joined the Fatherland Front and served as foreign minister in its first government.

Aleksandur Stoimenov Stamboliiski (1879–1923): Teacher; journalist; politician. Stamboliiski is a dominant figure in Bulgarian history. He led BANU from almost its beginning until his death in 1923, turning it into a mass organization of farmers and the country's most popular

political party. His opposition to the Balkan Wars and World War I swept him to power in 1919. He served as prime minister from 1919 to 1923. He introduced reforms to benefit the agricultural population. He strove to follow a policy of peace with his neighbors. In June 1923, his enemies organized a coup d'état against him and brought down his government. IMRO terrorists captured him and, after an orgy of torture, brutally murdered him.

Stefan Nikolov Stambolov (1854–1895): Revolutionary and politician. Stambolov participated in the April Uprising and was one of the leaders of the Liberal Party in the first years of Bulgarian independence. He organized the union of Eastern Rumelia and Bulgaria. He split from the Liberal Party and formed the Russophobe National Liberal Party. As prime minister from 1887 to 1894, he ruled by authoritarian methods but did much to establish Bulgaria's economic base. After his term, he was brutally attacked in the street by enemies and died from his wounds.

Aleksandur Tsolov Tsankov (1879–1959): Economics professor; politician. Tsankov was a member of the Social Democrats (Broad) but became a leader of the Democratic Alliance in the 1920s. He was adamantly opposed to the Communists and BANU. He served as prime minister from 1923 to 1926. Afterward, he formed his fascist National Socialist Movement and supported the Axis in World War II, although he opposed King Boris's government as a *subranie* representative. In 1944, the Nazis established him as the leader of a government in exile.

Dragan Kiriakov Tsankov (1828–1911): Teacher; publisher; politician. Tsankov worked for the independent church. After liberation, he was one of the leaders of the Liberal Party. A Russophile, he opposed Stambolov. Later he helped found the Progressive Liberal Party. He served in several important government posts, including as prime minister in 1880 and from 1883 to 1884.

Zheliu Mitev Zhelev (b. 1935): Philosopher. Zhelev was one of Bulgaria's leading dissidents during the Communist period. In 1989, he challenged the Zhivkov regime by establishing the Club for Glasnost and Democracy and then by helping found the Union of Democratic

Forces. He was selected as president of Bulgaria in 1990 even before the new constitution was written. Then he was elected as the first

president under the new constitution. His disagreements with the other leaders of UDF led to his break with the coalition. After leaving the presidency, he continued to play a minor role in Bulgarian politics.

Todor Hristov Zhivkov (1911–1998): Bulgarian Communist leader. Zhivkov was born to a farming family but started working life as a printer, as did Georgi Dimitrov. He joined the Communists in 1928. During World War II, he served in the resistance in Sofia and was promoted to the inner circles of the party. Following Moscow's policies after Stalin died, Chervenkov appointed him First Secretary. Zhivkov, a wily politician, outmaneuvered his boss and became leader of the party and country until 1989. He was able to defeat all challenges to his rule until then. He tried to ameliorate conditions in the country but in the 1980s ran into a series of economic and political disasters. With the collapse of the Communist system in Eastern Europe in the late '80s, he lost power as well. Afterward, charges of corruption and various political misdeeds were brought against him, but his only punishments were fines and periods of house arrest.

Liudmila Todorova Zhivkova (1942–1981): Educator; author. She was the daughter of Todor Zhivkov and was given a position on the Communist Party's Politburo and the Council of Ministers in charge of culture. An ardent Bulgarian nationalist, she promoted the country's culture around the world. She also sponsored a charity for improving the lot of children in the Third World. She believed in mysticism and held many patently un-Marxist ideas. Through her, liberalism was promoted in Bulgaria, but many corrupt persons took advantage of her naiveté. She aroused the ire of a number of orthodox Marxists as well as the Soviets and died under mysterious circumstances.

Glossary

Ancien Regime: European society and government ruled by the landed aristocracy before the French Revolution

April Plenum: Full meeting of the Central Committee of the Bulgarian Communist Party to introduce reforms following the death of Josef Stalin

Attack: Extreme right nationalistic Bulgarian political party

Axis: German, Italian, and Japanese alliance during World War II

autocephalous: autonomous church

baksheesh: Turkish for *gratuity* or *bribe*

Balkan Entente: Diplomatic alliance among Greece, Romania, Turkey, and Yugoslavia between World Wars I and II

BANU: Bulgarian Agrarian National Union, a Bulgarian farmers' economic and political association

Bashi-Bazouks: Irregular Turkish troops from the Caucuses stationed in Bulgaria during the Balkan crisis of the 1870s

BCP: Bulgarian Communist Party

bey: Turkish governor

black-red coalition: A government composed of political parties with widely differing agendas

Blitzkrieg: Lightening War; German rapid victories during the beginning of World War II

Bogomils, Bogomilism: The meek of God; medieval Christian heretics and heresy prevalent in the Balkans

boyars: Medieval Slavic princes

BRCC: Bulgarian Revolutionary Central Committee; a group of Bulgarian radicals preparing to free their country from the Ottoman Empire

BSCC: Bulgarian Secret Central Committee; another radical organization preparing to free Bulgaria from the Ottoman Empire

Bulgaroktonos: Bulgarslayer; title given to the Byzantine Emperor Basil II after his defeat of the First Bulgarian Empire

BWP: Bulgarian Workers Party; the Communists in the 1930s

BZNS: *Bulgarski Zemledelski Naroden Suiuz*; Bulgarian acronym for BANU

BZNS-Aleksandur Stamboliiski: Left-wing agrarian party after the fall of the BANU government

BZNS-Pladne: Alternate name for the *BZNS-Aleksandur Stamboliiski*

BZNS-Vrabcha 1: Centrist agrarian party after the fall of the BANU government

cheta: A guerilla band

chetnik: A member of a guerilla band

chiflik: A large, private farm

chitalishte: A reading room

chorbadzhi: Literally "a person who can eat expensive meat soup;" a derogatory expression for a wealthy person

CITUB: Confederation of Independent Trade Unions in Bulgaria; a post-Communist-era labor union group

Comintern: The Communist International; a worldwide association of Communist parties

Cominform: An international association of Communist parties established by Josef Stalin after World War II

communism: The last stage of society when, according to the philosophy of Karl Marx, all people will live in equal harmony

Concert of Europe: The group of Great Powers (England, France, Austria, Prussia, and Russia) that controlled Europe in the nineteenth century

Constitutional Bloc: Group of political parties opposed to the BANU government

Cordon Sanataire: Sterile border; the name of the buffer of East European countries between Germany and Soviet Russia established by the 1919 Treaty of Paris

Corecom: Special shops in Bulgaria where goods from non-Communist countries could be bought for hard currency

Cyrillic: Alphabet used by several Slavic languages including Bulgarian

devshirme: Child tax; practice of Ottoman authorities of gathering Christian children for the civil service, janissaries, and harems

Dunovists: A Bulgarian Christian mystical sect founded by Peter Dunov

etatist: Based on occupational strata, e.g., peasantry, urban laborers, etc.

Fatherland Front: Antifascist and antigovernment coalition during World War II; Bulgarian government ruling coalition from 1944 to 1989

Freikorps: German paramilitary groups formed after World War I

Glagolitsa: Medieval Slavic alphabet; a precursor of Cyrillic

GERB: Citizens for European Development of Bulgaria; a right-of-center political party

grand national assemblies: Enlarged Bulgarian parliaments elected for special purposes such as amending the constitution

gulag: Soviet prison camp for political prisoners

haiduk: Bulgarian highwayman

Hatt-ı Hümayun: Ottoman reform decree of 1856

Hatt-i-Sherif **of Gülhane:** Ottoman reform decree of 1839

il duce: Italian for the *leader*; popular title of fascist dictator Benito Mussolini

Ilinden Uprising: 1903 Macedonian revolt on St. Elijah's Day

IMRO: Internal Macedonian Revolutionary Organization; political association of Bulgarian Macedonians

Izvestia: Russian for *news*; Soviet Union newspaper

janissary: Ottoman infantryman

khan: Bulgar ruler

Komsomol: Communist youth organization

Krestintern: Peasant International; international association of agrarian parties sponsored by the Soviet Union

Little Entente: Alliance among Czechoslovakia, Romania, and Yugoslavia sponsored by France between World War I and World War II

metropolitan: An Eastern Orthodox bishop

millet: An Ottoman religious community responsible for many legal matters concerning members of its faith.

MRF: Movement for Rights and Freedoms; a chiefly Moslem political party in Bulgaria

NMSS: National Movement Simeon Second; a Bulgarian Political party supporting the candidature and policies of ex-king Simeon II

OSS: Office of Secret Services; American counterespionage agency; precursor of the CIA

Pan-Slavs, Pan-Slavism: Persons, ideology that maintain all Slavic peoples should be in the same nation-state

Pechenegs: Medieval Turkish people of Central Asia

personal rule: Direct rule of the state by Bulgarian monarchs

Pomak: Bulgarian Moslems whose ancestral language is Bulgarian

Pliska: First medieval capital of the First Bulgarian Empire

Podkrepa: Bulgarian labor union

Politburo: Political Buro; policy-making core of a Communist Party central committee

Pravda: Russian for *truth*; newspaper of the Soviet Union's Communist Party

Preslav: Second medieval capital of the First Bulgarian Empire

Quisling: A leader of a country occupied by Germany during World War II who worked with the Nazis

Raiffeisen cooperatives: A method of cooperative farming with a moral basis, popular in the early twentieth century

Reichstag Fire: The arson of the German parliament building in 1933

Reichswehr: The German army during the Nazi period

revisionism (socialism): Moderation of Marxist theory maintaining that socialism can be attained through legal means instead of revolution

revisionist camp: Countries opposed to the 1919 Treaty of Paris, especially Germany, Italy, the USSR, Austria, Hungary, and Bulgaria

RSHA: *Reichssicherheitshauptamp*; Imperial Security Chief Office, the German security bureaucracy during the Third Reich, run by the SS; included the secret police (*Gestapo*) and the department in charge of the Holocaust

SA *Stürm Abteilungen:* Storm Battalion; a Nazi paramilitary force; the Brown Shirts

Serdica: Ancient name of Sofia

show trial: A public trial of political prisoners

Slovo: The newspaper of the Constitutional Bloc

socialism: In Marxist political theory, the stage of society between capitalism and communism

slavophones: Persons of Greek nationality or supposed Greek nationality whose native language is a Slavic tongue

Sredetz: Medieval name of Sofia

spahi: Ottoman cavalry

Sublime Porte: The Ottoman government

subranie, subrania: The Bulgarian parliament; *subrania* is the plural

SS, *Schutzstafel*: Protective Echelon; Nazi paramilitary force; the Black Shirts

Sudetenland: A mostly German enclave in the western mountain region of Czechoslovakia

Tanzimat: Reform movement in the Ottoman Empire

tetraevangelia: A book of the gospels containing religious icons

Third Reich: The Third German empire under the Nazis, 1933–1945; the First Empire was the medieval Holy Roman Empire; the second was united Germany, 1871–1918

timor: An Ottoman estate ruled by the sultan

Treaty of Kuchuk-Kainardzhi: 1774 Treaty between Russia and the Ottoman Empire giving Russia the right to protect Christians in the Ottoman Empire

tsar: A Slavic title for a king or emperor, probably derived from *Caesar*

UDF: Union of Democratic Forces; a Bulgarian political coalition formed in 1989

Ustaše: Croatian fascist organization

Vlachs: A Balkan ethnic group related to Romanians

zadruga: A South Slavic communal farm

Zeta: Medieval Montenegro

Zveno, Zvenarist: Link; a Bulgarian political organization in the 1920s and 1930s; a member of the organization

Bibliographic Essay

There have been comparatively few books in English about Bulgaria until recently, when more American and other English-speaking scholars have entered the field. The following essay describes some on the subject that the interested casual reader might find useful.

The best general history of Bulgaria in English, and possibly in any language, is R. J. Crampton's *Bulgaria* (New York: Oxford University Press, 2007). Crampton also has a shorter version—*A Concise History of Bulgaria*, 2nd edition (New York: Cambridge University Press, 2005). Another interesting older work, originally published in 1919 and recently reissued, is Dimitur Mishev, *The Bulgarians in the Past: Pages from the Cultural History* (Chestnut Hill, MA: Adamant Media Corporation, 2007), which deals with the period from the Byzantine Era to liberation. Also see David Marshall Lang, *The Bulgarians: From Ancient Times to the Ottoman Conquest* (London: Thames and Hudson, 1976).

For the ancient period, there is R. F. Hoddinott, *The Thracians* (New York: Thames and Hudson, 1981), and for the Middle Ages there is the classic by Steven Runciman, *A History of the First Bulgarian Empire* (London: G. Bell & Sons, 1930), written by a respected Byzantinist. Dimitri Obolensky, another Byzantinist, has written about the

Bogomils in *The Bogomils: A Study in Balkan Neo-Manichaeism* (Cambridge, England: University Press, 1948).

For the Ottoman period, there is the American scholar Dennis Hupchick's *The Bulgarians in the Seventeenth Century: Slavic Orthodox Society and Culture under Ottoman Rule* (Jefferson, NC: McFarland, 1993) and Raina Gavrilova's *Bulgarian Urban Culture in the Eighteenth and Nineteenth Centuries* (Cranbury, NJ: Susquehanna University Press, 1999). On the Bulgarian revival period, an excellent study is Thomas A. Meininger's *The Formation of a Nationalist Bulgarian Intelligentsia 1835–1878* (New York: Garland Pub., 1987). Also see his *Ignatiev and the Establishment of the Bulgarian Exarchate, 1864–1872: A Study in Personal Diplomacy* (Madison: University of Wisconsin, 1970). James Franklin Clarke's *Bible Societies, American Missionaries, and the National Revival of Bulgaria* (New York: Arno Press, 1971) documents the church struggle. Clarke was the son of American missionaries and was born in Bulgaria. *Bible Societies* is his doctoral dissertation, written under the Harvard historian William Langer and published by the *New York Times*'s Arno Press series of reprints on the classics of Eastern Europe. A number of older books on Bulgaria are in the collection. A more modern study on the missionaries is Tatyana Nestorova, *American Missionaries among the Bulgarians 1855–1912* (Boulder, CO: East European Monographs, 1987).

The liberation struggle is described by Mercia MacDermott in *The Apostle of Freedom: A Portrait of Vasil Levski against a Background of Nineteenth Century Bulgaria* (South Brunswick, NJ: A. S. Barnes, 1969). MacDermott is an English author and teacher who sympathized with the Bulgarian Communist cause and is a great admirer of the Bulgarian nation and culture. She has lived in Bulgaria off and on for many years and has written many books on the history of the country with a nationalistic bias. Another book on Levski is Maria Nikolaeva Todorova's *Bones of Contention: The Living Archive of Vasil Levski and the Making of Bulgaria's National Hero* (New York: Central European University Press, 2009). Todorova, the daughter of the historian Nikolai Todorov, who headed the Bulgarian Academy of Sciences Institute of Balkan Studies, examines the role of the life of Levski, the dominant figure of Bulgaria's national history, in formulating the essence of Bulgarian nationalism. Mara A. Firkatian wrote about Rakovski in *The Forest Traveler: Georgi Stoikov Rakovski and Bulgarian Nationalism* (New York: P. Lang, 1996). A firsthand account of the Bulgarian liberation activity in English can be found in Zahari Stoianov and M. W. Potter's *Zachary Stoyanoff: Pages from the Autobiography of a Bulgarian Insurgent* (London: E. Arnold, 1913).

R. J. Crampton's first scholarly work was on the initial period of Bulgarian independence and is found in *Bulgaria 1878–1918: A History* (Boulder, CO: East European Monographs, 1983). On the role of Russia in Bulgaria's first years, see Karel Durman's *Lost Illusions: Russian Policies towards Bulgaria in 1877–1887* (Uppsala, Sweden: Uppsala University, 1988). A classic work on Bulgaria's first constitution is Cyril Edwin Black's *The Establishment of Constitutional Government in Bulgaria* (Princeton, NJ: Princeton University Press, 1943). Black, the son of the director of the American College in Sofia, was, along with Clarke, one of the first American Bulgarian specialists. Another classic work is Egon Corti, *Alexander of Battenberg* (London: Cassell, 1954). Duncan M. Perry examines Stambolov's role in the early decades of Bulgaria's independence in *Stefan Stambolov and the Emergence of Modern Bulgaria* (Durham, NC: Duke University Press, 1993).

On the Macedonian question, several older as well as more recent books are pertinent. H. N. Brailsford's *Macedonia, Its Races and Its Future* (New York: Arno Press, 1971) is another classic reprinted by Arno Press. Duncan Perry examined the early years in *The Politics of Terror, The Macedonian Revolutionary Movements, 1893–1903* (Durham, NC: Duke University Press, 1988). Laura B. Sherman related the history of the Ellen Stone affair in *Fires on the Mountain: The Macedonian Revolutionary Movement and the Kidnapping of Ellen Stone* (Boulder, CO: East European Monographs, 1980). See also Teresa Carpenter's *The Miss Stone Affair: America's First Modern Hostage Crisis* (New York: Simon & Schuster, 2003). Stoyan Christowe, a Macedonian immigrant and Chicago newspaper reporter, wrote several books about both Macedonia and America. In his *Heroes and Assassins* (New York: R. N. McBride & Company, 1935), he lauds IMRO as freedom fighters. Stephen Constant in *Foxy Ferdinand, 1861–1948, Tsar of Bulgaria* (New York: Franklin Watts, 1980) gives a rather unflattering picture of the Bulgarian monarch. In contrast, Nadezhda Stancheva Muir sings the praises of her father in *Dimitri Stancioff, Patriot and Cosmopolitan, 1864–1940* (London: Hutchinson & Co., 1957). Stancioff was Ferdinand's secretary. Lady Muir also helped publish her mother's memoir in English—Anna Stancioff, *Recollections of a Bulgarian Diplomatist's Wife* (London: Hutchinson & Co., 1930). Mari Firkatian wrote of both generations in *Diplomats and Dreamers: The Stancioff Family in Bulgarian History* (Lanham, MD: University Press of America, 2008). Lady Muir served in Aleksandur Stamboliiski's diplomatic service.

For the Balkan wars, there is a firsthand account of the events leading up to wars in Ivan Evstratiev Geshov's *The Balkan League* (London: J. Murray, 1915). Ernst Christian Helmreich has written *The Diplomacy of the Balkan Wars* (New York: Russell & Russell, 1969), and Richard C. Hall is the author of *The Balkan Wars, 1912–1913: Prelude to the First World War* (New York: Routledge, 2000). Hall is also the author of *Bulgaria's Road to the First World War* (Boulder, CO: East European Monographs, 1996).

For the BANU, the best work in English is John D. Bell's *Peasants in Power: Alexander Stamboliski and the Bulgarian Agrarian National Union, 1899–1923* (Princeton, NJ: Princeton University Press, 1977). Kosta Todorov's *Balkan Firebrand: The Autobiography of a Rebel Soldier and Statesman* (New York: Ziff-Davis Publishing Company, 1943) is an amusing if self-aggrandizing autobiography of one of Stamboliiski's associates. The American scholar and former president of the North American Bulgarian Studies Association Charles Moser has written a biography of his father-in-law, Gemeto, in *Dimitrov of Bulgaria: A Political Biography of Dr. Georgi M. Dimitrov* (Ottawa, IL: Caroline House, 1979). Irwin Taylor Sanders, who was an instructor at the American College in Sofia in the 1930s and later a foreign member of the Bulgarian Academy of Sciences, wrote *Balkan Village* (Lexington: University of Kentucky Press, 1949) based on his research of the village of Dragalevski outside of Sofia. Sanders's work helped establish internationally the field of rural sociology.

Stephane Groueff's *Crown of Thorns, The Reign of King Boris III of Bulgaria, 1918–1943* (Lanham, MD: Madison Books, 1987) is a favorable biography of King Boris. Joseph Swire's *Bulgarian Conspiracy* (London: Hale, 1939) deals with the terror of IMRO, the 1934 coup d'état, and the trial of Damian Velchev. Marshall Lee Miller writes about World War II in *Bulgaria During the Second World War* (Stanford, CA: Stanford University Press, 1975). On the fate of the Jews, see Frederick B. Chary's *The Bulgarian Jews and the Final Solution, 1940–1944* (Pittsburgh, PA: University of Pittsburgh Press, 1972). Tsvetan Todorov also writes about this in *The Fragility of Goodness: Why Bulgaria's Jews Survived the Holocaust* (Princeton, NJ: Princeton University Press, 2001); so does Guy H. Haskell in *From Sofia to Jaffa: The Jews of Bulgaria and Israel* (Detroit: Wayne State University Press, 1994).

On the history of the Communist Party, see Joseph Rothschild's *The Communist Party of Bulgaria, Origins and Development, 1883–1936* (New York: Columbia University Press, 1959); Nissan Oren addresses the subject in *Bulgarian Communism: The Road to Power, 1924–1944* (New York: Columbia University Press, 1959); John D. Bell, also, in *The Bulgarian Communist Party from Blagoev to Zhivkov* (Stanford, CA: Hoover Institution Press, 1986). Nissan Oren discusses the policies of BANU and the Communists in *Revolution Administered, Bulgarian*

Agrarianism and Communism in Bulgaria (Baltimore: Johns Hopkins University Press, 1971). Ivo Banac, ed., *The Diary of Georgi Dimitrov, 1933–1949* (New Haven, CT: Yale University Press, 2003) presents selections from the Communist leader Dimitrov's writings. J. F. Brown in *Bulgaria under Communist Rule* (New York: Praeger, 1970) unfavorably casts the Communist government of Bulgaria. For the Georgi Markov affair, see his own *The Truth that Killed* (New York: Ticknor & Fields, 1984), published posthumously, and Vladimir Kostov's *The Bulgarian Umbrella, The Soviet Direction and Operation of the Bulgarian Secret Service in Europe* (New York: St. Martin's Press, 1988). The disinformation about Bulgaria's involvement in Mehmet Ali Ağca's failed attempt to assassinate Pope John Paul II is written about in Edward S. Herman and Frank Brodhead's *The Rise and Fall of the Bulgarian* Connection (New York: Sheridan Square Publications, 1986). For a favorable view of Liudmila Zhivkova, see her own *Lyudmila Zhivkova: Her Many Worlds, New Culture and Beauty, Concepts and Action*, 2nd edition (New York: Pergamon Press, 1986), also posthumously published.

There have been a number of works about post-Communist Bulgaria. These include Vesselin Dimitrov's *The Uneven Transition* (London: Routledge, 2001) and the historian John Bell's *Bulgaria in Transition: Politics, Economics, Society and Culture after Communism* (Boulder, CO: Westview Press, 1998). Gerald Creed, an anthropologist specializing in rural Bulgaria, has written *Domesticating Revolution: From Socialist Reform to Ambivalent Transition in a Bulgarian Village* (University Park, PA: Penn State University Press, 1998), which won the John D. Bell Memorial Book Prize of the Bulgarian Studies Association (BSA) in 1998. See also Albert P. Melone's *Creating Parliamentary Government: The Transition to Democracy in Bulgaria* (Columbus: Ohio State University Press, 1998) and John A. Bristow's *The Bulgarian Economy in Transition* (Brookfield, VT: Edward Elgar, 1996).

There are a number of books on the Turks and Moslems in Bulgaria but few in English on the Roma. An early one is Huey Lewis Kostanick's *Turkish Resettlement of Bulgarian Turks, 1950–1953* (Berkeley: University of California Press, 1957). Since the revival process and the resulting migrations, several works have appeared. Ivan Palchev's *Ahmed Dogan and the Bulgarian Ethnic Model* (Sofia: Bulgarian Bestseller, 2002) concerns the founder of the Movement for Rights and Freedom. Kemal H. Karpat, a distinguished American professor of Turkish history, wrote *The Turks of Bulgaria: The History, Culture, and Political Fate of a Minority* (Istanbul: Isis Press, 1990). See also Bilâl Şimşir's *The Turks of Bulgaria 1878–1985* (London: K. Rustem, 1985) and Mary Neuburger's

The Orient Within: Muslim Minorities and the Negotiation of Nationhood in Modern Bulgaria (Ithaca, NY: Cornell University Press, 2004). Ali Eminov's *Turkish and Other Muslim Minorities in Bulgaria* (London: Hurst & Company, 1997) won the BSA's Bell prize for 1999.

For economic history, two excellent and highly regarded works are Nikolai Todorov's *Society, the City, and Industry in the Balkans, 15th–19th Centuries* (Brookfield, VT: Ashgate, 1998) and John R. Lampe's *The Bulgarian Economy in the Twentieth Century* (London: Croom Helm, 1986). For literature, see Charles A. Moser's *A History of Bulgarian Literature 865–1944* (The Hague: Mouton, 1972) and Atanas Slavov's *The "Thaw" in Bulgarian Literature* (Boulder, CO: East European Monographs, 1981).

Index

Note: Photographs, maps, and illustrations are indicated by italics